EMPOWERED EVANGELICALS

Empowered
<u>Evangelicals</u>

Bringing Together the Best of the
Evangelical and Charismatic Worlds

Rich Nathan
and Ken Wilson

VINE
BOOKS

Servant Publications
Ann Arbor, Michigan

Vine Books is an imprint of Servant Publications especially designed to serve evangelical Christians.

Although the stories in this book are true, all names and identifying characteristics have been changed to protect the privacy of those involved.

Published by Servant Publications
P.O. Box 8617
Ann Arbor, Michigan 48107

Cover design by A2 Graphics

95 96 97 98 99 10 9 8 7 6 5 4 3 2 1

Printed in the United States of America
ISBN 0-89283-929-5

Library of Congress Cataloging-in-Publication Data

Nathan, Rich
    Empowered Evangelicals : bringing together the best of
the Evangelical and charismatic worlds / Rich Nathan and
Ken Wilson.
        p.   cm.
    Includes index.
    ISBN 0-89283-929-5
    1. Evangelicalism—United States—History—20th
century.   2. Pentecostalism—United States—History—
20th century.   3. Spiritual healing.   4. Holy Spirit.   5.
Church renewal.   I. Wilson, Ken.   II. Title.
BR526.N29   1995
270.8'2—dc20   95-31941
                                                                         CIP

Contents

Dedication

To John Wimber
"Remember your leaders, who spoke the Word of God
to you. Consider the outcome of their lives and
imitate their faith."
We remember. We have considered. We are imitating!

Foreword

This is a book that should not have been needed. But it is needed, and in some quarters quite urgently.

It seeks to lead polarized people out of some tangles of negative and impoverishing opinion in which they are currently caught. One group sees the other as weak in the head, while the second rates the first as weak in the heart. Each forfeits some wisdom and maturity by declining to learn from the other.

Neither group, perhaps, is untouched by sinful pride, but both are to some extent victims of history. It is no wonder if disciples of Calvin, Owen, Baxter, Edwards, Hodge, Warfield, and Kuyper, with latter-day dispensationalists, fundamentalists, and Bible teachers, should look askance at a theologically loose and unstable-looking mass movement that lays special claim to the leading and life of the Holy Spirit; those whom they most admire had to fend off such movements themselves. Nor is it any wonder if adherents of a populist movement of renewal such as Pentecostal second-blessingism should suspect that intellectuals who critique them care more for notional orthodoxy than for knowing and enjoying God. But the tensions here are truly weakening, and need to be overcome.

Wilson and Nathan are pastors, not devotees of either

side but men with feet in both camps, and what they want to do is help these two sorts of Bible people to benefit from each other's insights and experience at the local church level. I applaud their venture. It would be a mistake to treat their upbeat, well-rounded presentations as implying that once their points are taken all problems are solved and all troubles are over, but following their lead will be a big step forward toward the unity in truth and power that our times oblige us to seek. They did not waste their talents when they wrote *Empowered Evangelicals,* and you will not be wasting your time when you read it.

J.I. Packer

Authors' Preface

The genesis of this book is found in a series of lectures Rich gave for approximately one hundred leaders of various charismatic and Pentecostal groups. During those lectures, he suggested that a synthesis of the best of the conservative evangelical and charismatic worlds offered the best combination of qualities for Christian people as we enter the next millennium.

These lectures focused upon several pairs of items: for example, worship and teaching the Word, using our emotions and using our minds, valuing the supernatural world and valuing the natural world. Rich suggested that Christianity would be much stronger and more biblical if the best emphases of conservative evangelicalism could be combined with the best emphases of Pentecostalism. The lectures, by God's grace, were well received, particularly among the younger leaders.

Before we begin, we must ask the readers' indulgence for our choice of labels. No one within the body of Christ is particularly fond of labels. It would be nice if we could simply refer to all those who claim Jesus as Lord as "Christians" and stop there. But the fact remains that there are real differences among Christians, and if we are to consider these differences, we are forced to use labels. Thus, let us explain the book's use of the labels "conservative evangelical," "Pentecostal," and "charismatic."

Many Pentecostal denominations such as the Assemblies of God, the Church of God (Cleveland, Tennessee), and the Pentecostal Holiness Church have been involved in the National Association of Evangelicals (NAE) since its founding in the early 1940s. Several Pentecostals have served as Presidents of the NAE, including Assembly of God General Superintendent Thomas Zimmerman. Moreover, most Pentecostal denominations have very conservative doctrinal statements regarding the inspiration and authority of the Bible. Thus, most Pentecostals *are* evangelicals.

Alister McGrath, an English theologian, listed six characteristics of evangelicalism. In his opinion, these include:

1. the supreme authority of Scripture,
2. the majesty of Jesus Christ,
3. the Lordship of the Holy Spirit,
4. the need for personal conversion,
5. the priority of evangelism,
6. the importance of Christian community.

Mainstream Trinitarian Pentecostals clearly fulfill these six criteria.[1]

Nevertheless, in popular usage, conservative evangelicalism generally refers to that portion of evangelicalism that is *noncharismatic*. In the United States, conservative evangelicalism would be represented by the leadership of Billy Graham and Carl Henry, the magazine *Christianity Today,* and seminaries such as Trinity Evangelical Divinity School, Gordon Cornwell Theological Seminary, and Fuller Theological Seminary. In England noncharismatic conservative evangelicalism is best represented by the leadership of John Stott and James I. Packer.

To complicate matters further, beginning in the 1960s many

distinctively Pentecostal practices such as speaking in tongues and a felt "baptism in the Holy Spirit" began to be widely experienced by people outside the historic Pentecostal denominations. Some of these practitioners were in nonevangelical, mainline denominations such as the Roman Catholic Church, the Episcopal Church, the United Methodist Church, and the American Lutheran Church. These people began to be known as "charismatics" or "neo-Pentecostals." Many, such as Larry Christenson, Dennis Bennett, and Michael Harper, have attempted to explain their experiences in terms of their denomination's traditions.[2]

Finally, there is a growing number of people who hail from noncharismatic conservative evangelical backgrounds but have adopted certain classical Pentecostal practices such as healing the sick, casting out demons, and receiving prophetic revelations.[3] Many of these people (we are among them) believe that the so-called "baptism in the Holy Spirit" happens at conversion and is not a second work of grace subsequent to the new birth. They also believe that tongues is simply one of many spiritual gifts and not the only evidence of a particular spiritual experience. Many of these people still see themselves as conservative evangelicals, theologically and culturally, and have sought to relate their experiences of the Holy Spirit's power to conservative evangelical beliefs. What should such people be called?

C. Peter Wagner, one of the leading church growth authorities in the world and professor at Fuller Theological Seminary's School of World Mission, calls such people "Third Wave" Christians. He does so because in the American experience, the practice of certain spiritual gifts moved from the Pentecostal denominations (first wave), to the charismatic movement (second wave), to conservative evangelical churches (third wave).

We very much appreciate Dr. Wagner's groundbreaking

work as he attempts to understand and label the characteristics of this latter group of Christians. However, we generally haven't adopted the term "Third Wave" for three reasons:

1. It takes into account only the experience of Americans in the twentieth century and has limited cross-cultural value.

2. The Holy Spirit's activity is better described as a continually flowing river since the day of Pentecost; three waves or two hundred waves hardly does justice to the Holy Spirit's continuing activity, even if confined to the United States.

3. The term "Third Wave" has been employed by futurists such as Alvin Toeffler and has a popular meaning completely different from the one intended by C. Peter Wagner.

So what label should be given to conservative evangelical who regularly heal the sick in the power of the Holy Spirit, ca: out demons, have a low-key perspective regarding tongue and regularly receive prophecies? We have chosen to call suc people "Empowered Evangelicals." Of course, immediate one might believe we are demeaning the experience of tho: who don't regularly practice healings or deliverance. Are Bil Graham or John Stott *unempowered*? Of course not!

Then why did we choose such a potentially misundersto term? Because we wanted to capture the emphases of the two worlds described in this book. Pentecostals and charismatics have historically emphasized *power*, thus the word "empowered." Conservative evangelicals have historically been concerned with the *evangel*—the good news of salvation that God has made known in Jesus Christ. Combining the concerns of Pentecostals and charismatics with the overriding concern of conservative evangelicals, we have chosen the term "Empowered Evangelicals."

Our prayer is that our book might be received in the irenic spirit in which it was intended, despite our occasional critique:

of what we see as possible weaknesses in the two worlds described. We intend to build a bridge, so that travelers from either world might grow to appreciate and love the strengths of the other world. If more churches choose, as a result of reading this book, to focus on preaching the evangel and couple that preaching with the practices of healing, prophecy, and intimate worship, we will feel that God has answered our prayer.

Rich Nathan and Ken Wilson

ONE

Looking for the Best of Both Worlds

"You can't have your cake and eat it, too." It's an old, familiar adage. Mothers have quoted it for decades, especially to teenagers who notoriously want the freedom of adulthood without the responsibilities. Sometimes we just can't have it both ways.

But sometimes we can. We can, for example, experience worship that includes "spirit and truth," heartfelt intimacy, and thoughtful biblical exposition. We can pray for healing, believing God will heal, and still leave room for God to be God. And we can hear God's voice and feel God's leading, yet still respect God's Word as the ultimate source of revelation. Yes, we can have the best of both worlds. In fact, we believe God wants us to.

As stated in the authors' preface, the genesis of this book is found in a series of lectures I, Rich, gave for approximately one hundred leaders of various charismatic and Pentecostal groups. During those lectures I suggested that a synthesis of the best of the conservative evangelical and charismatic worlds offered the best combination of qualities for Christian people as we enter the next millennium. (See the preface for an explanation of our use of labels.)

Conservative evangelicals, for example, have been strong in communicating our universal human experience of suffering, unhealed pain, and disappointment in a fallen world, and that much of our healing awaits the second coming of Christ. But conservative evangelicals have been weaker in communicating the corresponding New Testament message that Christians can, right now, "taste... the powers of the age to come" (Hebrews 6:5). Christians are not simply called upon to "be there" for the suffering. Christians can also pray for healing and should often see substantial transformation.

On the other hand, Pentecostal and charismatic Christians have been strong in teaching people to pray for healing. But they have been weak precisely where conservative evangelicals are strongest, in explaining why many who are prayed for do not get well. In many circles, Christians actually feel more guilty and further away from God after prayer for healing fails to work than they did before the prayer was offered.

In a very real sense, however, I was simply describing my own spiritual journey. I ultimately chose to straddle the conservative evangelical and charismatic worlds because I see the strengths of both worlds articulated in the Bible. But I zigzagged back and forth for a while—as did my coauthor, Ken—before finding my place. For me, it began with Judaism.

SPIRITUAL JOURNEY

I was raised in a conservative Jewish family in New York City. I went to a Jewish parochial school for five years, where I learned Hebrew. I was bar mitzvah, a rite of passage for thirteen-year-old boys that celebrates their entrance into manhood. But by and large we were only culturally Jewish, meaning that we kept very little of the religious law.

I believed in God until about age ten. In fact, I used to pray the *Shema,* the central prayer of Judaism which is taken from Deuteronomy 6:4. "Hear, O Israel: The Lord our God, the Lord is one." I used to pray that prayer while my parents were fighting, which was often, and then I would add, "Please, God, don't let my parents get divorced. Keep us together as a family." But my parents did get divorced, and in the furnace of the turmoil that was my home, my faith, such as it was, vaporized.

By the time I was a teenager, I was an avowed agnostic. Looking back, I am not sure if I ever had one intelligent conversation about God that took God as a serious subject of consideration for thinking people in the twentieth century. I considered religious people to be "hold-overs" from another era. On the rare occasions when somebody did talk with me about religion, I had the kind of reaction that you might have if someone were describing the wonders of astrology to you. I deeply suspected that religious people either were not very intelligent or not in touch with the last four hundred years of modern history.

My first encounter with a Christian. During my first week of college, I noticed an extraordinarily attractive woman in my Psychology 101 class. Summoning up my courage, I sat down next to her one day and began to engage her in conversation. Because I was an avid reader, I asked what she had read that summer, noting that I had read a number of different contemporary authors. She said that she had read a few books by C.S. Lewis. Since I had never heard of C.S. Lewis, I assumed that he was an obscure nobody and probably not worth reading.

After class I asked her if she might want to go out drinking with me that weekend. Actually, I don't remember if I asked her to go drinking or to smoke pot. But I do recall her reaction to my invitation. She immediately said, "Oh, I am sorry; I don't do that. I am a Christian." I responded, "So what? I'm Jewish!" I didn't have any idea at the time how her being Christian had any possible relevance to whether she drank or smoked. It was almost as if she had said, "I don't drink. I have blond hair." What difference did being a Christian make?

She then explained in great detail exactly what she meant by "being a Christian." I thought, "Oh, no. This girl is religious." Marlene had very strict rules regarding whom she would date. Since I was a non-Christian, I was definitely outside the realm of anyone she would date.

In spite of our differences, we became friends over the next several months, and I had the opportunity to watch my new Christian friend. I discovered that she was an incredibly nice person, nicer than any of my other friends. She was scrupulously honest and would often apologize for the least lapse in truth-telling. I also watched her relate to the unpopular students on campus. She could have gone out with any guy on campus, yet she chose to relate to men and women no one else would accept.

During the first few months of our friendship, Marlene often tried to talk with me about Jesus. Although I was interested in her, I was completely uninterested in her Christianity. Sometimes she carried on monologues about some aspect of Christianity. Because I didn't respond, she assumed that I was interested in what she was saying; so she would talk on and on until I cut her off. On occasion, if the mood struck, I argued with her about her beliefs. Because I was a good arguer, I could manipulate what she said and turn it against her. I thought that I was getting the upper hand in our interactions. In fact, God was using Marlene to draw me to himself.

God was also using Marlene to show me my own sinfulness. As I noticed her goodness, I tried to imitate it. But no matter how hard I tried, my "nice periods" lasted little more than an hour at a time. Before I knew it, I would slip back into my cynical, sarcastic, New York mode of relating. I began to recognize my wickedness—not simply that I occasionally *did* bad things, but that *I* was bad and totally incapable of changing myself.

One incident stands out in my mind as the turning point in my spiritual journey. After several months of friendship, Marlene and I were in her dormitory room studying. She was studying sociology. I was mainly studying her. After about an hour of quietly studying, I reached over to her and put my arm around her shoulder in an attempt to pull her down on the bed. She immediately jumped up from the bed and just about took my head off, saying, "You have completely misunderstood the nature of our relationship!" She went on to tell me how shocked she was that I would try to do something like that.

Because I was embarrassed and had been caught, I did what many non-Christian guys would do in that situation: I lied! I said to her, "Marlene, what did you think I was going to do?" She was so pure-hearted, she thought that perhaps she had mistaken my intentions. I couldn't believe she actually swallowed my feigned shock at her response.

I then said, "Marlene, I am surprised at you. I would never think of doing such a thing" (in the most innocent tones that I could muster). After a few minutes, I had completely manipulated the situation so that she ended up apologizing to me. Once I had drawn an apology from her, I let her off the hook by saying, "Don't worry, there is no offense taken. I completely understand how you might have misinterpreted my actions!"

After I left Marlene's room that evening, I was shaken. For the first time in my life, I realized that I was a really bad person. Here was a girl who was decent and trusting and I had attempted to take advantage of her. Then when she caught me,

I didn't even have the courage to honestly acknowledge that I had done something wrong. Whereas confession came so easily for Marlene, confession of wrongdoing was virtually impossible for me. I knew I needed help with the badness that I now felt inside me. Later on, I would recognize this incident as the "conviction of sin." At the time, I only knew that there was something deeply wrong with me.

Perhaps Marlene sensed that God was working in my life, or perhaps it was simply a sovereignly ordained invitation by God. Either way, Marlene invited me to the little Assemblies of God church that she was attending so that I might assist her teen group leader in a Passover service. She told me that they needed someone who knew something about Passover to say a few of the prayers. I later found out that her real intention was to get me to the Passover dinner so that I might hear a Jewish believer in Jesus describe the Passover in terms of what Christ had done for us.

His entire presentation made sense to me. Having gone through the Passover ritual for many years, it was suddenly infused with new meaning. It was as if the dry canal that had been dug in my life was filled with flowing water. By the end of the evening, I was certain of two things: the story of Jesus was true, and I wanted to become his follower.

For me, as a Jew, I knew that there would be no turning back. This new commitment that I made changed everything in my life. All of my Jewish friends quickly learned that something had happened to me. My parents and my sisters learned about it as well. My world went through a revolution. When I "joined up," I realized that there was a price to be paid. But because I knew that Jesus was true, I was very willing, at the time, to pay the price.

Jesus more than met me. For the first month after my Christian commitment, I was filled with joy and with a sense of God's presence. I *knew* I was born again! My friends thought that I had gone off the deep end, particularly since I no longer did drugs with them or went out drinking. Even my musical tastes began to change. I was becoming a different person.

The heavens open in California. The summer after my conversion, I drove out to California to build houses with my dad. Before I left, Marlene gave me a book to read called *They Speak With Other Tongues,* by John Sherrill. While I don't recall anything about the book now (or even if I would currently agree with Sherrill's arguments), at the time the book created a clear desire in me to receive the spiritual gift of tongues. One evening, after I finished reading the book, I took a long walk around a lake by my father's apartment. I said to the Lord, "I would like to become more intimate with you. You know it is my desire to pray better and to get to know you better. Please give me the gift of tongues." Then it seemed to me that the heavens opened, and I felt something like electricity go through my body. I began, without effort, to speak in a language that I had not previously learned. The experience lasted for about twenty minutes as I walked around the lake and spoke in this unknown language.

Showdown at the student union. When I returned to college in the fall, I was still excited about my newfound gift. Marlene was part of the only Christian organization on campus—InterVarsity Christian Fellowship—and I began attending meetings with her. At our campus, InterVarsity was made up of an ecumenical group of conservative Baptists, some students who attended an Evangelical Free church, a few Roman Catholics, and a few charismatics such as Marlene. At the time, I was not aware of all of the disagreements between these various groups. Nor was I particularly sensitive to the fact that some Christians did not believe in a modern-day expression of certain spiritual gifts. Since I had so little schooling in theology or even in the proper use of gifts, I prayed aloud in my newfound language. It didn't occur to me that I would offend anyone!

I then made another serious mistake, again quite innocently. Marlene and I also attended a little charismatic fellowship on Friday evenings, where a Pentecostal pastor occasionally spoke. Because I liked him, I thought that he would be a wonderful speaker at our InterVarsity meeting on campus. I recommended to the coordinator that he invite Pastor Fred to attend one of our meetings the following month.

When Pastor Fred came, he immediately offended most of the group by saying that he "hadn't prepared anything but he would simply speak as the Holy Spirit led." It was quite common in those days for charismatics to use that kind of language. In any case, he then gave a fairly well-prepared teaching. But he proceeded to give what he called a prophecy regarding the group, and then he walked around the room laying hands on the now stunned conservative evangelical students while praying over them in tongues.

I knew I was in trouble when most of the students silently walked out of the room, too upset to talk to Marlene or me about the evening's events. The faculty advisor for InterVarsity called a meeting of the entire group a few days later and said that we needed to get all of the issues out regarding Pentecostalism and see where the InterVarsity group at our campus was going to be headed. What had happened at the previous meeting had offended many students, and if it continued to happen, most of the students would not return.

I spent the next few days reading booklets and pamphlets produced by Marlene's church. The booklets attempted to prove from various passages that there was an experience called the "baptism in the Holy Spirit" that often followed conversion. That experience was, according to the pamphlets, always evidenced by speaking in other tongues. Having memorized the arguments laid out in these pamphlets, I went to the meeting at the student union, fully prepared to deal with the conservative evangelicals who were upset by the events of the previous week.

As I began to set forth my parroted arguments, the faculty advisor dismantled them one by one. He pointed out that in the Bible there was only *one* baptism (see Ephesians 4:5). He pointed out from 1 Corinthians 12:13 that every Christian is "baptized by one Spirit into one body whether Jews or Greeks, slave or free." He also pointed out from the Book of Acts a very different and, in fact, more convincing interpretation of the passages that I had presented. By the end of the meeting, Marlene and I were the clear losers, in terms of the Pentecostal theology that we were pushing. I became convinced that the faculty advisor and the rest of my friends in the InterVarsity group were, in fact, correct and that we had made a serious error.

Becoming a conservative evangelical. For the next several years, my Christianity took on a very different look. I learned how to do inductive Bible studies (always with a notebook and pen). I became the chapter president of our InterVarsity group and led small-group Bible studies for the next three years in my apartment.

I became an avid reader of Christian literature and theology, particularly theology from a Reformed perspective. I read every book suggested to me by my mentors. I didn't know at the time that I had only been exposed to a narrow stream of the Christian theological tradition. None of my mentors put me in touch with Christianity's mystical tradition or any revival literature. Nor did I ever read anything by a serious charismatic or Pentecostal writer. In my mind a two-tiered system of theology was being established. The upper tier was represented by solid, respectable, intelligent theologians who generally wrote from a noncharismatic, Reformed perspective. The lower tier was made up of authors that my InterVarsity friends and I had never read because we suspected they probably had very little to say. And what they did have to say was likely inaccurate.

I remembered my experience in California, and I knew that something dramatic had happened to me—something that was real and was from God. However, the issue of the charismatic gifts was growing much less important for me. The bulk of my Christian life was consumed with a growing conservative evangelical perspective of the Christian life that was mainly concerned with sound Bible teaching, seeing people converted, personal discipleship, and a classroom model of discipleship that emphasized reading and discussing but not necessarily "doing" or "experiencing" Christianity.

Looking back, I see that I was gradually slipping back into the worldview that I had possessed before I became a Christian. I increasingly adopted my friends' view that God was not to be felt or experienced today. My friends and mentors did not expect to hear from God, except through the written Word of God in the Bible. They never talked about charismatic gifts. For this reason, I began to believe that if charismatic gifts existed, they were "on the margin" of the Christian life and not very important.

We also weren't trained to experience spiritual phenomena except in totally naturalistic terms. For example, one time a girl from a very troubled background came to our small-group Bible study. During our time of conversational prayer, the girl fell to the ground and began to choke. We didn't know what was wrong with her. One of the students got up to get her a glass of water. I remember wondering while I watched her writhing on the ground if she had a demon. But no one that I knew spoke about such things, and I thought that perhaps I was being a little fanatical. Over the next few weeks, every time our group would begin conversational prayer, this girl would fall to the ground and begin to writhe and choke, while her eyes rolled up in her head. I became convinced that she did, in fact, have a demon. Not knowing what to do, I set up an appointment for her to meet with our conservative evangelical pastor. He determined that she had a troubled family background, and his approach was entirely psychological and therapeutic. (Indeed she may have had a troubled family history, but this did not account for what we witnessed.) Unfortunately, he probably didn't have a framework for dealing with a possible case of demonization. The girl was not helped, and she drifted out of our InterVarsity group.

A fresh encounter with the Holy Spirit. Nearly a dozen years passed from the time "the heavens opened" for me in California. Then the shape of my Christianity changed during the winter of 1985 at a Christian conference. A few of us picked up the conference speaker at the airport. He was to address a men's conference for the six or seven local churches that made up our particular church association. Our churches consisted of conservative evangelical baby boomers who, like me, had been saved in the late 1960s and the early 1970s. We were all theoretically open to the existence of charismatic gifts, but almost entirely lacking in charismatic experience.

We had a few hours before the men's conference to talk with the speaker over dinner. I used that time to subtly "check him out." In the course of conversation, I asked about his background and schooling. A person's academic credentials meant a great deal to me at the time. The speaker basically brushed me off, saying that he had done some academic work at the University of Southern California. I was, obviously, seeking more information about exactly what kind of academic work he had done at Southern Cal, but he didn't volunteer any more. Nor did he give me much information regarding the theological camp he identified with or the books he found most helpful in developing his own philosophy of ministry. In fact, he seemed particularly uninterested in attempting to impress me with his knowledge or credentials. I found the pre-meeting time with him frustrating because I couldn't place him on the map that I was attempting to draw.

The evening meeting went well. The speaker gave a decent presentation from the Bible about evangelism and the Holy Spirit. Nothing was theologically wrong with what he said, although several times I thought that he could have nuanced his points better. Overall, I thought his presentation was solid and entirely acceptable to me as a conservative evangelical. He ended his teaching abruptly with the statement that he was now going to hold "a clinic time" and demonstrate the power of the Holy Spirit, of which he had just spoken. He said that we should all keep our eyes open and watch what happened. The atmosphere was very unemotional; he certainly was not a dynamic, razzle-dazzle kind of speaker. Indeed, he read most of his material from an outline and delivered it in a matter-of-fact tone. But now it was "clinic time"—a term that I had never heard before, nor did I anticipate what it would mean.

He asked the audience of about two hundred men to stand, and he said that he was going to "invite the Holy Spirit to come." I didn't understand what he meant since the Holy Spirit is omnipresent and I assumed he was already at the meeting. The man prayed very simply, "Holy Spirit, come," and then we waited silently for about a minute. I began feeling a bit uncomfortable. I wasn't exactly sure what he was looking for or aiming at in terms of effect. After about a minute's waiting, the speaker said, "The Holy Spirit is beginning to touch people over on the right side of the room." I looked over to the right side of the room to see what particular phenomenon the speaker was referring to. I saw a man who was obviously shaking.

The speaker told us all to sit down and invited the trembling man to come forward. He could barely walk because he was shaking so violently. The speaker told us to look at this man who was shaking. He pointed out that one of the ways you could tell that the Holy Spirit was doing something was through a physical phenomenon. According to him, these phenomena could include shaking, glistening on a person's face, or a sense of peace on the person.

I was becoming increasingly uncomfortable with the whole scene. On an emotional level, I did not enjoy watching someone shake, nor did I appreciate any person being used as an object lesson in front of a whole group. I moved from a neutral, somewhat questioning position to increasing hostility as the speaker explained his view of various Holy Spirit-created phenomena.

Then the speaker asked the man who was shaking to hold up one of his hands and to bless the audience. The man held up a trembling hand and said over the group, "I bless you. I bless you in the name of Jesus." Then it happened! It was almost as if a lightning bolt leaped off the man's hand and struck one of my closest and dearest friends from our church. This friend was someone I had known for almost a decade. Until that moment, I would have described him as rock-solid, very conservative, not the kind of person to be easily caught up in the emotion of a group. He had his master's degree in chemical engineering and was the plant manager of a large chemical company in Columbus. But when the man with the trembling hand began to bless the group, my friend also began to tremble violently. I didn't know the man who was initially brought forward, so I had no idea about his emotional stability. But I did know my friend, and I knew him to be emotionally stable. Yet here he was, his whole body shaking.

After that, pandemonium broke out in the room. A few men began to cry. Others fell down. Still others began to shake. As I observed the different phenomena that were breaking out around me, I stepped back to the stage area where the speaker had been. I did not like what I was observing. I was uncomfortable with emotional displays. I didn't understand why well-educated men were reacting this way. I decided that I was not going to allow myself to be carried away with this kind of emotionalism.

Then without warning, I began to feel a heavy weight pressing down upon my head. Since I was standing ten or fifteen feet from the nearest person, I knew that no one was touching me. Yet I felt like a gigantic hand was pushing me down toward the ground. I began wondering whether I, too, was being carried away with the emotion in the room, so I sat down and told myself to "get a grip on it." I thought that I would be able to relax and regain my composure if I simply sat down. Unfortunately for me, sitting down wasn't sufficient. The great weight I felt continued to press me toward the ground. My response seems laughable now, but I put my elbows in back of me on the stage to brace myself so that I wouldn't be pushed down any further. By putting my elbows in back of me, I thought I would be able to push myself back up. Still, as much as I pushed up, this tremendous weight kept pushing me back down. One of my old friends from a sister congregation saw me attempting to push up against the weight that I was feeling, and he very gently said to me, "Rich, why are you resisting the Holy Spirit so violently?"

I broke! I began to cry as I suddenly realized that my emotional opposition to what was going on, both in the room and to me, was in fact opposition to the work of the Holy Spirit. Somehow, despite my early intimacy with the Holy Spirit's presence, I had lost my ability to appreciate and respond to his presence. Thus, when God wanted to reduce me to dust and ashes before him, I, like the apostle Paul, chose to "kick against the goads" and resisted the Spirit's movement.

PUTTING THE PIECES TOGETHER

After telling the story of this men's conference, I must quickly say that I do not believe that every person needs to have a dramatic experience like me, or forever be consigned to second-class Christianity. God works differently in all of our lives. Just as our salvation experiences vary radically, despite our common belief in Christ, so our lives in Christ will also vary in terms of the number and intensity of our spiritual experiences.[1] It seems to me that the Christian life is like a giant mosaic in which God fits colored tiles in different places in our lives. All Christians try to make sense of the mosaic of their lives. Here is how I currently fit the pieces of my life in Christ together.

Despite all of the conservative evangelical friends I had made and literature I had read over the years, I never became anti-charismatic. I simply had no place for my experience or for my understanding of the spiritual gifts in the rest of my theology. It was as if the spiritual gifts mentioned in 1 Corinthians 12 and 14 were tied to the bulk of my theology like a balloon tied to a large cement block. My early experience of the gift of tongues was thoroughly unintegrated into the rest of my Christian life. So by the time I went to that men's conference, I had culturally and theologically taken on all of the beliefs and practices of my noncharismatic conservative evangelical friends.

From them I had learned to respect reading and education. I learned to value the historical-grammatical approach to interpreting the Scriptures and gained a passion for accuracy in theology. I learned to value world missions and evangelism. In fact, leading the lost to Christ became my lifelong passion. My friends taught me that one of the most basic aims of the Christian life is to see others get saved. I still believe that evangelism and world missions are a primary target for me and for the church I now pastor.

But I also picked up some of my conservative evangelical friends' negative baggage. I didn't realize at the time that my conservative evangelical friends neglected major blocks of biblical teaching about experiencing God. They didn't speak very much about personal intimacy with God and they placed a low value on worship. Singing hymns was really just a warm-up to why we really went to church—to hear excellent expository teaching.

My friends also didn't teach me to value supernatural guidance, although I did know a few people in our church who claimed to "hear from God." While I respected those people and sensed a reality in their spiritual experiences, I figured that I was wired differently than they were. They seemed to be the creative, artistic types. In contrast, I had a very rational, analytical mind. After college I went on to law school and then to teach law at Ohio State University. I simply figured that those who reported hearing words or seeing visions from God had experienced something intended only for them—things that would never happen to *me*.

As a result of the men's conference, I realized I needed to take a fresh look at my Christianity. On the one hand, I didn't and still don't see a second baptism in the Holy Spirit clearly laid out in the Scriptures. I certainly didn't and still don't believe that tongues are a necessary evidence for the Spirit's baptism, or that tongues are necessary for being involved in other spiritual gifts. Moreover, my conservative evangelical training has put me on edge regarding the seeming credulity of some Pentecostals. I didn't and still don't like some of the overuse of spiritual-sounding words such as "anointing," and I didn't and still don't enjoy an overly emotional atmosphere, although my definition of "overly emotional" has radically changed since that men's conference. I continue to be wary of emotional manipulation and what feels like spiritual hype. In sum, conservative evangelicalism has put in me a desire for something solid, something real. I am interested only in experiences that are clearly found in the written Word of God.

On the other hand, in reflecting on the Scriptures in recent years, I am more open to the possibility that my previous Christian experience was somewhat deficient. The more I study the Bible, the more I see that biblical Christianity is thoroughly supernatural in its orientation. Demons often manifested themselves when Jesus was present, and these demonic manifestations were not explained away as mere psychological or emotional responses (the way my pastor explained away the demonized student's problems). Why shouldn't Christians today be as thoroughly supernatural in orientation as the church in the Book of Acts? I now realize that I also didn't have much room in my first decade of Christianity for experiences of God's Spirit—at least not the kinds of spiritual experiences that people in the Bible had. Most of my approach to God was intellectual and mental. The notion that God's Spirit might produce an overwhelming sense of awe so that a person would cry out like Isaiah, "Woe to me, I am undone!" was considered theoretically possible, but not realistically expected by anyone I knew.

While I was in the process of reevaluating my Christianity, I believe that God allowed me to meet John Wimber of Vineyard Ministries International to provide me with a new model of conservative evangelicalism. In my reassessment, I was looking for someone who believed all the things that I did about the Bible. These would include the Bible's infallibility, the deity of Christ, justification by grace alone through faith alone, the substitutionary atonement, the physical resurrection, the imminent return of Jesus Christ, *and* the priority of evangelism and world missions without the Pentecostal add-ons of a necessary second baptism in the Holy Spirit or speaking in tongues as the doorway to an experience of other spiritual gifts. As I attended some of his meetings, I found

John Wimber to be nonhyped in his teaching style. I never felt emotionally manipulated, but I did realize that I was being presented a different kind of conservative evangelicalism than I had been exposed to previously.

For example, much of John's teaching was from the Gospels. The epistles, and particularly Paul's letters, had been the primary source of my faith and practice and were placed above the Gospels. In other words, the conservative evangelical churches that I attended preferred theology over historical narrative. Moreover, Jesus was presented as an example to me only in relation to his character and his nonsupernatural activities such as teaching or evangelism. I began wondering whether Jesus could be a model for me, not only of nonsupernatural things, but for supernatural things as well. Until I began rereading the Gospels, I honestly did not see that there were dozens and dozens of verses in which Jesus' teaching was inextricably tied to supernatural healings or to demonic expulsions. Essentially, I had learned to cut New Testament sentences in half, holding on to the teaching part of Jesus' ministry without the demonstration of works of power.

I now see that deeds and demonstrations of the Spirit's power are a vital part of Christianity. Again, no conservative evangelical I ever met teaches that Christianity was meant to be simply words. But the utter neglect of teaching on such common gospel subjects as healing, deliverance, and hearing directly from the Holy Spirit made these subjects seem superfluous compared to the main body of my faith and practice.

THE CONSERVATIVE EVANGELICAL ASSISTED BY CHARISMATIC POWER

I feel as if I am being asked by God to walk through a forest into which a path has not been clearly blazed, at least not by the predominant theological schools in the United States today. As I talk with younger conservative evangelicals, I find an enormous hunger and desire for intimacy with God and biblical spiritual experiences. I regularly meet people who are hungry to worship God, who are passionate about hearing God's voice, and who long to see some demonstration of the Holy Spirit's fullness whether in physical healing, healing of emotional traumas, or deliverance from demonic oppression.

I also meet many charismatic and Pentecostal people who long for rationality in their faith, who want to hear solid preaching of the Bible based on sound interpretive methods, and who are tired of being promised unbroken triumphs in a world filled with obvious pain and suffering. Many charismatics also reject emotionalism and struggle with the theological packaging of spiritual gifts and even the "style" of their church's worship. In sum, I continually meet people who have come to the place in their lives where they are looking for the best of the conservative evangelical world and the best of the charismatic, Pentecostal world. They want conservative evangelical theology in the main, but they also want certain charismatic practices and experiences. They want evangelism to be a priority and they want that evangelism fueled by the power of the Holy Spirit.

By God's grace, I have been able to walk this tricky high-wire act in the context of a church community that loves God and wants all that he has for us. We started with about a hundred young conservative evangelicals. It probably helped that we and the church were young. We had the energy to clean up lots of messes and the flexibility to experiment within the bounds of Scripture, but without the added pressure of 150 years of church tradition or standing committees!

The conversion from a more typical conservative evangelical background to this new synthesis took us several years. Along the way we found that many of our assumptions regarding such issues as the place of worship or the supernatural in the church needed radical reassessment. But there were other areas, such as healing, deliverance, and hearing God's voice, that needed more than reassessment. They had been so neglected that they were entirely missing from our church's practice. Fears, discomfort, cultural biases, and legitimate theological questioning all needed addressing as we moved forward. But God has been gracious in this journey and has been merciful with us as we slowly (sometimes very slowly) moved forward.

Today, a decade after that men's conference, we now number over two thousand. And we are more committed than ever to "the Scriptures [and] the power of God" (Matthew 22:29).

Can we have the best of both worlds? Can a bridge be built that brings the two worlds together? We believe it can. To us, the most exciting aspect is the marriage of the conservative evangelicals' historic target—the salvation of the lost—with charismatic power to get the job done. Imagine a church that experiences joyful intimacy with God, that regularly sees sick people healed, that tunes in to God's voice and worships with body, emotions, and Spirit, but employs the power of the Spirit not for a "spiritual buzz" but for evangelism and world missions! Imagine churches that experience powerful spiritual life, but channel that life toward the world. We call such churches *empowered evangelical* churches. It is to encourage the planting and multiplying of empowered evangelical churches that we have written this book.

TWO

Evangelicals and Charismatics: Children of Revival

Until I reached college, I, Ken, didn't have much interest in family history. The reminiscences of older relatives and those dusty scrapbooks with photographs of dour-faced, tight-collared ancestors held no fascination for me—at least, not until I wanted to understand why our family functioned the way it did. Why did some relatives have little to do with the rest of the family? How did issues like divorce, alcohol abuse, and religious faith play themselves out in previous generations? What accounted for the characteristic strengths and unexplained tensions in our family?

When I experienced conversion to Jesus at the age of nineteen, I received a warm letter from my Great Uncle Stuart, about whom I knew precious little. He wrote that he had been praying for my salvation every day since my birth. My father's response to my newfound faith, though gracious, wasn't nearly as enthusiastic. As I probed the family's religious history, I discovered two branches on my father's side: devout Plymouth Brethren and the black sheep of the family who chafed under the Brethren yoke. My great-uncle was from the devout

35

branch; my grandfather was the black sheep. (My own father, I learned, wrote a spirited defense of atheism at the age of thirteen.) Without my realizing it, my conversion was touching some tender family nerves. My father and I have subsequently come to appreciate our Brethren heritage, but we're both keenly aware of the danger of religious judgmentalism that his father experienced. We've been touched by the family history.

Any time we join in fellowship with a body of Christians, we're walking into a family with a long history. Each church has a fascinating heritage of heroism, courage, faithfulness—and conflicts, controversies, and family tensions. Each church has a story it can't help telling: a combination of the brightest Shakespearean comedy and the darkest tragedy, all rubbing shoulders with the gospel story. We hear the echoes of these stories from the pulpit every Sunday; they are played out in the activities of the church. Whether we understand the source of these inherited tensions or not, we can usually feel them. Why does this church respond to sickness as it does? Why does the pastor teach certain things about what it means to receive the Spirit? All these are profoundly influenced by the congregation's family history, its story.

The issues that we're concerned with in this book have been the subject of a boiling pot of debate, bold experimentation, divine intervention, and varied human interpretations covering several generations. In order to learn from the best of the evangelical and charismatic worlds, we'll need to know a little bit about the family history of each tradition. In the process, we'll discover how much the two camps have in common.

CONSERVATIVE EVANGELICALS AND CHARISMATICS: CHILDREN OF REVIVAL

When we took my son to a nationally renowned headache institute, we learned that the traditional categories for diagnosing headaches (tension, migraine, cluster) weren't holding up to a developing understanding of head pain. Instead of sharply differentiated categories, specialists are viewing head pain along a continuum in which the categories tend to blur.

The same could be said for the labels that we've used for theologically conservative Christians. Twenty years ago, churches were either charismatic or noncharismatic—and never the twain should meet. But things are changing and the categories are blurring. When our church moved to a new town, the local Baptist minister asked me if we were charismatic. "Depends on what you mean by 'charismatic,'" I replied, which led to a stimulating and enjoyable conversation. In the heat of earlier controversies, more energy went into drawing sharper lines. But the story of the conservative evangelical and charismatic movements reveals more blending of these categories than one might think.

Conservative evangelicals and charismatics have many things in common, including a history of revivals. In fact, the history of these two streams is *primarily* a history of revivals. The common themes are a stirring of religious fervor, a renewed emphasis on the fundamentals of Christian faith, and an awakening to the presence and power of the risen Lord Jesus. Revivals stir believers, stimulate conversion of nonbelievers, and often result in social reforms in the broader society.

Protestant Reformation: the great-grandaddy of revivals. The Protestant era began with a widespread revival in Europe: the Protestant Reformation. The Reformation ushered in the hallmarks of evangelical faith and practice: the necessity of conversion, salvation by faith apart from works, the priesthood of all believers, and the need for the ongoing reform of the church. This latter emphasis established the concept of revival as part of the genetic code of the Protestant movement. Like other revivals before and since, the Reformation was marked by conflict and controversy, not simply from the established church of the time, but within the various expressions of those seeking reform. Some of the sharpest Reformation controversies took place among Lutheran, Reformed (Calvinist), and Anabaptist approaches to reformation.

The cycle of revival continued in the seventeenth century among the Puritans in England, Ireland, and Scotland. Consider the following account of an outbreak of revival during that era: "There was so convincing an appearance of God, and downpouring of the Spirit, even in an extraordinary way, that did follow the ordinances, especially that sermon on Monday June 21 [1630] with a strange unusual motion on the hearers."[1]

The Great Awakening. The eighteenth century witnessed a revival in England and North America called "the Great Awakening." George Whitefield, a young Anglican clergyman with a powerful voice, took the daring step of addressing the unchurched in open field meetings, a radical violation of the British sense of propriety among churchmen. In his journal, Whitefield recalled a typical scene:

The open firmament above me, the prospect of the adjacent fields, with the sight of thousands of thousands, some in coaches, some on horseback and some in the trees, and at all times affected and drenched in tears together, to which was added the solemnity of the approaching evening, was almost too much for, and quite overwhelmed me.[2]

Estimates of these open-air crowds numbered in the tens of thousands—listening to Whitefield without the benefit of electrical sound systems.

Whitefield also worked closely and at times disputed sharply with John and Charles Wesley, the founders of Methodism.

In the United States, Jonathan Edwards became the leading

theologian and defender of the Great Awakening. Edwards delivered his well-crafted, tightly reasoned sermons in a voice filled with conviction but lacking Whitefield's animation. He read portions of his lengthy sermons through thick glasses. Despite his lack of excitement, the effect on his hearers was dramatic. At times, the reserved New England parishioners interrupted his homilies with shrieks, sobbing, falling over, and shaking. These "manifestations" were never encouraged by Edwards, but he defended them as genuine effects of the Spirit on his listeners. To varying degrees, Whitefield and the Wesleys witnessed similar phenomena during the course of their ministries.

The Great Awakening is a wonderful reminder that charismatics are not the only Christians with a history of unusual phenomena attributed to the Spirit's presence. These people who occasionally cried out, shook, trembled, and fell over (perhaps even rolled!) were not particularly interested in charismatic gifts of the Spirit such as tongues, prophecy, and healing. If we saw them carrying on today we might be tempted to bet the mortgage that they were wild-eyed charismatics. We would lose the mortgage.

One Great Awakening deserves another. The Second Great Awakening of the late eighteenth and early nineteenth centuries, though not as widespread as its namesake, still had immense impact. The abolitionist movement and the underground railroad were fueled largely by those touched by the fires of this revival.

Charles Finney, a Presbyterian law clerk, was one of the chief voices in this awakening. Finney is regarded by many as the father of modern evangelistic techniques, paving the way for such noted evangelists as D.L. Moody, Billy Sunday, and Billy Graham. His experience of the Spirit's power, an empowering for ministry that sounds strikingly similar to the charismatic "baptism in the Spirit," demonstrates the common heritage of conservative evangelicals and charismatics. Finney wrote:

> The Holy Spirit descended upon me in a manner that seemed to go through me, body and soul. I could feel the impression, like a wave of electricity, going through and through me. Indeed it seemed to come in waves and waves of liquid love.... It seemed like the very breath of God.... I wept aloud with joy and love; and I do not know but I should say, I literally bellowed out the unutterable gushings of my heart. These waves came over me, and over me, and over me, one after the other, until I recollect I cried out, "I shall die if these waves continue to pass over me." I said, "Lord, I cannot bear any more."[3]

D.L. Moody, for whom the Moody Bible Institute and Moody Press were named, did not hold to a charismatic view of baptism in the Spirit either, but he had an experience which rivals Finney's before him and the experience of Pentecostals after him.

> One day, in the city of New York—oh what a day!—I cannot describe it, I seldom refer to it; it is almost too sacred an experience to name. Paul had an experience of which he never spoke for fourteen years. I can only say that God revealed Himself to me, and I had such an experience of His love that I had to ask Him to stay his hand. I went to preaching again. The sermons were not different; I did not present new truths, and yet hundreds were converted. I would not now be placed back where I was before that blessed experience if you should give me all the world.[4]

Holiness and Healing. In addition to Moody's evangelistic campaigns, two other movements, the Holiness and Healing movements of the nineteenth century, provided the historical background to the modern day Pentecostal and charismatic movements. Historians trace the modern Holiness movement (which gave birth to over a hundred holiness denominations) to a series of camp meetings that began after the Civil War with the declared purpose of promoting Christian holiness. During this time people began to speak of an experience subsequent to conversion called "baptism in the Spirit." The term was not unknown prior to the Holiness movement, but it became part of the everyday vocabulary during that time. The chief effect of this Spirit baptism was an "entire sanctification" which gave the believer a secure victory over sin. Holiness camp meetings were anything but staid affairs, witnessing many of the same manifestations that characterized earlier revivals.[5]

Many of those influenced by these holiness teachings also began to teach about divine healing, including A.B. Simpson, Ethan Allen, and Maria B. Woodworth-Etter. Miraculous healings of physical ailments were reported through their ministries. Visible manifestations of the Spirit's power were also characteristic, like this description of one of Woodworth-Etter's meetings:

> Many of the most intelligent and best dressed men would fall back in their seats, with their hands held up to God, being held under the mighty power of God. Men and women fell, all over the tent, like trees in a storm.[6]

Once again, it is clear from church history that charismatics don't have a monopoly on the market of spiritual experience.

TWENTIETH-CENTURY REVIVALS

The twentieth century—referred to by some as the "Post-Christian era"—has, in fact, been a time of widespread spiritual ferment. Statistician David Barrett has traced the impact of three waves of renewal in the twentieth century: Pentecostal, Charismatic, and Mainstream (or Evangelical) Church Renewal (dubbed a Third Wave of renewal by C. Peter Wagner.)[7] Together, these three waves account for 21 percent of worldwide Christianity.[8]

The birth of modern Pentecostalism (resulting in denominations such as the Church of God in Christ and the Assemblies of God) is frequently traced to an event at the Bethel Healing Home in Topeka, Kansas, led by Charles Parham. Parham's personal history exemplifies the impact of revivals in the church. As a one-time Methodist minister, he had roots in the First and Second Great Awakenings. However, he left the Methodist church after developing an interest in the teachings of the Holiness movement and in the prospect of divine healing. (Parham was greatly weakened by viral encephalitis as an infant and suffered recurring bouts of rheumatic fever.) His Bethel Healing Home was a center for the teaching of the Holiness and Healing movements.[9]

Happy New Year! On the eve of the twentieth century, Parham prayed for a woman named Agnes Ozman to receive the baptism of the Holy Spirit. "I had scarcely repeated three dozen sentences," Parham recounts, betraying a predilection for long prayers, "when a glory fell upon her, a halo seemed to surround her head and face, and she began speaking in the Chinese language, and was unable to speak English for three days."[10]

Although speaking in a language unknown to the speaker (also called "glossolalia" or "speaking in tongues") was an occasional occurrence, it was not part of the Holiness experience of Spirit baptism, which was more closely identified with an empowering for service and holiness. But Parham and his students began to connect baptism in the Spirit with speaking in tongues. Miss Ozman's experience inspired a series of meetings in which most of the students at Parham's school, including Parham himself, began to speak in tongues.[11] The experience was viewed as a new Pentecost.

The Pentecostal movement didn't gain powerful momentum, however, until 1906, when a black preacher named William Seymour led a series of meetings which became known as the Azusa Street Revival in California (near Los Angeles). Historian John Nichol described Azusa Street as a "veritable Pentecostal mecca to which pilgrims from all over the world came and from which the news of supernatural signs and wonders was broadcast."[12]

The Azusa Street meetings were a sight to behold. Observers describe a remarkable mix of blacks and whites, men and women, from many different church backgrounds, all joined in worship marked by extremes of joy, sorrow for sin, fillings with the Spirit, and healings from physical ailments. William Seymour, the uneducated leader of the meetings, could be seen seated near the front with a paper bag over his head to allow for undistracted prayer in preparation for the service.[13]

The Pentecostal revival is arguably one of the most widespread and sustained experiences of revival in church history, with dramatic growth internationally, and over 193 million adherents by 1990.[14] (This figure does not include subsequent revivals spawned by the Pentecostal movement.) Pentecostals incorporated emphases of previous revivals, including the importance of a new birth, power for service, witness, holiness, and divine healing, but their distinctive doctrine is a baptism in the Holy Spirit subsequent to conversion, evidenced by speaking in tongues. With the restoration of tongues, Pentecostals also emphasize the present-day availability of all the gifts of the Spirit referenced in the New Testament.

The early Pentecostals were reluctant to form new denominations. They viewed themselves as Baptists, Methodists,

Anglicans, or Lutherans, who had discovered the ancient secret of Pentecostal power. Over time, however, many of their churches repudiated Pentecostal experience and doctrine. The Pentecostal Church of the Nazarene (a holiness church that did not hold to the Pentecostal's view of Spirit baptism) voted in 1919 to remove the word "Pentecostal" from its name, to distinguish itself from the growing Pentecostal movement.[15] Eventually, denominations that embraced the Pentecostal distinctives began to form, including some older holiness denominations and the Assemblies of God, which formed in 1914.[16]

Post-war ferment. The end of the Second World War and the beginning of the Cold War brought a renewed spiritual hunger in the Western world. Church membership in the United States rose dramatically in the 1940s. A young evangelist named Billy Graham reached thousands of young people through Youth for Christ rallies. Graham eventually left Youth for Christ for a wider harvest field. His crusade in Los Angeles in 1949—with the conversions of an Olympian, a war hero, and a notorious mobster—drew national attention, launching his ministry of mass evangelism into a new orbit.[17]

Graham's simple message—prefaced with an authoritative "the Bible says," and backed by a well-run organization—effectively reached millions of people. In 1973 Graham spoke to a crowd of over a million people in Seoul, South Korea. In 1995 he spoke to one billion people via satellite hook-up. Graham is widely recognized as the leading spokesman of the modern evangelical movement, stimulating the growth of churches like the Southern Baptists, now the largest Protestant denomination in the United States.[18]

As conservative evangelical churches were growing rapidly, the Pentecostal world was touched by the ministry of the healing revivalists and what was called the "Latter Rain" movement. The healing revivalists included Oral Roberts, William Branham, Jack Coe, and Kathryn Kuhlman. The Latter Rain movement began in Saskatchewan, Canada, in 1948 and was marked by healing, personal prophecies, and a form of worship called singing in the Spirit (corporate singing with participants improvising in the same musical key, in either English or tongues). Interestingly, the old-line Pentecostal denominations did not embrace the Latter Rain movement, viewing some of its practices (especially personal prophecy) as aberrant.[19]

Charismatic movement. By 1960 the blessings of the new Pentecost were safely quarantined within the Pentecostal churches, with only limited contact between these churches and the wider church. Pentecostal churches continued to grow, especially in the underdeveloped countries, as did conservative evangelicals like the Southern Baptists. Though both groups stressed the need for conversion and the authority of the Bible, evangelicals had little to do with Pentecostals. Meanwhile, the mainline churches (such as Episcopal, Lutheran, and Presbyterian) were facing a crisis of faith as their leaders began to question the fundamental teachings of Christianity in an attempt to accommodate the insights of modern science, philosophy, and psychology.

On Sunday, April 3, 1960, the quarantine between Pentecostals and mainline Protestants was breached. Dennis Bennett, rector of St. Mark's Episcopal Church in Van Nuys, California, surprised his parishioners by sharing from the pulpit the news that he had received the gift of tongues. It wasn't received as good news. He spoke of his experience in each of the three morning services. After the second service, his associate resigned and a board member sought Bennett's resignation, which he gave at the third service![20]

The stir caused by this dramatic turn of events within the

reserved Anglican tradition sparked a new interest in Pentecostal phenomena within the mainstream churches, especially among Episcopalians, Presbyterians, and Lutherans. Lay people, pastors, and theologians alike were awakened to the power of the Spirit through what came to be known as the charismatic movement. But this time, there was a concerted effort to interpret Pentecostal experience (including speaking in tongues) within the framework of the various church traditions. Those involved in charismatic renewal were adamant about remaining within their respective denominations. Theologians provided sophisticated apologetics for the exercise of the gifts of the Spirit consistent with their own church doctrine.[21] Baptism in the Spirit was often viewed as a renewal of the Spirit's power granted through baptism and confirmation. Speaking in tongues, while considered a normal part of being filled with the Spirit, was not considered a requirement for genuine Spirit baptism among charismatics.

By 1967, the emerging charismatic movement (from the Greek "charismata," a word for the spiritual gifts) was introduced to Roman Catholics, among whom it spread like wildfire. Catholic charismatics formed prayer groups and lay communities using contemporary songs for worship, "singing in the Spirit," and "prophecies" (primarily messages of encouragement, spoken in the oracle form of the Old Testament prophets to a prayer group, rather than the "personal prophecies" of the Latter Rain movement). In contrast with the early Pentecostals, most Catholic charismatics were comfortable and even skilled in bringing organization to the movement. They published magazines, wrote books, formed local, national, and international service committees, sponsored conferences, and worked hard to relate the values of the movement to the Catholic hierarchy. In 1975 Pope Paul VI celebrated mass with a conference of Catholic charismatics, in which St. Peter's Basilica was filled with charismatic worship, including prophecies spoken by lay people from the altar.[22] Classical Pentecostals, conditioned by the rejection of the mainstream church hierarchies, could only stand back in wonder.

Jesus Freaks. The late 1960s saw another expression of revival which included charismatic and noncharismatic elements, called the "Jesus Movement." The movement included the young post-war baby boom generation, who were filling high schools and colleges at the time. Participants were sometimes called "Jesus Freaks." This generation flavored the movement with a great deal of suspicion, even hostility, toward the institutional church. One of my Jesus Freak friends approached a Lutheran bishop who was wearing a crucifix around his neck. He pointed to the crucifix and asked the bishop, "Do you know the man who hung on that cross, Bishop?" Those involved in revivals are not known for their tact.

The Jesus movement gave birth to "Contemporary Christian Music," a style that spans soft pop to hard rock and beyond. The movement also reflected a growing cross-pollination of conservative evangelicals and charismatics. Local expressions of the revival were charismatic or noncharismatic depending on local leadership, as a variety of approaches exercised influence.

EVANGELICALS AND THE HOLY SPIRIT

In 1977, John Wimber left his position as a church growth consultant with the Fuller Theological Institute of Evangelism and Church Growth (a well-known evangelical institution) to pastor a local church. Though Wimber did not travel in Pentecostal or charismatic circles, he became convinced that the gospel should be preached as Jesus declared it, with healing for the sick and demonized. By this time, some professors at Fuller's School of World Missions had observed the dramatic growth of Christianity in the third world through Christians addressing disease and demonic oppression in the power of the Spirit. They observed the gospel spreading more effectively when it was accompanied by biblical signs and wonders. The observation challenged their traditional evangelical thinking and began a period of reassessment. Wimber felt the same approach to preaching the gospel was needed in the United States.

After months of praying for the sick, with little to show in the way of healing, Wimber and his associates were close to giving up. One morning Pastor Wimber prayed with a woman new to the church who was ill with a high fever. As Wimber prayed for healing, the fever left, and the woman felt suddenly better. No one was more surprised than John Wimber. After this, remarkable physical healings and encounters with demonized individuals began to take place and the church began to grow.

In 1982, Wimber taught a course called "Signs and Wonders and Church Growth" at the Fuller's School of World Missions. The course was the most popular in the seminary's history, as Wimber led the class in praying for the needs of students, with sometimes dramatic results. Needless to say, the course sparked a raging controversy within the bastion of evangelical scholarship. But professors like C. Peter Wagner and Charles Kraft became outspoken proponents of the notion that God wants to spread the gospel and grow the church through teaching accompanied by signs and wonders. It marked the beginning of a major reassessment of the power of the Spirit that continues among evangelicals around the world.

C. Peter Wagner has described this phenomenon as a "Third Wave" of the Holy Spirit's influence in the twentieth century, following the Pentecostal and charismatic movements.

Wagner notes several distinctions of this Third Wave of renewal, estimated by David Barrett to include some twenty million Christians worldwide:

1. Belief that the baptism of the Holy Spirit occurs at conversion (see 1 Corinthians 12:13) rather than as a second work of grace subsequent to the new birth.

2. Expectation of multiple fillings of the Holy Spirit subsequent to the new birth, some of which may closely resemble what others call "baptism in the Spirit."

3. A low-key acceptance of tongues as one of the many New Testament spiritual gifts that God gives to some and not to others. Speaking in tongues is not considered the initial physical validation of a certain spiritual experience but rather a gift used by some for ministry or prayer language.

4. Ministry under the power and anointing of the Holy Spirit as the portal of entrance into the Third Wave rather than a spiritual experience as is typical of the first two waves. The context of ministry is most commonly a body of believers rather than individual activities such as those of a faith healer.[23]

CHARISMATICS AND EVANGELICALS: COMMON GENES

Although charismatics and conservative evangelicals have been isolated from each other at various points in history, they share a common heritage as the children of revival. Obviously, both share the evangelical distinctives: the new birth, a high view of Scripture, the priesthood of all believers. But as the children of revival, both also share what are often viewed by contemporary Christians as Pentecostal or charismatic distinctives.

We've already seen how many of the revivals that gave birth to evangelical churches were marked by phenomena commonly thought of as charismatic. The ministries of John Wesley, George Whitefield, Jonathan Edwards, Charles Finney, and the Methodist camp meetings in the nineteenth century looked more like a Pentecostal tent revival at times than a present-day conservative evangelical church service.

Evangelical heroes like D.L. Moody and Charles Finney bear witness to a powerful immersion in the Spirit's power that looks a great deal like the charismatic "baptism in the Spirit" minus tongues. Divine healing didn't wait for the Pentecostal movement. A.B. Simpson and others were healing the sick through the power of the Spirit long before that time. In other words, there are some charismatic skeletons in the conservative evangelical closet.

A broader cultural perspective also reveals the common heritage. Much of what white North American or European evangelicals consider charismatic behavior is common in African-American churches that hold no charismatic doctrines. Hand clapping, dancing, and shouts of joy are standard fare in these churches, where nary an unknown tongue is uttered.

REVIVAL-EXCESS-REACTION SYNDROME

If Pentecostals and conservative evangelicals have so much in common, what accounts for the polarization between the camps? Ultimately, the answer lies rooted in the human condition. Rivalry, envy, and animosity come naturally to human beings. But there is also an oft-repeated pattern seen during revivals and their aftermath that adds fuel to the fires of controversy among friends: revival-excess-reaction.

By definition, a time of revival brings a great release of religious energy. This increased power can be seen in individual conversion and sanctification, and on a broader scale, in major social reforms. But the energy released in times of revival can also lead to excess. Tares grow up along with the wheat. In the enthusiasm generated by revival, there is often a low premium placed on discernment. As excesses multiply, reactions are provoked, and campaigns are launched to "remove the tares that threaten the wheat," provoking counter-reactions. Over time, positions harden, increasing the polarization between camps. Redemption is indeed a messy business.

The modern Pentecostal movement is no exception. The excesses that so frequently accompany revivals provided more than enough fuel to ignite a backlash to this "new Pentecost." Pentecostals framed their new experience of the Spirit's power in a way that was guaranteed to polarize other Christians: they claimed that speaking in tongues is the definitive and essential sign of Spirit baptism. No tongues, no baptism in the Spirit. This was William Seymour's first message to the Nazarene mission in California that called him as an associate pastor. The holiness congregation was predictably offended by the implication that they were not baptized with the Spirit (as they firmly believed they were). Seymour was literally locked out of the church.[24] It's taken a long time to unlock the door.

The Pentecostal movement, with its perceived and real excesses, eventually provoked the spread of cessationist theology—the view that the charismatic gifts, divine healing, and miracles ceased with the ministry of the original apostles. Twelve years after Seymour began his Azusa Street ministry, a professor at Princeton Seminary named Benjamin Warfield published *Counterfeit Miracles*. While some Protestant Reformers believed that the age of miracles ended with the apostles, Warfield developed this teaching and, more importantly, popularized it. His book exercised immense influence among conservative Christians. Several local churches and denominations adopted formal doctrinal statements condemning Pentecostalism, emboldened by the arguments of Warfield's book. By the middle of the twentieth century, dispensationalism, a theological system that embraced cessationism, was the dominant perspective among evangelicals.

The polarization of doctrinal positions led to a profound isolation between Pentecostals and non-Pentecostal evangelicals. In the earlier years of publication, *Christianity Today*, the magazine of modern evangelicalism, largely ignored the Pentecostal world. Pentecostals avoided evangelical institutions, including seminaries, making cross-pollination difficult. After all, why would any self-respecting Pentecostal want to be influenced by those who were not "Spirit-filled"? We can only stand back in the face of all this controversy and say, "What a shame!"

BEYOND POLARIZATION: A NEW SYNTHESIS?

Perhaps time is God's trump card when it comes to reversing the effects of polarization. The animosity between charismatics and evangelicals has faded with time. Several factors seem to be conspiring to promote reconciliation between the camps. The erosion of institutional loyalty among the baby boom generation is one factor. Opportunities for charismatics and evangelicals to rub shoulders have multiplied through the proliferation of para-church campus ministries and neighborhood Bible studies with no church sponsorship. The rising pressure of secularism helps us appreciate what we hold in common in spite of our differences. Pentecostal and Baptist believers met in Romanian prisons where it was difficult to be choosy about picking prayer partners. In North America, charismatics and evangelicals found themselves standing together in the public arena over issues like the sanctity of human life. Radio and television made avoidance of exposure to "the other side" nearly impossible.

So as the end of the twentieth century approaches, it's no wonder that evangelicals are taking another look at the experience of Pentecostals and charismatics. We have things to learn that we may only be able to learn from each other. That's one of the central themes of this book.

Now that the dust of controversy spanning several decades is finally settling, what can evangelicals and charismatics learn from each other? In particular, how can we draw from the best of the evangelical and charismatic worlds?

WHAT GOD HAS JOINED TOGETHER

As evangelicals take another look at the power of the Spirit, it is important that we hold together certain truths that God has joined together, but which the church sometimes tends to separate.

Word and Spirit. For too long evangelicals have emphasized the Word over the Spirit, while charismatics have emphasized the Spirit over the Word. But the Word and the Spirit belong together. The following saying is a handy summary:

If we emphasize the Word without the Spirit, we *dry up*.
If we emphasize the Spirit without the Word, we *blow up*.
If we hold the Word and the Spirit together, we *grow up*.

We won't gain more of the Spirit by having less of the Word. And we won't depend less on the Word by having more of the Spirit. We need as much of both as we can have. This means that as evangelicals consider the lessons of Pentecost, we must maintain as strong an emphasis as ever on the priority of Scripture. If our honest reading of Scripture tells us to avoid a particular charismatic approach, then avoid it we must. But if the Scripture leads us to incorporate things that we used to consider charismatic, then incorporate them we must.

Passion and patience. The fires of revival always fan the flames of passion. We fall more in love with the Lord Jesus and we care more deeply for his kingdom. But if history is any guide, we also know that the fires of renewed passion without renewed patience lead those who taste renewal to become even more frustrated with and critical toward those who have not tasted the same new wine. Of course, this is in keeping with the devil's script. Those who haven't experienced renewal sense the spirit of judgment among those who have, and they keep an even greater distance from them, thus inhibiting the Spirit's work through the body.

Patience is passion, seasoned with grace, expressed through intercession, sustained over time. If you are the pastor of an evangelical church and some of your members experience a renewal in the Holy Spirit, you realize you have a potential blessing and a potential curse on your hands. If those who have been renewed gain a deeper love for the church, and they commit themselves to sustained intercession for renewal and a gracious disposition to those who haven't had the same experience, blessing will surely follow—and you will be more open than ever to the Spirit's work in your church. But if those who are renewed form a revival club, and reinforce each other's frustration with how dead the rest of the church is, your heart toward them will not be strangely warmed. If you allow the Spirit to increase your passion while resisting his efforts to increase your patience, your spiritual renewal will be a mixed bag of benefit and boondoggle to the rest of the church.

Openness and Discernment. My seventy-year-old father, who would not describe himself as a charismatic, was listening to one of his friends speak in disparaging terms about an outbreak of renewal near his hometown. "Wait a minute," Dad implored. "You don't have to go to one of those meetings where people are doing things that make you feel uncomfortable, but we do have to stay open to what God may be doing." An honest reading of the Scriptures and church history demands that we maintain an open attitude toward the work of the Spirit to renew the church. God is God and he does whatever he pleases in the way that pleases him. The mere fact that we feel uncomfortable, or that there is a mixture of wheat and tares, doesn't mean God is not at work.

But along with a posture of openness we must also exercise discernment. "Do not put out the Spirit's fire; do not treat prophecies with contempt. Test everything. Hold on to the good. Avoid every kind of evil" (1 Thes 5:19-22). As a friend of ours, Steve Nicholson, has said, "A work of the Spirit cannot be quenched by discernment; in fact, discernment is necessary to keep the fire of the Spirit burning." Some people seem to think that genuine openness to the Spirit and discernment are incompatible. But the work of the Spirit demands discernment, since the Spirit interacts with human beings who are anything but perfect. It's essential that we understand what is from God and what is not—so that we can embrace the former and reject the latter.

The fact that conservative evangelicals can learn something from charismatics, and that charismatics can learn from conservative evangelicals, doesn't mean we have to adopt everything the other side offers. So with openness we must also hold on to discernment.

WANTED: AN EVANGELICAL APPROACH INFORMED BY CHARISMATIC EXPERIENCE

In many cases, the Pentecostal or charismatic experience of the Spirit's power is something conservative evangelicals can be especially attentive to. Even when we disagree with various charismatic teachings or practices, we must ask ourselves, "Is there a reality to which the charismatic experience nevertheless bears witness?"

For example, if we discern that Jesus is indeed healing the sick through supernatural means, we have a responsibility to learn how to pray for the sick in the power of the Spirit. We don't have to pray for the sick like a Pentecostal faith healer prays for the sick. We don't need to adopt any charismatic approaches that don't square with Scripture as we understand it, but we do need to develop approaches that do justice to the Spirit's power and remain true to our understanding of Scripture. That's what we're looking for—the best of both worlds.

FOR DISCUSSION

1. Modern Christians often don't place a great deal of value on church history. Why do you think that is? What are the advantages of understanding a history of revival? What impact would a better appreciation for church history have in our present experience?

2. Trace your own spiritual genealogy from the perspective of the authors' review of revival history. Which movements do you think have had the most impact on your life?

WHEN SEEKING A CHURCH

1. A healthy church will have some sense of her history. Are the historical roots of the congregation valued and communicated?

2. What strengths and limitations does the particular historical background of a church bring?

3. Does the church's response to contemporary expressions of renewal and revival seem primarily either reactive or blindly promotional? Or is there an attempt to thoughtfully discern current movements within the church?

FOR PASTORS

1. Do you know where your own church fits within the history of revivals? Which revivals have had the most impact on the people in your church?

2. Consider doing some further study of revivals that preceded the modern Pentecostal movement, with an eye toward understanding what role the leadership of pastors played in the fruitfulness of revival.

3. Consider teaching on the history of revivals, drawing from biblical and church history examples and providing guidelines for responding to contemporary works of renewal.

FOR FURTHER STUDY

Christian History, a magazine published by *Christianity Today*.

Keith J. Hardman, *The Spiritual Awakeners* (Chicago: Moody, 1983).

Stanley M. Burgess and Gary B. McGee, eds., *Dictionary of Pentecostal and Charismatic Movements* (Grand Rapids, Mich.: Zondervan, 1993).

Earle E. Cairns, *An Endless Line of Splendor* (Wheaton, Ill.: Tyndale House, 1986).

THREE

Power and Pain

Anyone who watched television in the United States on Saturday afternoons during the 1960s and the 1970s will be familiar with the opening theme of ABC's "Wide World of Sports." We can still vividly remember the announcer intoning, "The thrill of victory...." We then would be shown scenes of Sugar Ray Leonard knocking out an opponent or the U.S. Hockey Team's miraculous victory over the Russians or an ice skater's perfect double toe loop.

But we always knew what was coming right after "the thrill of victory... the agony of defeat." Then we were treated to that horrible scene of the skier careening down the side of a ski jump. Even after watching that unfortunate skier somersault down the ski jump and off the track countless times, something inside of us would tense up each time we saw it again. Somehow that picture created a powerful connection with us. We could see ourselves rolling down the hill to the horror of all the bystanding fans.

In many ways the Christian life is summed up by the opening words of "Wide World of Sports." Is there anyone who has walked with Christ for more than a few days who doesn't know both the thrill and the agony? Like us, you probably love the part of Hebrews 11 where the heroes of faith "shut the mouths of lions, quenched the fury of the flames, and escaped the edge of the sword... became powerful in battle and routed foreign armies."

But there are other heroes of the faith mentioned in Hebrews 11. "Some faced jeers and floggings. Still others were chained and put in prison. They were stoned. They were sawed in half. They were put to death by the sword. They lived in sheepskins and goatskins—destitute, persecuted, and mistreated."

The Christian life is a life of thrill and of agony, victory and defeat. But why must it be so?

THE THRILL OF VICTORY

I, Rich, have a dear friend in my church named Mike. When Mike was five years old, he began to suffer from epileptic seizures. Over the next two decades, Mike was taken to the emergency room on dozens of occasions because he fell as a result of a seizure and cracked his head or bloodied his face.

Growing up with epilepsy caused Mike unimaginable social embarrassment. Consider what it would be like if you were an insecure, extremely self-conscious adolescent, wanting nothing more than to fade into the woodwork and to be noticed by no one. Add to that adolescent self-consciousness this thought: about three times a week you find yourself looking up from the ground in the school yard, only to realize that you have had another grand mal seizure and half of your classmates are standing around, staring at you. Mike can vividly remember scenes like these every year from kindergarten through college.

Yet, despite the dozens of pills he took each day, and despite the constant trips to the emergency room, Mike's epilepsy got so bad that he was experiencing, at a minimum, three grand mal seizures and hundreds of petit mal seizures *each week*.

Because of the severity of his disease, his job at a hospital was in jeopardy because the hospital judged him to be a significant danger to himself and to patients. His neurologist suggested that Mike undergo a radical operation involving severing the hemispheres of his brain to reduce the intensity of his seizures. Such an operation almost certainly meant several years of physical therapy to fully recover. Even then, Mike's seizures would only be controlled, not eliminated.

When Mike came to me, as his pastor, asking for my counsel regarding the doctor's advice, I encountered a man who was devastated. He was devastated physically, his face puffy and his eyes blackened from a recent fall. He was devastated vocationally because he was about to lose his job. And he was devastated spiritually because he could not see God in the midst of all his suffering. What would you do if you met Mike and he asked you for counsel and help regarding his future?

A few friends and I began to pray for Mike's healing. From the outset we saw significant power as we prayed for him; we experienced certain physical sensations that I have learned often accompany the healing presence of God. On several occasions we felt extraordinary amounts of heat on our hands as we prayed for Mike. On other occasions we felt as if a "force field" descended around Mike. Consequently, we were encouraged to continue to pray because of these signs that we believed to be indications of God's healing presence.

Nevertheless, despite over a dozen lengthy prayer sessions during the next few months, Mike's grand mal seizures continued unabated. He was not healed as a result of our prayers and his time to make a decision regarding the radical surgery was running out.

About that time, I was planning to attend a conference in New York led by John Wimber, and it occurred to me that I might ask John to pray for Mike's healing. I knew from past experiences that John was often used by God to heal the sick.

And so I called John and he agreed to set up an appointment with Mike.

He was excited about the possibility of receiving prayer from John Wimber, but Mike, like the rest of us, was also apprehensive. What if it didn't work? Where would that leave him? What would his lack of healing mean regarding God and God's will for Mike's life?

We spent a significant amount of time in prayer before we went to the conference, asking God to intervene on Mike's behalf. Then, at the conference, we met with John and another man. They began to pray for Mike, laying hands directly on Mike's head and back.

Mike received prayer for about an hour. Everything seemed to slow down for Mike. His subjective impression was that the prayer only lasted for a few minutes. In Mike's own words, it felt like a tornado was rushing through his body while John was praying for him. At the end of the prayer time, John told Mike to check out his condition with his neurologist, but that he believed Mike was "90 percent healed; the next 10 percent will come slowly over time."

Since that prayer session with John nearly six years ago, Mike has never experienced another grand mal seizure—not even one! His neurologist said, after reading his EEG, that Mike appeared to have experienced about a 90 percent improvement in his brain wave activity. His neurologist attributed the radical change in Mike's condition to a sudden and instantaneous change in Mike's brain due to his growing older. He did not explain Mike's experience of God's presence during prayer or give much credence to the possibility of divine healing.

Because of Mike's changed condition, he was gradually weaned off most of his medication. Today Mike has a driver's license and has been driving without limitation for two years. He obtained a job promotion. Mike is also happily married. I had the privilege of performing Mike and Susan's wedding last year. In short, Mike is an example of someone who has experienced in this life "the thrill of victory."

AND THE AGONY OF DEFEAT

About the same time I was praying for Mike, I met a little girl in my neighborhood who was dying of leukemia. The children at my daughter's elementary school were going around the neighborhood raising "Pennies for Pamela" so that little Pamela could have a bone marrow transplant, which was the last option for saving her life.

Some time after Pamela's bone marrow transplant, I knocked on the door of her home and introduced myself to her mother as a neighbor and a pastor of one of the churches in the neighborhood. Pamela's mother looked very suspicious, obviously wondering why I had shown up at her door uninvited.

I said to Pamela's mother, "I am not looking for anything from you or from your daughter. I am not interested in using your pain. My daughter is in your daughter's class at school and asked me to come by and pray for Pamela. I would consider it a real privilege if you would let me meet your daughter and pray with you for Pamela's healing." For some reason, perhaps because it was obvious that I was sincere, she let me in.

Over the next several months I had the opportunity to meet with Pamela and pray for her many times. I also had the opportunity to watch God draw Pamela's mom to a saving knowledge of Jesus Christ. Pamela's mom, in turn, explained the message of salvation to Pamela and she, too, received Christ as her Savior.

The initial results of our prayer time were encouraging.

Pamela's liver was shrinking back to its normal size. Her blood count was improving dramatically. Then summer came and I left town for two weeks for our family's vacation. Before I left I arranged for a few women from our church to drop by Pamela's house and continue to pray for her in my absence.

The day I returned home, I was rushed to the hospital with a blood clot in my leg. The doctors had no idea why I had suddenly developed this blood clot. They thought that I might have injured myself as a result of my long-distance running regime. One evening while I was lying in my hospital bed, watching the evening news, the newscaster on the television reported: "Now for some sad news. Little Pamela, for whom children around the city have been collecting pennies, died this morning after a several-year battle with leukemia."

I was devastated. I began to weep uncontrollably there in my hospital bed as I stared at Pamela's picture on the screen. How could this happen? Everything seemed to be turning around for Pamela! Her blood counts were improving. Why did I have to go away on vacation? Why was I lying there in the hospital? My questions unanswered, I checked myself out of the hospital a few days later against my doctor's orders, and I had the extraordinarily depressing task of performing little Pamela's funeral. When I saw her small casket being lowered into the ground, I broke down in tears.

That funeral was a profoundly unsettling experience for me. For several months I found myself in a state of extreme depression and turmoil. How could I pray for someone's headache when God wouldn't answer my prayers for a little girl dying from leukemia? Who cared if someone lost a job when I had to watch a mother lose her little girl? Testimonies that were designed to bring encouragement only deepened my sense of alienation and bitterness toward the Lord.

What sense can I make of the nearly simultaneous experience of the thrill of victory and the agony of defeat? We know of no Christian who doesn't need to come to some resolution regarding the inescapable fact of suffering and pain in this world. After the honeymoon period of conversion begins to wear off (assuming you had a honeymoon), everyone experiences the shock of waking up and realizing that while things have changed, they have not changed totally. Some of our sin patterns continue unbroken right through conversion. Some of our relationships remain unhealed. We still lose jobs, fail exams, experience fender-benders and worse, and get sick without healing. For every Mike, we all know a Pamela; for every Peter that is released from prison, there is a James who is martyred in prison. Every Christian knows, through personal experience, that the Christian life is lived on two tracks, power and pain, victory and defeat. But how shall we make sense of it? Our understanding of power and pain is rooted in the biblical message of the kingdom of God.

THE KINGDOM OF GOD IN THE OLD TESTAMENT

Throughout the Old Testament, God is continually referred to as "the King." He is the King of Israel (see Numbers 23:21). But he is no local deity since he is King over all the earth (see Psalm 96:10; Psalm 97:2,3). God is regularly pictured with all of the accoutrements of kingship, including being seated on a throne, having a royal scepter, being waited upon by thousands of heavenly attendants, and receiving tithes which were considered the king's portion.

But even though God was considered to be the King, the prophets predicted a day when he would manifest his kingship in the world and show himself to people as the King (see Isaiah 24:23; Zechariah 9:9ff; 14:9ff). The prophetic hope for the coming kingdom was variously expressed in the Old Testament. It was clearly tied to a descendant of David who would reign upon David's throne forever and ever (see Isaiah 9:6-7; Isaiah 11). The hope was also expressed apocalyptically as being tied to a heavenly Son of Man who would come and establish God's kingdom, bringing God's reign into human history (see Daniel 7:13-14).

Thus, the Jews looked forward to a day when God would break into history and defeat the enemies of God and Israel, end wars, reestablish the borders of Israel, destroy death, and raise the dead. We can imagine the stir, then, when Jesus of Nazareth came claiming to be the one who was bringing in the long sought-after kingdom of God.

Jesus and the kingdom. That Jesus understood his ministry as a fulfillment of the Old Testament promises regarding the kingdom of God is absolutely clear. In his inaugural address in which Jesus summarized his ministry, he read portions from Isaiah 61 and 62 about the coming of an Anointed One who would preach good news, free prisoners, heal the blind, release the oppressed, and proclaim the year of the Lord's favor. After reading this messianic text, Jesus solemnly declared, "Today this scripture is fulfilled in your hearing" (Lk 4:21). And when John the Baptist wondered if Jesus was, in fact, the Messiah prophesied about in the Old Testament, Jesus cited the messianic prophecy in Isaiah 35 claiming to fulfill that prophecy by his own ministry (see Matthew 11:2-6). But the strongest statement of Jesus regarding the inbreaking of the kingdom of God in his ministry is found in Matthew 12 when Jesus declared, "But if I drive out demons by the Spirit of God, then the kingdom of God has come upon you."

The disciples clearly believed that Jesus was the anointed King who was sent by God to establish God's kingdom (see Matthew 16:16). But their understanding of Jesus' mission seemed to include only the thrill of victory. They regularly rejected the notion that the kingdom of God also included a wooden cross and the death of their beloved King. Thus, we see even Peter taking Jesus aside and rebuking him after Jesus explained that he "must go to Jerusalem and suffer many things at the hands of the elders, chief priests and teachers of the law, and that he must be killed and on the third day be raised to life" (Mt 16:21-23).

That the kingdom of God had come in the person of Jesus was believed and embraced by his followers. But the form of the kingdom and, specifically, the idea that Jesus did not break the Roman yoke off Israel's neck, remove the presence of sin, wipe away every tear, destroy poverty, and throw death and Satan into hell was not embraced by the disciples until after they watched Jesus' bloody death and then experienced the power of his resurrected life. It was only then that they realized that the kingdom of God prophesied about in the Old Testament was to enter into this world through *two comings* of the Messiah, and not just one.

Whereas the Jews believed that all of the blessings of the kingdom of God would arrive in one coming of the Messiah, we now know that the coming of the kingdom, God's reign and rule over all of his enemies, is a *two-stage event*. In his first coming, Messiah *defeated* the enemies of God. In his second coming, Messiah will *destroy* the enemies of God.

In Jesus' first coming, Satan, sin, and death were judged and condemned at the cross (see Colossians 2:13-15; John 12:31). In Jesus' second coming, Satan, sin, and death will be removed from the new heavens and the new earth and be thrown into the lake of fire (see Revelation 20:10, 14).

WHAT TIME IS IT NOW?

We presently live at a time between the first and second comings of Messiah, which could be expressed this way: *the kingdom of God has come, but is also coming!* The theologian Oscar Cullman compared it to the time in World War II between D-Day and VE-Day. From the moment of D-Day it was clear that the Allies had won and that the Germans were defeated. Nevertheless, a long mop-up operation needed to be fought for the next year, which included some of the fiercest battles in the entire war.[1]

So it is today. Satan is a defeated foe who knows that his time is short. Nevertheless, he prowls around like a roaring lion seeking someone to devour (see 1 Peter 5:8). And in this real war, we see real casualties in the church and in the world.

While it is true that the sting of death is removed in this age (see 1 Corinthians 15:55-56), nevertheless the presence of death is not removed. Therefore, we Christians still mourn for those who die, but we don't mourn as those who have no hope since we look forward to the second coming of Christ and the resurrection of the dead (see 1 Thessalonians 4:13,14). Many people have described the present age as the time between the *already* and the *not yet* of the kingdom of God. As God's people, the church is caught between the ages.

What can we expect now? It is important to grasp the profound idea that in Jesus Christ the kingdom of God has truly invaded this world and has not simply "drawn near." In other words, there has been a true change of affairs affecting the present evil age even though the present evil age was not entirely destroyed or removed. It is absolutely the case that the most profound change took place on the wooden cross at Calvary where Jesus bled and died for the forgiveness of our sins. All evangelicals, whether charismatic or noncharismatic, agree that Jesus' mission at his first coming was chiefly "to give his life as a ransom for many" (Mt 20:28).

But it is no denigration to the chief mission of Christ, that is, the salvation of sinners, to state that Jesus' first coming was not exhausted by this central fact of the forgiveness of sins. Jesus *also* came to bring about the invasion of the kingdom of God, namely God's rule and reign in eternity, into our present time and space. Thus, it should be no surprise that in Jesus' first coming, the things awaiting eternity—namely, the healing of the sick, the recovery of sight for the blind, the end of poverty and hunger, the reconciliation of broken relationships, the deliverance of demonized, the raising of the dead—were all brought by Jesus into human history. In Christ, *eternity broke into time.*

Again, lest we be misunderstood, we believe that the *center* of what Christ came for was his death and resurrection for the forgiveness of sins. But we don't believe that the full purpose of Christ's ministry and coming is exhausted by the forgiveness of sins. While atonement is his chief and central work, it was not the only work accomplished by Christ's first coming. His first coming also included bringing a piece of eternity into time through the proclamation and demonstration of the kingdom of God.

Jesus is like a glorious marathon runner who takes the torch of the kingdom of God from the Father's hand and carries it into this world, into our age, lighting the torch of eternity in our time. The torch was passed to the apostles, who were commissioned to do and proclaim the very same things that Jesus was doing and proclaiming. Jesus gave the twelve disciples the authority to drive out evil spirits and to heal every disease and sickness, commissioning them to "preach this message: 'The kingdom of heaven is near.' Heal the sick, raise the dead, cleanse those who have leprosy, drive out demons. Freely you have received, freely give" (see Matthew 10:1, 7-8).

Jesus also gave the same commission and authority to the seventy-two, a group of followers obviously broader than Jesus' core of twelve disciples (see Luke 10:1, 8-16). And the apostles not only proclaimed the gospel by preaching and healing, but they also taught the disciples they made to proclaim the gospel by preaching and healing. Such nonapostles as Stephen, Philip, Ananias, and congregations such as the ones in Galatia, Corinth, Philippi, and Jewish Christian congregations (in the Book of Hebrews) all experienced and practiced the ministry of the kingdom, which included not just the proclamation of the forgiveness of sins but also the healing of sickness and the driving out of demons.[2]

We presently can experience the thrill of eternity, which includes having our sins carried away and having "tasted the goodness of the word of God and the powers of the coming age" (Heb 6:5). Nevertheless, in this time before the second coming, we are like Paul: "Hard pressed on every side, but not crushed; perplexed, but not in despair; persecuted, but not abandoned; struck down, but not destroyed. We always carry around in our body the death of Jesus" (2 Cor 4:8-10).

Our experience of the thrill is always tempered by our knowledge of the agony, and our belief in the power of God always runs side-by-side with our experience of pain and suffering. Empowered evangelicals make sense of power and pain, therefore, through the grid of the *already* and *not yet* of the kingdom of God. It is our belief that we will not see *total healing* of our racial and ethnic divisions until the holy city Jerusalem comes down from heaven (see Revelation 21:10), but we can experience *substantial healing* of our divisions now (see Ephesians 2:14-17). Likewise, we will not experience the eradication of disease until the second coming of Christ (see Revelation 21:4). Nevertheless, we can expect many mental and physical healings (see James 5:13-16). And even the resurrection of the dead, which will be fully accomplished at Christ's second coming, should occasionally, though rarely, be seen in this age (see Matthew 10:8; Acts 9:40-42; 20:7-12).

The lens of the *already* and the *not yet* of the kingdom enables us to understand the empowered evangelical's problems with the healing beliefs and practices, both of traditional Pentecostals on the one hand and of conservative evangelicals on the other. As we trace through some of the beliefs and practices regarding healing of Pentecostals and conservative evangelicals, we would remind our reader that our descriptions of various teachings and practices are in no way meant to be pejorative toward our brothers and sisters. Indeed, it would be the opposite of the unifying purpose we are seeking to accomplish to merely caricature various groups' positions.

We also want to remind our readers that, by and large, we tend to emphasize the negative edges of both Pentecostals and conservative evangelicals in order to state what we consider to be the broad middle position which, indeed, is held by many Pentecostals and conservative evangelicals. Nevertheless, in order to state what we consider the broad middle to be, we must expose the extreme edges of the playing field.

DIFFICULTIES WITH THE CHARISMATIC POSITION

The empowered evangelical critique of the traditional Pentecostal view of healing can be summarized as follows:

1. the claim that healing is in the Atonement,
2. the prominence of techniques and formulas in healing prayers, and
3. the exaltation of one individual healer over and against a healing church.

But the ultimate issue from the perspective of kingdom teaching is the overemphasis on the *already* of the kingdom to the neglect of the *not yet.*

Is healing in the Atonement? Occasionally, Pentecostals have taught that healing in this life is guaranteed in the Atonement every bit as much as forgiveness is guaranteed. "By his stripes we are healed" (Isaiah 53:5, KJV) is a common quotation over the doorways of Pentecostal churches and in Pentecostal books on healing and in many worship songs in Pentecostal churches. Some Pentecostals may be included in Paul's rebuke found in 1 Corinthians 4:8, "Already you have all you want! Already you have become rich!"

The guarantee of physical healing in this life through the Atonement leads, we believe, to several unfortunate results. First, since according to this teaching God *always* purposes to heal (based on Isaiah 53:5), then *the failure to be healed after prayer must rest on our shoulders.* In other words, because healing is guaranteed by the death of Christ, then the only explanation for a person not being healed is that the person being prayed for or the person praying has failed to meet one of the necessary human conditions for healing. Practitioners of healing are then forced to search around for the human basis for healing not taking place—in the worst case scenario, the sick person's lack of faith or hidden sin.

We do not believe that healing is guaranteed every time we pray for somebody to get well. Our understanding is that the *not yet* of the kingdom of God represented by the second coming of Christ means that we will not always experience healing in this world. While healing is a part of the kingdom introduced by the first coming of Christ, *it is not a guaranteed part of the kingdom.* Many people continued to be sick even though prayed for by the apostles. Paul left Trophimus sick in Miletus (see 2 Timothy 4:20). Epaphroditus almost died from an illness and was, apparently, not supernaturally healed (see Philippians 2:25-27). Paul prescribed wine for Timothy's stomach and frequent illnesses instead of supernatural healing (see 1 Timothy 5:23). And Paul himself does not appear to have been supernaturally healed from his mysterious ailment in Galatia (see Galatians 4:13-14).

Some attribute these cases of the failures to heal to the gradual disappearance of the healing gift during the last phases of the apostolic age.[3] Others might attribute it to a lack of total faith in the heart of the apostle or some block regarding sin in the church or in the life of the person being prayed for. Empowered evangelicals would generally attribute the lack of healing that we see to the *not yet* of the kingdom of God.[4]

What then is our understanding of healing "being in the Atonement"? The empowered evangelical view of the relationship between healing and the Atonement of Christ is simply to say that healing, like every kingdom benefit, comes in and through the cross of Jesus Christ. Since Jesus is our mediator and his sacrificial death alone gives us access to the throne of grace, anything we receive from God—whether our daily bread, the forgiveness of sins, physical healing, or our resurrection bodies—comes through the cross of Christ.

Nevertheless, our understanding of the two comings of Christ shapes our perception regarding what is guaranteed now and what is guaranteed only as a result of the second coming of Christ. We believe that *we can guarantee* to all who come to Christ in simple trust and repentance the forgiveness of sins 100 percent of the time without fail. No undiscovered sin in the person's background, demonic principality, unrepented of sin in the church, or any other human or demonic power can in any way keep a person from being totally forgiven all of the time when that person turns in repentance and faith to the cross of Christ.

But we can make no such guarantee regarding physical healing. The benefit of physical healing brought into this age in the kingdom ministry of Jesus is only partial, not total. The *not yet* of the kingdom means that not everyone will be healed even if they have perfect faith. And even regarding those who do get healed, all of them will surely die if Christ does not return first. Thus, holding onto the *not yet* of the kingdom enables us to avoid the common pastoral problem of blaming the victim for not receiving healing. One day we will all be totally healed—physically, psychologically, relationally—but that day is not yet. In the meantime, our efforts, though essential, will produce partial, imperfect results. But partial, imperfect results are better than none!

The problem of techniques and formulas. At times, because some charismatics believe that healing is guaranteed, healing practices can sound formulaic and somewhat technique-oriented. As it is presented in its simplest form, some Pentecostal teachings sound like: "If you do 'x' (believe, confess all of your known sins, rebuke the devil, etc.), then God *must* heal you." We see two problems with this approach.

First, because we do not believe that God has promised or guaranteed perfect healing in this age, we do not believe that God *must* heal. Empowered evangelicals do not believe that God *must* do anything. Instead, as the psalmist declares: "Our God is in heaven; he does whatever pleases him" (Ps 115:3). Empowered evangelicals believe that it is important to hold on to our belief in God's freedom to do whatever pleases him. This doesn't mean that God will act capriciously or in violation of his Word, but we must not pin promises to God that he has not made or limit him to our view of what is good or helpful either for ourselves or God's kingdom. God alone knows what is good and helpful. And whatever happens, whether thrill or agony, we know (or should know) that "in all things God works for the good of those who love him, who have been called according to his purpose" (Rom 8:28). Room for mystery and the freedom of God must be preserved in our practice of healing.

Second, we see little biblical support for specific techniques in the practice of healing. Some Pentecostals have taught that healings of certain categories of illnesses can be obtained through certain specific steps or practices done by the sick person and the person praying for them. Occasionally the technique might include such things as making sure the person has repented of every known sin or has spent a day in fasting and prayer. A techniques orientation might also suggest that back problems are to be prayed for differently than leg problems because of the healer's experience in the past regarding the healing of backs.

While empowered evangelicals agree that it is always a good idea to confess one's sins and that fasting and prayer for a period of time can result in physical healing, what we find in the Gospels is an amazing lack of predictable order or technique regarding healing. Indeed, the one pattern that is discernible in Jesus and the apostles' healing practices is that *no pattern is discernible!* On occasion some material like spittle or mud was used. On other occasions, the healing was accomplished by a simple word of command. Sometimes the person was commended for his or her faith. Other times there was no mention of faith. And still other times it seems as if faith was present in the people bringing the sick person to Jesus.[5]

Further healing was accomplished by the touch of the healer and at other times it was accomplished through the touch of the person being prayed for. On one occasion no touch is mentioned and the healing took place at a long distance. While a person's sin is sometimes forgiven before the healing, in many instances no mention is made of sin until after the person is healed.[6] In short, empowered evangelicals believe the variety of patterns in the Scripture suggest that it is inappropriate to teach a technique for healing beyond simply telling people to attempt to discern what God wishes to do in an individual situation. (See the appendix on page 265 for John Wimber's healing prayer model.)

One healer or a healing church? Another unfortunate result of some charismatic healing meetings is the exaltation of one individual, who has a "healing gift," to the almost complete exclusion of the entire church as the healing agent of God. *The whole church* has been commanded to do *everything* Jesus commanded the apostles to do (see Matthew 28:20). There is no biblical reason to exclude healing from "the everything I have commanded you" in the Great Commission any more than we would exclude witnessing or prayer. Moreover, *the whole church* is told by Paul that *"whatever* you have learned or received or heard from me, or seen in me—put it into practice" (Phil 4:9). Part of the "whatever" is healing. We believe that certain people do have healing ministries and will be more frequently used to heal the sick than other people (see 1 Corinthians 12:28) just as some people will be more gifted in evangelism. Nevertheless, every individual in the whole church can pray for others and occasionally see healings even if the whole church is not uniquely gifted with a healing ministry. To facilitate the whole church learning to pray for the sick, our church has frequent training classes on subjects such as spiritual gifts, healing, prayer, and learning to hear God's voice. Every Sunday, lay people who have completed our training classes pray for the sick. We also encourage lay people to regularly pray for the sick in their small groups, and to help them by participating in ministries such as our food pantry and our ministries in prisons, and those with the AIDS virus.

In concluding this section on certain charismatic problems with healing ministry, we must point out that we have learned a great deal from Pentecostal and charismatic writers regarding healing and are much indebted to these movements for our own theology and practice of healing. Moreover, despite our difficulties with some charismatic practices regarding healing, at least healing is prayed for and practiced in charismatic churches. The idea that the kingdom has come already in the person of Christ is sincerely taught and believed. In the case of healing, our more significant problems rest not with some charismatic teaching but with some conservative evangelical teachings.

CONSERVATIVE EVANGELICALS: MODEL? WHAT MODEL?

We must state lovingly that if empowered evangelicals occasionally struggle with some charismatic models regarding healing, we more seriously object to some conservative evangelical teachings that completely overlook divine healing despite its prominence in the Gospels and the Book of Acts. Many conservative evangelicals have simply never been trained in church regarding *how* to pray for the sick. Thus, we end up praying only for the toughest cases, for friends and loved ones who are dying or for whom physicians have given up hope. Is it any wonder that conservative evangelicals see few people healed, when the only exposure to healing prayer is, generally, prayers offered for the terminally ill?

How many services have you attended where the prayer for sick people sounded something like: "Dear Lord, guide the surgeon's hands during Pete's operation.... And bring your comfort to Jean and her family following a car accident."

We certainly believe in the providence of God to guide surgeons' hands and to bring his comforting presence to the families of the sick and dying. In other words, it isn't wrong to pray in such a fashion, but we ought to follow the apostolic pattern of prayer, just as we ought to follow the apostolic practice of evangelism, as a general rule. And we certainly encourage people to use all available medical means to get well. But empowered evangelicals also believe that the intervention of God goes *beyond* the use of natural medicine and goes *beyond* God simply "being with" people and situations. Empowered evangelicals believe in the *actual transformation* of people and situations through the direct intervention of God, *apart* from natural means every bit as much as *through* natural means. Thus, we believe that it is imperative for people to be taught to have some expectation that God will heal directly, supernaturally, and to model prayers for the sick that go beyond guiding the surgeons' hands.

Why Jesus heals. It is commonplace in some conservative evangelical teachings to assume that Jesus healed only as a proof of his Messiahship. Thus, it is assumed that Christ healed as a sign that he was the Anointed One, the Son of David. At times, various Scriptures do suggest that Christ's healing activity was designed to be a sign that he was the fulfiller of Old Testament prophecy (see Luke 7:20-23). (Nevertheless, the healing works of Jesus are often attributed to nothing other than *the compassion* of Christ for those who are struggling.) It is not at all the case that Jesus healed simply to prove to a sick person that he was the Messiah. The primary motive attributed to Jesus is the Greek verb *splanchnizomai*, which is best translated as "compassion." This word originally referred to the innards of a person—the liver, the intestines, the stomach. What compassion means, then, is that when Jesus came upon sick people, he felt pity for them in his "guts." Healing flowed from the deepest part of Christ. Have you ever felt pity and compassion for a sick person in your guts? Have you ever had a visceral response to someone's hurt or illness? Perhaps that was God's signal to you to pray for the person's healing.

Thus, people can be physically healed today simply because God is good and wishes to be good to them and not because of any necessary proof or authentication of the gospel. Indeed, a sick person may already believe the gospel and may need no further verification. Nevertheless, God may choose to be good to him or her through healing. On the other hand, an unbelieving person who is healed may continue in unbelief. God simply is good to the just and unjust alike (see Matthew 5:45).

Sanctification through sickness? Conservative evangelicals have, at times, adopted a perspective of illness which can be traced to the end of the Roman persecution of the church in the fourth century. In most of the writings of the New Testament and most of the writings of the early church fathers, passages regarding suffering are most commonly associated with suffering via the persecution (often physical) of Christians by the world. This suffering through persecution was believed to have a sanctifying effect in the life of the believer. Thus, Peter described believers as going through painful trials and as a result of these persecutions "done with sin" (1 Pt 4:1). It may be that persecution causes a person to look to God more strongly, and as a result of increased dependence on God, an individual is made holy. However, after the elimination of physical persecution from many Christians' lives, biblical passages on suffering were often reinterpreted to the more common experience that believers had, namely illness and disease. While empowered evangelicals would not object to a secondary application of suffering passages to sickness and illness, we believe that this is not the primary import of most passages regarding trials and sufferings. Further, empowered evangelicals believe that a "sanctification through sickness" position can, at times, lead a person away from asking God for physical healing. It is, of course, the case that God can and does use anything, including illness, to make his people holy! Indeed, God can use any consequence of the Fall, including divorce and church splits, to make us holy, but such is not the norm. Indeed, we would be remiss in our practice of Christianity if we did not pray *against* such things and *for* God's purpose of holiness to be brought into our lives *apart from sinful and broken situations.* Far better for us to be made holy through prayer and Bible reading, fellowship, worship, and obedience to the commandments of God than through the brokenness caused by the Fall, such as illness or broken relationships.

Again, empowered evangelicals believe in the sovereignty of God and certainly view sickness as a potential occasion for sanctification. But we would see sickness chiefly as a consequence of the *not yet* of the kingdom and the universal human experience of fallenness and not primarily as being sent to us by God to make us holy.

But I don't have the gift of healing. If you become convinced that healing is a part of the kingdom of God, which invaded this world through the first coming of Jesus Christ, you might adopt the position like that of many conservative evangelicals: "Well, I believe that God can potentially heal people because I see healing in the Gospels and in the Book of Acts. And I certainly believe that God can do anything he wants. I also see that some may be gifted with the gift of healing, *but I don't have the gift of healing.*"

Empowered evangelicals believe that while some may more regularly be used by God to heal the sick, that does not exclude the rest of us from praying for physical healing for the sick on a regular basis. By way of analogy, there are very few of us, if any, who have the gift of evangelism at the same level as Billy Graham. Indeed, only a small percentage of us are even called to be evangelists (see Ephesians 4:11). Nevertheless, we are all called upon to share our faith and we know that if we regularly share our faith, occasionally someone will respond to our less than powerful presentation of the gospel and be converted.

In the same way, we may not be uniquely gifted in praying for the sick, but if we pray often enough, we will see a few people get physically healed. Our own experiences are exactly this. We have discovered that if we take lots of swings at the ball, we will occasionally get a hit even though we more commonly strike out. The fact that we now regularly pray for the sick, whereas we didn't in the past, means that we are going to see more people physically healed at present than we did when we didn't pray for anyone.

Could it be that the reason you have rarely or never seen people physically healed is because you don't pray for people to be physically healed on a regular basis?

LESSONS IN THE AGONY OF DEFEAT

The church that prays for the sick must be trained to deal with failure every bit as much as success. Nothing will stop a person from praying more often than having no capability to deal with the regular experience of failure. If a church simply sends people out to pray for the sick without the knowledge that many of the folks they pray for will not get well, the church will guarantee that the folks it sends out will not pray for the sick for long.[7]

The experience of the church in this age is that of "seeing through a mirror dimly." We "know only in part" (1 Cor 13:12, 13:9, KJV). Things are not simple in this age since we live between the *already* and the *not yet*. But knowing in part is better than not knowing at all! *We know* that God understands suffering because the nails that went through the hands of

Jesus went through the hands of God. *We know* that whatever happens, whether a person is healed or not, God promises to work situations out for good for those who love God and are his children (see Romans 8:28). The "good" promised in Romans 8:28 is, of course, not necessarily our immediate good, nor always our apparent good. Continued sickness will not always seem good, but God promises to use even our continued sickness for our ultimate good. Therefore, Christians can always say, "I believe God will use this situation for my good even though I can't currently see how."

We also know that all healing, however wonderful, is both partial and temporary. One day people will be totally healed, but that day is not now. We may be healed of a blind eye and still suffer from a cold. And even Lazarus eventually succumbed to death.

What we *don't know* is why some people are healed and some people are not. Certainly healing is not the result of merit or holiness or personal worth or even, from our perspective, the fact that a healing will result in a strong witness to families or friends. Sometimes Jesus simply does not tell us in this life why somebody remains ill (see John 9:1-3). We also do not know the precise interaction of faith, expectancy, hearing from God, and God's action in our lives.

That faith must be present to receive anything from God is a scriptural fact (see Hebrews 11:6). To obtain healing, or anything else from God, we must believe that God *is,* that God *is good,* and that God *will be good* to us if we pray to him! But the exact proportions of faith and God's activity are not always apparent. Sometimes it seems to us that we are full of faith and God does not heal. At other times we simply pray without the feeling of faith, because we know we should, and God does miraculously heal. We do not know the precise mixture necessary of the human and divine components or why certain prayers work sometimes and others do not. This is why, by the way, we prefer the term "divine healing" rather than "faith healing," since it emphasizes God's activity and not our faith!

HEALING AND EVANGELISM

Throughout this book we will point out the value of coupling the conservative evangelical target of evangelism and world missions with charismatic power. Nowhere is this coupling more biblical than where healing is concerned. Certainly, the gospel message alone has saving power apart from any physical healing (see Romans 1:16). Certainly too, the power we chiefly celebrate is the power of the cross (see 1 Corinthians 1:17). Not everyone who experiences healings or any miracle will necessarily believe or be saved! (See John 10:25-26.) Nevertheless, physical healing can often serve as *a door opener* to people's reception of the power of the gospel message. Thus the gospel message spread quickly through entire cities in the Book of Acts through the accompanying presence of healings (Acts 9:32, 42). And if reports from China and the Muslim and Hindu worlds are to be believed, the gospel is spreading like wildfire in two-thirds of the world, in part because it is often accompanied by physical healing.

Why is physical healing a helpful encouragement for unbelievers to believe in the gospel for salvation? First, healing communicates supernatural reality to the message we preach. Certainly, the resurrection of Christ should be evidence enough. Yet there are many "Thomases" who do benefit by some visible sign of God's reality and presence.

But more than God's power, physical healing often communicates a message of God's love and concern. We have seen several nonbelievers turn to Christ for salvation after being physically healed because they realized that if God loved them enough to heal them, he must love them enough to save them.

Physical healing functions very much like an act of service. And even if a nonbeliever is not healed (which is our ultimate fear), we have found that people still believe that God loves them, since his representatives (we Christians) love them enough to pray for them.

FOR DISCUSSION

1. How do the authors explain the experience of the thrill and the agony? Have you experienced both sides of the Christian life? Discuss how you have explained your experience of disappointment.
2. According to the authors, why did Jesus heal? Do you agree? Why or why not?
3. Why don't you pray for the sick more often? What would encourage you to pray for the sick?
4. What is the relationship between healing and the Atonement according to the authors? Do you agree?
5. What is the relationship of healing to evangelism and world missions in the Bible, according to the authors? Do you agree?

WHEN SEEKING A CHURCH

1. Does the church seem to have a balanced message—one emphasizing both thrill and agony—in its approach to ministry?
2. Does the church teach people to pray for the sick? If it does, how does the church approach those who are not healed? Are people blamed for not being healed or are they always loved and encouraged to remember God's love for them?

3. Is God free to do whatever he pleases in the church, including divine healing or choosing not to heal?

FOR PASTORS

1. Consider doing a series on healing and the kingdom of God from the Gospels. Try to not "spiritualize" the healings, but instead, treat them as they were written—as *physical* healings.
2. Since going outside one's familiar surroundings can serve to stretch us, consider attending a seminar or conference with several of your key leaders on the subject of healing. Consider inviting someone with whom you are comfortable theologically to do a conference at your church on the subject of healing.
3. Do the people in your church know how to pray for the sick? How can this skill be developed?
4. Do the people in your church know how to deal with failure or disappointment? How can you better equip them to deal with failure? Consider testimonies from people in your church on experiencing "the thrill of victory" and coping with "the agony of defeat."

FOR FURTHER STUDY

Don Williams, *Signs, Wonders, and the Kingdom of God* (Ann Arbor, Mich.: Servant, 1989).

John Wimber, *Power Healing* (San Francisco: Harper and Row, 1987).

George Ladd, *The Presence of the Future* (Grand Rapids, Mich.: Eerdmans, 1974) and *The Gospel of the Kingdom* (Grand Rapids, Mich.: Eerdmans, 1959).

FOUR

The Supernatural and the Natural

In the 1940s two researchers conducted an interesting experiment regarding people's ability to perceive unexpected facts. The researchers presented the subjects with a series of playing cards and asked the subjects to identify the cards. Most of the cards were normal, but some were deliberately made unusual: for example, red spades or black hearts.

The subjects of the experiment were shown a single card and then asked to identify what they had seen. When shown the "normal" cards, the subjects always responded correctly. The subjects shown the unusual cards, however, almost always "saw" normal playing cards! They responded without any hesitation or questioning: The card was "fit" into a category that corresponded to the subjects, prior experience of playing cards. In a very real sense, the subjects had not even seen anything different than what they had expected.

Only when the researchers increased the exposure time to the unusual cards did the subjects begin to hesitate and display any awareness that they were viewing something out of the ordinary. Even then, the subjects desired to fit what they were seeing into their prior expectations. Exposed, for example, to a red five of spades, one of the subjects said, "That is the five of spades, but something is wrong with it. It has a black border."

Further increases in the exposure time resulted in even more hesitation and puzzlement until finally, and often quite suddenly, most subjects understood what was going on and were able to correctly identify the unusual playing cards. After doing this with two or three cards, most subjects were able to rapidly identify other unusual cards. A fascinating side note was that several subjects were never able to adjust their prior categories or expectations. Even at forty times the average exposure necessary to recognize normal cards, several subjects were simply unable to correctly identify the unusual cards. One of the subjects exclaimed: "I couldn't make the suit out, whatever it is. It didn't even look like a card that time. I don't know what color it is or whether it is a spade or a heart. I am not even sure, now, what a spade looks like."[1]

Importance of paradigms. According to Thomas Kuhn's famous study of the progress of science, science moves ahead not simply by the gradual accumulation of additional discoveries, but also by revolutionary changes that Kuhn calls "paradigm shifts." According to Kuhn, a paradigm is not a theory or hypothesis, but a way of looking at the world that is influenced by cultural prejudice, as well as by scientific observation and experience.

In other words, scientists, like the rest of us, do not view the world "as it is," but through the lens of previous assumptions, prejudices, prior experience, and the authority of teachers and mentors. This is not to suggest that starting with certain given assumptions is bad or wrong. If it were, we would have to go back to ground zero every day in terms of the entire way we interact with the world around us. It is not necessary to repeatedly discover that you cannot walk through a wall. One bump on the head or a stubbed toe is sufficient to "prove" to you that walls cannot be walked through.[2]

Of course, scientists are not the only ones affected by this issue of paradigms. All of us look at the world through a set of assumptions and expectations. An easy way to think about a paradigm is to compare it to a pair of glasses that one wears when looking out at the world. Often, in fact almost always, one is not even aware that he or she is wearing a pair of glasses. The world is thought to be seen as it is instead of being filtered through our glasses.

A paradigm is simply the way that a person perceives reality. Defined this way, we can quickly see that no two people wear exactly the same glasses all of the time. For example, if you have been married for more than one day, you have come to the realization that something in your spouse's brain often misfires when it comes to recollecting conversations. This misfiring particularly takes place regarding areas of dispute such as in-laws, money, sex, and the proper way to squeeze a tube of toothpaste.

The lens through which one looks at life is shaped by one's gender, education, and culture. It is important to understand that few of us had mothers who sat us down and said, "Now, honey, this is the paradigm (set of assumptions or worldview) through which we, here in this household, look at material things, relationships, and causal connections between events." The idea of a paradigm is that it is not explicitly taught, but is rather an *unstated assumption*. It is something that a culture, a family, or a group considers to be a given. A paradigm can become such a self-evident proposition that it "simply goes without saying." Thus, like the glasses that a person wears, one is not even aware that a lens exists through which the world is viewed until it is called into question.

Because paradigms are often received through cultural conditioning, we can see other cultures' paradigms better than we can see our own. A great illustration can be seen in the movie *The Gods Must Be Crazy*. In the movie, a Coca-Cola bottle was dropped from an airplane. A primitive sub-Saharan African tribe that had had no previous contact with the West saw the bottle falling from the sky. Because the tribesmen had no prior experience with airplanes, they assumed that the bottle had been dropped from the sky by one of their gods. Working on this assumption, they reasoned that the gods must have placed the bottle in their midst for a purpose. The movie then proceeds to tell the story of how the tribe discovered the hidden meaning of the gods' purpose for the tribe—all because of a Coca-Cola bottle.

Our point is that none of us sees objectively. We all have cultural lenses or paradigms through which we see the world. The church is no different.

CONSERVATIVE EVANGELICAL PARADIGMS

Many conservative evangelicals have adopted a number of paradigms that we see as unbiblical. Often, conservative evangelical believers are: (1) deistic, (2) naturalistic, (3) rationalistic, and (4) technique- and control-oriented.

Many conservative evangelicals are deistic. Deism was a view that became popular during the seventeenth century as a result of the Enlightenment. Deists believe that God created the world in such a way that it precludes him from getting involved in the day-to-day management of world events. *The Evangelical Dictionary of Theology* puts it this way: "Deism reduces God's function in creation to that of first cause only. According to the classical comparison of God with a clock maker... God wound up the clock of the world once and for all at the beginning, so that it now proceeds as world history without the need for his further involvement."

Clearly, deism is an entirely unbiblical view of God. In the Bible, God intervenes in the affairs of men and women, giving guidance through prophets, dreams, visions, pillars of fire, angelic visitations, earthquakes, and floods. He also upholds the world through his providence. Yet, despite the obvious unbiblical assumption that deism holds, namely that God does not intervene, many conservative evangelicals often look at the activity of God through a deistic pair of glasses.

Contrary to the biblical view of God, who is always involved in the lives of men and women in this world, many modern conservative evangelicals view God like a *Star Trek* adventure in which God, on extremely rare occasions, beams down into this world. A prayer is answered, a person is saved, a job long sought for is obtained, but then God beams back up, and the world continues to operate according to unchangeable laws set up by God at creation.

Many conservative evangelicals are naturalistic. Again, as a result of the Enlightenment, conservative evangelicals have been taught to interpret the world naturalistically. This means that the natural universe, the universe of matter and energy, contains all that is truly Real. Of course, conservative evangelicals believe in reality beyond matter and energy. Few conservative evangelicals would doubt the existence of angels or demons, much less of God. Nor would most conservative evangelicals doubt the possibility of healing or the possibility that somebody might receive supernatural guidance. Nevertheless, the supernatural realm is viewed as being less "real" than the natural realm.

To prove this, one need only compare the skepticism with which a claim of supernatural healing is received compared to a claim of healing by natural (medical) means. For example, if a person reports that as a result of prayer, a tumor under his arm disappeared, our naturalistically inclined minds might immediately raise questions such as: Are you sure you had a tumor? How long did you have the tumor? Did it somehow disappear as a result of a change in your body's chemistry? Are you sure that the tumor is gone? Are you simply deluding yourself into believing that the tumor is gone and you really ought to see a doctor? Of course, we might be too polite to raise such questions with a person who claims to have been healed as a result of prayer, but we certainly might think of them.

Consider, by way of contrast, a report by the same individual in which he tells us that a tumor was removed from under his arm as a result of an operation. Would we even imagine that he had no tumor or that another explanation for the tumor's disappearance is probably in order? Would we wonder in our minds if the person was deluded regarding the success of the operation?

The fact is, according to most western conservative evangelicals, "Reality" (with a capital "R") means the reality we can see, touch, and smell. All of our questions and doubts tend to be resolved in favor of a naturalistic interpretation over a supernatural interpretation of life's events. Indeed, it takes a very conscious effort for western conservative evangelicals to remove the naturalistic lenses and "to see" what people in other cultures or in the culture of the Bible saw.

Many conservative evangelicals are rationalistic. The post-Enlightenment culture has gained an understanding of the natural world primarily through the use of reason and intellect: The world, we believe, is accurately mediated to us through our intellects and our reason, rather than intuition and emotion. The priority that westerners place on human reason and the corresponding devaluation of emotion, intuition, and experience is called rationalism. Western conservative evangelicals are regularly told not to base their relationship with God on their experience, but on the truth!

While we heartily agree that we ought to base our relationship with God on the truth, why do we implicitly assume that our experiences would not be a vehicle for communicating the truth to us? Indeed, experience and feelings are so often called into question that one might begin to believe that only human reason was left untouched by the Fall. But every part of our being, including our reason, has been corrupted as the result of the Fall.

There is no inherent reason to trust human intellect any more than we trust human intuition. Indeed, some of the most corrupt people who have ever lived have been highly intelligent but have used their intelligence in a perverted and God-rejecting way. Nevertheless, the idea persists in evangelical circles that feelings, experiences, and intuition are, by definition, suspect while reason is not.

Many conservative evangelicals place a high value on technique and control. Os Guinness, in his fascinating book *No God, But God,* helpfully explores the effect of the modern age upon the church. Guinness writes:

> More and more of what formerly was left to God, or human initiative, or the processes of nature, is now classified, calculated, and controlled by the systematic application of reason and technique. What counts in the rationalized world is efficiency, predictability, quantifiability, productivity, the substitution of technology for the human, and—from first to last—control over uncertainty.[3]

Quoting social scientist Philip Rieff, Guinness sums up the church's preoccupation with control, saying, "What characterizes modernity, I think, is just this idea that men need not submit to any power—higher or lower—other than their own. In other words, there is no need for God, even in the church."[4]

Consider the way that worship is often engineered to create an inspirational effect for the congregation. Inspiration, of course, was formerly something left to the domain of God. In the New Testament, worship was anything but totally planned. Indeed, it appears that the Holy Spirit was the chief administrator of New Testament worship: "Now to each one the manifestation of the Spirit is given for the common good. To one there is given through the Spirit the message of wisdom, to another the message of knowledge by means of the same Spirit.... All these are the work of one and the same Spirit, and he gives them to each one, *just as he determines*" (1 Cor 12:7-8, 11, emphasis added).

Of course, we legitimately plan time for our worship, offering, and message in our main worship times. But must every single detail be pre-programmed? Forgetting for a moment whether we have faith to believe that individuals in our churches might spontaneously be given spiritual gifts, or even if we believe such gifts exist, when is time set aside for spiritual gifts to be employed during a worship service? When exactly during one of our modern worship services would a person read a Scripture or deliver a tongue and interpretation or a prophecy if every minute of the worship service has been pre-engineered before the meeting?

On a more personal level, how much room is there in our own lives for the Holy Spirit's guidance and redirection of our plans and our ambitions? Isn't it the case that many times we open our leaders' meetings in prayer and close our meetings in prayer, spending the vast percentage of our meeting oblivious to what God might be saying as we make our plans? In essence, while we say that Jesus is the head of our church, we are easily tempted to ask Jesus to bless our human control of the church.

Consider also the modern job description of a pastor, which in most large churches requires the same kinds of management skills that you would expect from the business world model of a CEO. Unfortunately, pastors may not be expected to be able to cast out demons, heal the sick, or even evangelize the lost; but in the effectively-led large church, pastors will be expected to draft a meaningful mission statement for the church, articulate the church's values and vision, delegate authority, preside over boards and committees, set reasonable goals and timetables for acheiving those goals, manage budgets, and write job descriptions. Are our standards of measuring large church pastors really derived from the Bible?[5] Even our training of seminarians tends to place a premium on human technique and control.

Don Williams writes:

In my "enlightenment" theological education, I was trained to control everything. Paul's dictum to do all things "decently and in order" is lived out by us Presbyterians to a fault. Thus, I was given exegetical tools with which to manage the Bible, theological tools with which to manage the faith, homiletical tools with which to manage my sermons, psychological and sociological tools with which to manage people and business tools with which to manage the church. Today's seminary curriculum is far advanced in the application of the scientific method to the professional clergy.[6]

What are the effects of adopting a supernaturalistic paradigm on the life of a church? The impact of what we believe is biblical paradigm cannot be overstated. A supernaturalistic paradigm is a worldview in which God, angels, and demons regularly interact and affect the world of people and material through such means as signs and wonders, healings, prophecies, visions, visitations, dreams, blessings, and curses.

Consider the matter of *physical healing*. Working with naturalistic assumptions, the first thing that a Christian might do when suffering from a backache is to call a physician or reach for the aspirin bottle. Working with a supernatural paradigm, the same Christian might, *first of all,* ask for prayer for physical healing and might occasionally discover that the backache was caused by an afflicting spirit. (If afflicting spirits can cause deafness and blindness in the Bible, which we naturalistically assume have only physiological causes, why not backaches?)[7] If we pressed the matter of divine healing further, we might begin to have seminars in our churches teaching people how to pray for the sick. We might begin to employ special parts of our church services specifically for healing prayer. We might even form prayer teams to go into hospitals to pray for patients. And we certainly would pay more attention to healing passages in the Gospels, asking ourselves what we can learn from such passages that would be valuable for our own practice of physical healing.

Consider also the matter of *guidance* and how we teach young disciples to discern the will of God for their lives. Much current conservative evangelical practice would confine the means of guidance to such things as the study of the written text of Scripture, obtaining godly counsel, and evaluating whether the decision is in accordance with our created desires and natural gifts.

In addition to these very legitimate means of discovering God's will, a supernaturalistic paradigm would add the possibility of a prophetic word such as that given by Agabus to the apostle Paul, or the possibility of a vision as in the case of Peter, or the possibility of receiving guidance through a dream as in the case of Jesus' father Joseph (see Acts 21:10-11; Acts 10:9-17; Matthew 1:20; 2:13, 19, 22). Why, in light of the extraordinary number of occurrences of dreams, visions, and prophetic words in the Bible, do we not train young disciples to anticipate the possibility of being guided by such means? Why do we not further train disciples to be able to interpret dreams or visions or to distinguish between true and false prophecies? Perhaps our naturalistic assumptions regarding how guidance might be received have controlled our discipleship training more than we ever realized.

A third area in which a supernaturalistic paradigm would radically affect our practice is *evangelism*. Currently, most conservative evangelistic practice and training regarding witnessing techniques focus primarily upon the logical presentation of gospel facts, as well as the ability to answer the questions that unbelievers frequently ask, in a reasonable and orderly way. Of course, presenting the facts of the gospel and answering questions of an unbeliever are primary skills that must be developed in our training of young witnesses. But why not add to our witnessing training programs the expectation that God might also wish to give to the evangelist a spontaneous insight or illustration that would give the gospel message more impact? Isn't that what the Holy Spirit did with Jesus when he was given insight regarding the particular sins of the woman at the well? Such leadings from God can often break through an individual's defenses so that they can "hear" the gospel facts for all that they are worth.

Perhaps, too, our presentation of the gospel message through a supernaturalistic framework would occasionally involve prayer for the healing of an unsaved person's physical condition. Like timely prophetic words, physical healings can serve to propel the message of the gospel forward by giving it supernatural validation and maximum impact.[8]

Finally, many evangelicals may need to revise their understanding of the word *disciple* to include following in healings, in deliverances, and in signs and wonders. What other than an anti-supernatural paradigm accounts for our restricting the scope of following Jesus to imitating Jesus' character or imitating Jesus' teaching?

For example, our college fellowship was fond of defining discipleship as follows: we were told that to be a disciple means "to be with him [Jesus] and to be sent out to preach [the gospel]" (Mk 3:14). Discipleship, therefore, included spending time with Christ and sharing our faith in Christ. What we weren't told was that the text that was quoted was cut off to exclude the supernatural element of deliverance. The text actually reads: "He appointed twelve—designating them apostles—that they might be with him and that he might send them out to preach *and to have authority to drive out demons."* For Jesus' followers, the ability to heal and to cast out demons was as much a part of their followership as preaching.[9] Yet these supernatural elements are neglected by many evangelicals today.

In sum, a church that wished to replace its naturalistic and rationalistic paradigms with a more biblical paradigm would find a significant number of its assumptions regarding the way to train, the way to witness, the way to worship, the way to lead and the way to counsel called into question.

THE TWO RULES OF ALL PARADIGMS

There are two rules that we need to understand if we wish to explore our own assumptions more deeply. (1) We do not see what we "know" should not be there. (2) If we do see, we constantly try to fit what we see into existing assumptions (we see what we want to see, or at least what we think we should see).

We do not see what we "know" should not be there. Recall the playing card experiment mentioned at the beginning of this chapter. In that experiment, the subjects, through prior conditioning, could not "see" unusual cards such as red spades.

Harvard theologian Krister Stendahl said, "It is not so much what we don't know, but *what we think we know* that obstructs our vision."[10] For example, after a leader falls into immorality, many people will often come forward saying, "How is it that we didn't see the warning signs of his unfaithfulness?" Often the warning signs were there to see: the leader's behavior was becoming erratic, he seemed to be flirtatious with young women, he had lapses for which he was unable to account in his schedule, even his sermons began to focus more on the problems of a double life due to immorality. Nevertheless, because everyone "knew" that the leader could not be immoral, they did not "see" the evidence mounting against him.

African-Americans often complain that black churches in the inner city are virtually invisible to white conservative evangelicals. Because of prior conditioning, white conservative evangelicals will often look at an inner-city neighborhood and wonder why no church is present in the neighborhood. Of course, the church is present, namely an African-American church, but it is not seen because the white observers are looking for a church that resembles their expectation of church life in the suburbs. A church must be a free-standing building with a parking lot surrounding it, having lots of green space, perhaps with a playground in the back and a parsonage next door. A church building does not look like a storefront or a warehouse or an apartment or a private residence.

Applying this problem of seeing to the realm of the supernatural, Charles Kraft, in his book on worldviews and a person's experience of the supernatural called *Christianity With Power,* brilliantly exposits the ninth chapter of John. From

John 9 Kraft finds numerous instances of people's prior assumptions blinding them from seeing the facts. For example, the Pharisees "knew" that "the man [who healed the blind man] could not be from God, for he does not obey the Sabbath law." They did not investigate whether Jesus was from God. That possibility was foreclosed by their prejudiced assumptions. Because of this knowledge, the Pharisees were also not willing to believe that the man was born blind. Nor were they willing to believe that Jesus was the Messiah because, as they said, "We know that this man who cured you is a sinner." Further, the Pharisees knew that they were not blind and that they would certainly recognize the signs accompanying someone who was from God.[11]

How does all of this apply to segments of the conservative evangelical church today? Consider the popular teaching that Bible miracles only appear in clusters around fresh periods of biblical revelation.[12] Bible miracles are said to occur almost entirely around the period of Moses and Joshua, Elijah and Elisha, and during the time of Jesus and the apostles. If one is taught this perspective, it is difficult to see that every part of the Bible is thoroughly supernatural and filled with the miraculous.

For example, the Book of Genesis is filled with the miraculous activity of God. In Genesis chapters 6-8, God destroys the earth by sending a miraculous flood that covers the entire earth. In Genesis 11, God supernaturally intervenes to destroy the Tower of Babel. God repeatedly speaks to Abraham in ways that we would consider today "supernatural"—through dreams, angelic visitations, and visions. The same kind of supernatural communication was given to Isaac, Jacob, and Joseph. Likewise, the birth of Isaac to his aged parents, Abraham and Sarah, is obviously nothing short of a miracle. Genesis is no less than fifty chapters that record the miraculous. Yet it falls outside of the paradigm of

Moses and Joshua, Elijah and Elisha, and Jesus and the apostles.

One could easily multiply the examples of the miraculous tenfold beyond these. Suffice it to say, one can hardly imagine a clearer example of the inability to see what we "know" is not there than the often-repeated—but utterly erroneous—teaching that biblical miracles are almost entirely clustered around three eras of biblical history.

If we do see, we constantly try to fit what we see into existing assumptions. At the beginning of this book, the story was told of the woman who kept falling to the ground, growling and choking, every time our college Bible study group prayed. The pastor to whom we took the woman believed our story: that the woman did, in fact, fall to the ground and would begin choking. However, his naturalistic assumptions precluded his interpreting her falling or choking as a demonic manifestation. Instead, he sought out a psychological explanation for what we witnessed.

Likewise, Mike, who had epileptic grand mal seizures for twenty-five years, never had another one after receiving prayer for healing. The physicians who had previously treated Mike did not doubt his long history of epileptic seizures; nor did they doubt that his seizures had suddenly stopped without reoccurrence. Their explanation, however, was that Mike's brain "out grew" them. That another possibility for Mike's healing existed, namely the prayers of a Christian, was not considered worthy of consideration by the physicians who had been trained in naturalistic explanations for physiological occurrences.

The Bible contains many wonderful examples of people who saw things but reinterpreted them according to their prior understandings. Again, we want to note that what we are talking about here are people who do *see* the facts, but *reinterpret* the facts according to their prior assumptions. For example, in John 12:28 the Scripture clearly tells us that God the Father spoke to Jesus and a crowd saying, "I have glorified [my name] and will glorify it again." The objective fact was that God the Father spoke from heaven. Nevertheless, John records, "The crowd that was there and heard [God's voice] said it had thundered; others said an angel had spoken to him" (Jn 12:29). The prior beliefs of the crowd forced the voice from heaven into more acceptable paradigms, namely either thunder or an angelic voice. How might this apply to us today?

Conservative evangelicals will often comment as they look back at their experiences of witnessing that they have regularly had examples or pictures simply pop into their mind that turned out to be greatly beneficial in presenting the gospel. Yet because of naturalistic assumptions, many conservative evangelicals have assumed that these spontaneous impressions or pictures were simply bursts of human inspiration or intuition. Perhaps they *were* entirely human, but how might a thoroughly supernaturalistic Christian interpret spontaneous insights that have tremendous power in drawing a person to salvation? Would not a supernaturalistic Christian regularly consider that those insights might have been given by God?[13]

RECOVERING THE NATURAL FOR CHARISMATICS

If the problem with many conservative evangelicals is the emphasis on naturalistic assumptions to the exclusion of the supernatural, the opposite problem exists for some charismatics. Supernaturalistic explanations are offered for every occurrence, even when a perfectly reasonable naturalistic explanation is available to entirely account for the occurrence.[14] What is necessary for some charismatics is a recovery of a view of God as being not only the God of signs and wonders, but also *the God of creation and providence.*

What does it mean for some charismatics to recover a view of God as a God of creation and providence? This renewed view of God would affect such things as the typical view of charismatic teaching of spiritual gifts, the charismatic practice of healing, the items highlighted in testimony times, as well as a more esteemed view of work and the arts in charismatic churches.

A more complete view of spiritual gifts. In a good deal of charismatic teaching, a sharp distinction is drawn between the supernatural gifts of the Spirit such as miracles, tongues, and healing, and more natural gifts such as administration, service, and teaching. But why draw a distinction between the gifts of the Spirit at all, classifying some as supernatural and some as natural? We are reminded in 1 Corinthians 12:6 that there are different kinds of working, but the same God works all of them in all people. Certain kinds of gifts are not implicitly elevated above others. In fact, Paul's entire argument in 1 Corinthians 12 is dismantled by the implication that God is more present in certain kinds of gifts than others.

A specific example of where charismatics (and our own church, the Vineyard) may give an overly supernatural interpretation of spiritual gifts and implicitly devalue more natural giftings concerns the charismatic interpretation of the "word of wisdom and word of knowledge." In 1 Corinthians 12:8 Paul writes: "To one there is given through the Spirit the message of wisdom, to another the message of knowledge by means of the same Spirit." There is no way to know, precisely, what Paul was referring to by a message of wisdom or message of knowledge since this is the only time this exact phrasing is used in the New Testament.

The typical charismatic interpretation of these gifts is that they involve the ability to receive a special, spontaneous revelation from the Holy Spirit and, on that basis, to give words that give wisdom or knowledge in a specific situation. The wisdom or knowledge is not based on information currently available to the person using the gift but derives solely from the Holy Spirit's immediate inspiration. But another possible interpretation is available for the word of knowledge and word of wisdom. Perhaps these gifts are simply the ability to speak a wise word or a knowledgeable word of counsel in a situation without any particular supernatural burst of insight. The counsel may come from one's Christian experience or a deep understanding of the Scriptures.

We prefer this latter possibility for two reasons. First, Paul's desire that the body value *all* of its gifts would seem to work better if nonmiraculous gifts were included in the gift list in 1 Corinthians 12. Since the Corinthians only seem to value the supernatural gifts, it would seem reasonable for Paul to include the more natural gifts in his list of giftings. He would, therefore, be suggesting to the Corinthians that both natural and supernatural gifts be equally valued as originating with the Holy Spirit.

Second, the spontaneous burst of insight, giving information that was not previously available to the speaker, is normally called something else in the Bible, namely prophecy.[15] A reevaluation would bring due honor to gifts of organization and, among other things, gifts of service, hospitality, teaching, and scholarship. Then the "big eyes" in the body would stop being able to say to the hands, "I don't need you." Nor would "the ear" ever be able to say again, "Because I am not an eye, I do not belong to the body" (1 Cor 12:16:21).

Learning to appreciate medicine and counseling. Many Christians live, according to the late Francis Schaeffer, as if God had created a two-story universe.[16] In the two-story universe the upper story is the realm of the supernatural, including God, angels, and demons. The lower story is the realm of the natural, including people, matter, and energy. Conservative evangelicals have primarily occupied the lower story while many charismatics have lived as if real Christianity meant trying to move into the upper story! But a more biblical view suggests that God fills both the upper and lower stories of the universe and that there is regular interaction between the two floors. Indeed, one should hardly speak of a two-tiered universe at all since that language is nowhere to be found in the Bible.

A biblical worldview is far more holistic and unified than either many conservative evangelicals *or* charismatics believe. What this means for charismatics is that the God of creation may choose to use medicine or the created body's own healing properties to heal a person's illness as much as he chooses to use prayer to heal a person's illness. There is no more or less of God simply because God chooses to use means other than direct intervention to bring about a healing. Indeed, the very skill that physicians have is affirmed by the Bible to come from God.[17] It must be noted that on the far-out fringes of the charismatic movement some leaders have discouraged the use of medicine and people have reportedly died. But such "fringe" leaders are rare. We have met thousands of charismatics, but never any who did not visit a doctor when a doctor was needed. Nevertheless, there can sometimes be a failure to appreciate medicine as a gift from God because of the emphasis on divine healing.

A more unified view of reality, as opposed to a view of a two-story universe, also has implications for the approach to deliverance taken by some charismatic pastors, therapists, and lay counselors. One need not always look for a supernatural basis for a client or a church member's psychological or emotional problems. Not every problem is the result of a demon, a family curse, or a person's past involvement in the occult. Many problems that individuals have are simply the result of God's law regarding sowing and reaping. We have often encountered people who have sown weeds for years in their lives and are now looking for a supernatural explanation concerning why they are reaping a crop of weeds instead of fruit. It can be extremely liberating for people to hear a simple explanation of natural consequences flowing from their actions and their need to take personal responsibility for choices made rather than exhaustingly search for the secret or demonic roots of their problems.

Recovering the value of the arts, work, and scholarship. Many charismatics—as well as many conservative evangelicals, for that matter—having lost a view of God as Creator, have also lost an appreciation of the arts, work, and scholarship. It is interesting to note that artistry and craftsmanship are specifically called gifts of the Holy Spirit in Exodus 31, where we read:

> Then the Lord said to Moses, "See, I have chosen Bezalel son of Uri, the son of Hur, of the tribe of Judah, and *I have filled him with the Spirit of God, with skill, ability and knowledge in all kinds of crafts*—to make artistic designs for work in gold, silver and bronze, to cut and set stones, to work in wood, and to engage in all kinds of craftsmanship. Moreover, I have appointed Oholiab son of Ahisamach, of the tribe of Dan, to help him. Also *I have given skill* to all the craftsmen to make everything I have commanded you."

Imagine for a moment the explosion of creativity that might take place in a church if church leaders promoted the visual or performing arts as much as they did other spiritual gifts. Imagine what would happen if churches held seminars and training sessions for the performing arts. Not only would this bring about a fresh appreciation of the arts in the Christian community, but it would serve to inject Christian values into the artistic community—a community that is often bereft of a viable evangelical Christian witness. Work and the discipline of scholarship can, likewise, be invested with meaning through the recovery of a view of God as Creator.

Because many charismatic church members have been implicitly taught the two-tiered universe worldview, they often feel that work and the discipline of study lack real meaning and purpose since God is not really present in those things. Such a view leads individuals to a sense of emptiness and boredom at work and in school and a tendency to view church and religious activities as the only place of meaningful service to God. We have found that teaching on work and scholarship as places of activity for God, in and of themselves, and not merely opportunities to evangelize our coworkers or fellow students, helped individuals in our churches to approach work and school with fresh joy, purpose, and enthusiasm.

LEARNING TO BE NATURALLY SUPERNATURAL

Much of the struggle that conservative evangelicals have with some charismatic churches is not primarily theological as both sides tend to believe, but rather is a struggle over *ministry style* and *presentation*. It is here, in the area of ministry style, that some charismatics could lessen the divide with their conservative evangelical brethren by learning to do ministry in a more *naturally supernatural* way. Again, the challenge that we offer is expressed in great love and a desire for unity in the church and is not intended to be overly critical or judgmental in tone.

When we suggest that the style of some charismatic ministry could be more naturally supernatural, we mean that some churches, pastors, and conference speakers ought to stop the self-promotional tone in their marketing of ministries. Is it really necessary for conference brochures to have pictures of fire bolts exploding off the speaker? Or large captions calling the conference "Extravaganza '96"? How many life-changing conferences can a person attend in a year? How many once-in-a-lifetime experiences ought a person to expect? Everything that we do as churches need not be the biggest, the best, the most stupendous, or the most essential. Simple helpfulness to individual attenders ought to be sufficient to sell a conference. And during our ministry times, must we attempt to "set the mood" by offering six or seven testimonies of extraordinary miracles before we pray for the sick? Neither do we need piano music playing quietly in the background or flamboyant styles of speech and dress in order to provoke the Holy Spirit to act on our behalf.

What we see in Jesus' style of ministry is what John Wimber has helpfully labeled a "naturally supernatural" style. Jesus did not, generally, hold miracle services; miracles "naturally" occurred as people brought the sick to him to be healed. Sins were revealed in the course of normal conversation. I don't believe Jesus changed his voice or dress or body posture as he performed signs and wonders. Instead, the supernatural became part and parcel of the workaday world in which Jesus brought the kingdom of God.

Is it any wonder that church members feel terribly intimidated and unsure of themselves as they attempt to "do supernatural ministry" in their own lives? How can the average church member possibly recreate all of the trappings of a conference setting which have been modeled as essential for healing the sick or delivering the demonized? If the person standing up front would instead model for the congregation a style of ministry that could be taken to the workplace or the marketplace or a hospital or one's own home, then we believe that we will see what charismatics and Pentecostals have always longed for and taught: "the true equipping of the saints for the work of the ministry." Supernatural ministry would then be for every Christian in every setting and would not need to take place in special conferences by special people!

HOW TO CHANGE A PARADIGM IN ONESELF

Here are some tips in changing your worldview to a more biblical one:

1. Recognize that you have a worldview—that is, a set of lenses through which you look at life, the Bible, and God. Before your vision can be corrected, you must first understand how your own lenses distort your worldview. Do some reading about worldviews. Study prominent worldviews in the west such as deism, rationalism, and the continual demand for technique and control. Ask yourself how these unbiblical paradigms have affected your practices and beliefs.

2. Deliberately expose yourself to worldviews different from your own. A wonderfully enlightening experience for any Christian is to participate in a short-term mission trip to a non western culture. You will immediately become aware of the fact that people do not universally look at family, the relationship of men and women, sexuality, possessions, hospitality, God, demons, healing, or any one of a thousand other subjects through the lenses you wear. Short-term mission trips or involvement with internationals in your community are helpful in revealing your own assumptions about life, as well as allowing you the opportunity to challenge those assumptions through conversations with non-Westerners.

3. Test your theological assumptions by the Word of God. We do not need to reformulate for ourselves from ground zero the orthodox distinctives that have been hammered out over centuries such as the Trinity, the divine and human natures of Christ, justification by faith alone, or salvation by grace alone. But there are many theological assumptions, especially regarding supernatural ministry, that need to be tested in the light of Scripture alone. For example, is it the case that Bible miracles only appear in clusters to signal fresh written revelation, as some suggest? Do people in the Bible often receive guidance through means other than counsel, study, and circumstance? Do healings occur in the Bible on a regular basis apart from the use of medicine and the body's own healing mechanisms? When reexamining theological assumptions it is important to remember that even the greatest theologians were not free from cultural biases and nonbiblical assumptions. Go to the Word of God regarding supernatural ministry and see what it says!

4. Spend more time in the Gospels, taking special note of the details surrounding Jesus' healing and deliverance ministries. Begin to read the accounts of the miraculous in the Gospels not simply as proofs that Jesus was God's Son, but rather as a model for your own ministry. Ask yourself questions that perhaps you have not asked yourself before, such as: If you were confronted with a deaf person and had to pray for his or her healing, how would you do it? How did Jesus do it? What were Jesus' assumptions regarding healing? What are your assumptions? In what settings did Jesus perform miracles? Where do you expect miracles to take place?

5. Find people whose ministries and styles you wish to imitate and learn from them. Whatever background or theological tradition you come from, there are people whose styles of ministry conform to your own deeply held values. Often you may be able to respect a person's ministry as being valid and from God, but you simply find yourself unable to use that person as a model because of insurmountable cultural differences. Find somebody who is further ahead in supernatural ministry whose style you can emulate.

6. Pair up with somebody who wants to grow in the same direction you do. Changing paradigms is difficult work to do alone. It is far easier when you have the encouragement of another person to keep on reading, learning, growing, and practicing than when you have to self-initiate all changes.

7. Recognize that conditioning and cultural assumptions are very stubborn and are not replaced in our minds by a once-for-all decision. The disciples of Jesus needed to be told regularly that the Christ had to suffer and die. They certainly heard the message regarding Messiah's suffering and death and, perhaps, at points began to grasp it, but the change of their worldview regarding the work of Messiah was a slow and painful process. So it is regarding the change of our own worldviews from deism to theism and from naturalism to biblical supernaturalism. In this regard, we must adopt a lifestyle of repentance and regularly make choices regarding how we will interpret the evidence. Changing a biblical paradigm is not a choice to believe *against the evidence*. Rather, it is a choice to allow for the real possibility of a supernatural explanation for an occurrence.

8. Practice! Practice! Practice! A worldview is not changed simply by the adjustment of one's thoughts or by reading and intellectualization alone. Our beliefs often follow *what we practice and do*. You do not really believe in the supernatural until you begin to make a regular practice of praying for the sick or delivering the demonized. Just as you do not fully know the power of the gospel message alone to save until you have shared your faith with many people, so you will not know the power of Jesus Christ to heal unless you pray for lots of people. Practice the changes. Practice your new worldview.

FOR DISCUSSION

1. What do the authors mean by deism, rationalism, and naturalism? How have these philosophies affected your Christian experience?

2. What experience of God do you think you might have had, but not seen because of your prior assumptions?

3. Do you find a genuine sense of purpose in your job or in education? Why or why not?

4. Which of the authors' recommendations for changing a paradigm is most possible for you in the near future? How can you practically implement some of the recommendations?

WHEN SEEKING A CHURCH

1. Does the church practice supernatural Christianity, including prayer for divine healing, deliverance, and the expectation of guidance through prophecy and dreams? Does the church respect and encourage natural gifts such as medicine, scholarship, and the arts as gifts of God?

2. Does the church practice the supernatural in a natural style? Are you comfortable with the church's style? If you are uncomfortable, are you being stretched toward a more biblical form of Christianity—or a form you don't see in the Bible?

3. Does the church equip and train you to practice the supernatural aspects of Christianity?

FOR PASTORS

1. Consider teaching on worldviews prominent in the western world, particularly deism, naturalism, rationalism, and technique-orientation. Don't be afraid to point out how these philosophies have affected members of your church.

2. Are you satisfied with your church's practice of biblical Christianity, particularly in its supernatural aspects? How might you encourage change and growth in your church in this regard? Consider the recommendations made at the chapter's end. Which ought to be priorities for you? For your church?

3. Consider teaching on the value of work, the arts, and scholarship beyond simply being a vehicle for Christian evangelism. Consider hosting workshops for the performing arts and for Christians in the workplace.

FOR FURTHER STUDY

Charles H. Kraft, *Christianity with Power* (Ann Arbor, Mich.: Servant, 1989).

Jack Deere, *Surprised by the Power of the Spirit* (Grand Rapids, Mich.: Zondervan, 1993).

Gary S. Greig and Kevin N. Springer, *The Kingdom and the Power* (Ventura, Calif.: Regal, 1993).

Thomas S. Kuhn, *The Structure of Scientific Revolutions* (Chicago: University of Chicago Press, 1970).

Doug Sherman and William Hendricks, *Your Work Matters to God* (Colorado Springs: NavPress, 1987).

FIVE

Presumption, Fatalism, or Faith?

We all have different ways of asking for things. My (Ken's) mother, for example, hated to ask for anything directly. If she wanted someone at the table to pass her the broccoli, she would say, "Does anyone else want any more broccoli?" Once everyone declined, she would pipe up, "Well, then, I suppose I might have some more." Rich's father, on the other hand, didn't beat around the bush. You never had to wonder if he wanted the broccoli or not.

Conservative evangelicals and charismatics ask for things differently. The differences go beyond the styles of prayer to matters of approach and substance. My first intercessory prayer meeting involved evangelical friends in Detroit. One by one, individuals spoke out their requests to God. Prayers for certain things, like the salvation of a family member, were uttered without equivocation. "Lord, reveal yourself to my younger brother!" But other prayers were more tentative. "Father, if it be your will to heal my mother, heal her to the glory of your name. If not, I ask you to give her courage and faith to endure what she's going through."

Our Pentecostal friend from India took a different approach. When Benjamin prayed for physical healing, he prayed with the same confidence that he would pray for the forgiveness of sins. He often prayed as if it were a gift already given and he merely had to "appropriate" it. When healing didn't come, he prayed harder, sometimes to the point of frustration. Once, when he couldn't seem to shake a lingering virus, he told me, "Ken, I don't understand it. The devil should leave my body!"

To the conservative evangelical, the charismatic approach to prayer often seems to border on presumption. At worst, it sounds like ordering God around. To the charismatic, on the other hand, an evangelical's approach seems laced with as much fatalism as faith. An approach that draws from the best of both worlds provides for an active, expectant faith that doesn't fall into either presumption or passive fatalism. By examining some of the distinctive evangelical and charismatic approaches to faith, we will attempt to draw from the strengths of each perspective.

CONSERVATIVE EVANGELICAL AND CHARISMATIC SLOGANS

People involved in Alcoholics Anonymous know the power of recovery slogans—short phrases that are meant to help keep life in perspective. You've probably heard most of them: "Let go and let God," "One day at a time," "Easy does it." These are code phrases packed with meaning for the recovering alcoholic.

Christians have their slogans too—well-worn phrases that represent and summarize an accepted approach within the tradition: "If it be thy will," "Seek the Giver, not the gifts," and "Conversion is the greatest miracle." Charismatic slogans sound a different note: "Ask whatever you will," "Receive your inheritance," and "If you ask for bread, would he give you a stone?" First, we'll consider the conservative evangelical mottos.

"Lord, if it be thy will." We have rarely heard a conservative evangelical pray for healing without adding the proviso "if it be thy will." The request for healing is often paired with an alternative request, in case God chooses not to heal—perhaps for character building or increased endurance in the face of suffering.

Jesus himself prayed along these lines in the Garden of Gethsemane when he was groping for an alternative to his impending arrest and execution: *"My Father, if it is possible, may this cup be taken from me. Yet not as I will, but as you will"* (Mt 26:39). Another biblical reference may be found in the letter of James, where the author advises against presumption.

> Now listen, you who say, "Today or tomorrow we will go to this or that city, spend a year there, carry on business and make money." Why, you do not even know what will happen tomorrow.... Instead, you ought to say, "If it is the Lord's will, we will live and do this or that." As it is, you boast and brag. All such boasting is evil.   **James 4:13-16**

Of course, this latter text has more to do with planning than praying.

On the face of it, we can hardly argue with adding "if it be thy will" to any prayer. But we wonder if the practice of preceding virtually every request for supernatural intervention with this phrase doesn't reflect a form of fatalism that is far from biblical faith. At times it sounds as though the person praying thinks it may be proper to ask, but feels it would be presumptuous to expect any affirmative response from God.

The Bible clearly teaches us to pray with the understanding

that God acts in response to prayer he has inspired. When Jesus urged his disciples to "pray in his name," he was urging them to pray as his representatives, as those who have an understanding of his will. Certainly it would be the height of presumption to do or say anything "in his name" without a corresponding conviction that it is just what Jesus would want in the situation.

Through prayer we become participants with God in his work in the world. In other words, prayer changes things. God doesn't change, but we believe that God changes circumstances and changes us through our prayers. Prayer makes a difference because prayer is a means God has provided to bring the influence of his kingdom. This reflects the fact that we were created to be partners with God; we were meant to represent him and his interests, to seek to understand his purposes and cooperate with them. Of course God remains God while we are only and forever his creatures.

In order to pray "in his name," we have a responsibility to actively seek to understand his will. Too often, we pray halfheartedly because we lack any conviction regarding God's will in a given situation. The phrase "if it be thy will" doesn't excuse us from the responsibility to seek him so we can pray according to his will. At worst, the practice of sprinkling our prayers with "if it be thy will" may simply be a cover for deeply felt unbelief regarding God's probable activity in a given area such as healing, for example.

Some time ago, I visited a man in the intensive care unit who had had a severe reaction to medication, plunging him into a deep coma. His body was unresponsive to pain, and his kidneys had shut down. The physicians felt that should he recover, it was likely he would "be like a vegetable." Under the circumstances, it wasn't clear how we should pray. So we prayed for direction. Over time, we grew in our conviction that we should pray for a full recovery, so we began to do just that.

Over the course of a few days, we spoke to the comatose man of our love and God's love, and we prayed for his complete recovery. To the amazement of the doctors, he woke up from the coma without any ill effects. Shortly thereafter he gave his life to Christ.

Certainly there have been other occasions when we felt convinced that God wanted to heal someone, prayed with that conviction, and were disappointed by the results. Our discernment may have been wrong; it's certainly been wrong about other things. But the fact that we have no assurance of infallibly discerning God's will in every situation doesn't relieve us of the responsibility to actively seek his will so that we can pray, to the best of our knowledge, according to his will.

It's worth noting how Jesus used this phrase when he prayed. The one case where it is recorded, during his agony in the Garden of Gethsemane, was an extraordinary situation. Jesus came to Jerusalem, knowing that "the Son of Man must be rejected and suffer many things." He had already instructed his disciples in the necessity of dying in order to bear much fruit. But the awful cruelty of the cross, not to mention the inconceivable prospect of bearing the sins of the world and suffering the wrath of God as a substitute for sinners, was a weight nearly too much to bear. In this state of mental and spiritual anguish, Jesus wrestled with the Father's will over the necessity of the cross. Of course, there's no way we can know his interior state accurately, but it is reasonable to assume that when he prayed "Thy will be done," he understood what that will entailed. The phrase was, in all likelihood, an expression of his anguish, more than his uncertainty.

Neither Jesus nor his disciples left us with a model of intercessory prayer that made liberal use of the proviso "if it be thy will" to cover uncertainty regarding the things we ask for. Of course, we must always leave room in all of our prayers for the possibility of God freely choosing to do other than what we pray. But the prayers of the Bible, rather than striking a tentative note, are bold—even when they express frustration and anguish.

"Seek the giver, not the gifts." When I was a brand-new Christian encountering Paul's teaching on spiritual gifts for the first time, I asked many questions. What are spiritual gifts? How would a person go about getting some? I was told, "Seek the giver, not the gifts." Actually, I am thankful for that advice. It certainly communicated the absolute priority of Christ's person above all else. As people with hearts that tend toward idolatry, we are always in danger of elevating matters of lesser importance to a position of primary importance.

Over time, I realized that my conservative evangelical friends were responding to an overemphasis among some charismatics on spiritual gifts—especially the gifts of tongues and prophecy, which were matters of no little controversy at the time. They felt that all the excitement over charismatic gifts obscured the preeminence of Jesus and the good news of the gospel. And, of course, that's the problem with most any controversy: it draws the participants into focusing on a particular issue beyond what the issue itself calls for.

But the phrase "Seek the giver, not the gifts" deserves closer examination. As stated, the advice is not biblical. St. Paul explicitly urged us to "eagerly desire spiritual gifts, especially the gift of prophecy" (1 Cor 14:1). This echoes his earlier encouragement to "eagerly desire the greater gifts" (1 Cor 12:31). Perhaps it would be better (though less pithy) to say, "Seek the gifts because of the giver, but never instead of the giver."

The motto "Seek the giver, not the gifts" also reveals a passive, even fatalistic approach to asking for the things God has to give. My wife, Nancy, never tires of observing my own reluctance to ask for anything—especially a personal favor.

(Before knowing her, at least I had the pleasure of taking pride in my self-sufficiency, but her comments are finally sinking in!) But the Bible encourages us to ask.

The Psalms, for example, are filled with David's passionate supplications. He asked for mercy, justice, vengeance, provision, and for his heart's desires. Jesus urged his disciples to "ask and it will be given you; seek and you will find; knock and the door will be opened to you" (Mt 7:7). The repetition is equivalent to our exclamation point: he really means it! James put it succinctly: "You do not have, because you do not ask God" (James 4:2). Freedom to ask God—for our daily bread, for spiritual gifts, for his imminent return, for more of the kingdom, for all that we need—is an effect of the "Spirit of sonship." If we don't understand that we're children of God, we will be much more reluctant to ask. The more we accept our position as heirs, the more freely and actively we will ask.

Too often, conservative evangelicals have selectively adopted a passive approach to asking that borders on fatalism. "If God wants to heal, he can do it. If he wants me to have the gift of miracles, he can give it to me any time he likes." This approach is selective, because it is normally restricted to areas which conservative evangelicals feel are "beyond their comfort zone." For example, many evangelicals no longer hold to the cessationist teaching which relegates the miraculous gifts of the Spirit to the apostolic era. They acknowledge that healing and the biblical gifts of the Spirit are—theoretically, at least—available today. But they adopt a passive approach to spiritual gifts.

The timidity is understandable, since we all approach the unfamiliar with a degree of caution. But it's not a place to settle down for the long haul. A fatalistic approach that says "whatever will be, will be" is a betrayal of the evangelical heritage. After all, inspired by the Scriptures, conservative evangelicals have led the way in asking for laborers to come into the harvest, for the salvation of souls, and for the return of Christ.

What conservative evangelicals can contribute to the discussion is a clear focus on the biblical goal for issues such as divine healing and spiritual gifts. The goal is clear: that Jesus be glorified and his influence on earth extended. Our interest in these things must always keep the goal in view, so that our preoccupation is always with "the giver, not the gifts."

"Conversion is the greatest miracle." For many years it has been common for conservative evangelicals to dismiss charismatic interest in miracles and other supernatural phenomena by pointing out that "conversion is the greatest miracle of all." It's absolutely true; conversion *is* the greatest miracle of all. According to the Bible there's nothing more depraved, corrupted, or darkened than the human heart. "Desperately wicked" was Jeremiah's depiction of it, and for good reason. The cause of every other evil in the world can be traced to the rebellion that took hold in the heart of humankind.

The Bible makes it clear that the conversion of sinners is nothing short of a resurrection, a raising of someone who is dead in his or her sins to life. When Jesus said, "The dead will hear the voice of the Son of God and those who hear will live" (Jn 5:25), his words apply spiritually to the miracle of conversion, just as they apply to the physical miracle of bodily resurrection at the end of the age.

As a teenager I can recall saying to God, "God, if you exist, I don't need you." I then proceeded to curse God in a way that causes me deep grief to this day. The most chilling thing about this episode is that it worked. For four or five years after that time, I cannot recall any serious thought of God. I cannot claim that I was provoked to this action by some gross fault of the church. My Christian upbringing in the Episcopal church wasn't particularly dynamic, but neither was there anything so offensive to provoke that kind of response. I do recall reading some books that were a factor in my act of rebellion, but they appealed to something already in me. So to think that I would become interested in Jesus and experience a new birth by the Spirit of God is nothing short of miraculous.

But to say that conversion is the clearest demonstration of God's power says nothing about less significant demonstrations. The pathway to the big miracle of conversion is often lined with less significant demonstrations of power. Five months into our first pregnancy, my wife began to have severe uterine bleeding. We rushed her to the hospital, where she was admitted. Several days of serious bleeding passed. At one point the obstetrician came in and told us nothing else could be done; we would lose the baby sometime soon. A friend of ours from high school, someone we called at that time a "Jesus Freak," came to visit us. Without our knowledge, he went home that night and called some Christian friends and asked them to pray for us. That night, the bleeding virtually stopped. Four months later my wife gave birth to a healthy baby boy. We named him Jesse, after Jesse Owens. I had been a runner in high school, and I wanted to avoid an Old Testament name since names like "Joshua" were becoming fashionable around that time. To my great chagrin, my father informed me that Jesse was the father of King David.

After Jesse was born, my mother-in-law, a staunch Missouri Synod Lutheran, insisted that we have Jesse baptized. So we began to talk with some clergymen about the meaning of baptism, primarily to humor her. In the process we began to consider Christianity. During this time it came to our attention that several Christians were praying for us the night Nancy's bleeding stopped. (We hadn't known this before.) Furthermore, while standing in line at the grocery store, I leafed through one of those baby name booklets. According to the booklet, "Jesse" means "God exists." Suddenly the power of Christ's kingdom became credible to me—and not long thereafter we became Christians. Conversion is the greatest miracle, but God used the prayer of Christians for the lesser miracle of healing to demonstrate the reality of his kingdom—thereby opening my heart to his existence.

Sometimes conservative evangelicals think that since the miracle of conversion is available to all who believe, we would have no need for less significant demonstrations of God's power. The reasoning seems to be: If God is already giving us the greatest gift, why would we need the lesser gifts of healing or other demonstrations of power? The biblical reasoning seems to be just the opposite: If God is willing to perform the greatest miracle (conversion), what would make us think he is unwilling to perform lesser demonstrations of his power? "He who did not spare his own Son, but gave him up for us all—how will he not also, along with him, graciously give us all things?" (Rom 8:32).

CHARISMATIC SLOGANS

We should keep in mind that both the conservative evangelical and charismatic traditions (as we are using those terms) constitute very broad streams within Christianity, with many variations. The slogans we've been considering represent trends at a popular level within their respective traditions. Evangelical and charismatic biblical scholars would likely feel that the slogans don't represent the best of their respective traditions. But our concern is with the popular tendencies within the two worlds that we are considering—the perspectives that shape local churches and their members.

"**Ask whatever you will.**" The "faith movement," represented by teachers like Kenneth Hagin and Kenneth Copeland, is a particular stream within the broader charismatic tradition. Many charismatics would differ with some of the teachings of the faith movement. The faith movement itself has many different voices, but a central text for the movement is from the Gospel of Mark.

> "Have faith in God," Jesus answered. "I tell you the truth, if anyone says to this mountain, 'Go throw yourself into the sea,' and does not doubt in his heart but believes that what he says will happen, it will be done for him. Therefore I tell you, whatever you ask for in prayer, believe that you have received it, and it will be yours." **Mark 11:22-24**

At its best the faith movement has alerted the church to the immense importance that Jesus attaches to faith in God. However, this emphasis can degenerate into a "name it and claim it" mentality that bears little resemblance to biblical faith and an uncanny resemblance to human selfishness and presumption. In its irresponsible forms, believers name their hearts' desires (a luxury car, for example) and "claim" this gift "by faith." Faith in this context means the conviction (expressed through a rigorous mental discipline and careful attention to one's speech) which excludes any doubt that the car will, in due time, be given. Sometimes people will even speak of the car as if it has been given already and the recipient is simply "awaiting delivery."

While this approach places a high value on the believer's authority and the power of faith, it often runs roughshod over a few important considerations: human depravity, God's sovereignty, and some simple rules of biblical interpretation.

One of the rules of interpreting Scripture is that the individual parts of Scripture must be interpreted in the light of the whole of Scripture, with the understanding that God does not contradict himself. If this text is taken out of context, it is easy to see how a person might think that Jesus is telling us that if we identify something that we want to have happen and convince ourselves that it will happen (without entertaining any doubt whatsoever), it surely will take place. This, by the way, is not the teaching of responsible faith movement leaders. But sometimes the careful distinctions of teachers are lost on their hearers. The reader can see how, taken to the extreme, the believer begins to assume a position of virtual sovereignty. Of course, that's just what we crave. As the song from the movie *The Lion King* says, "Oh, I just can't wait to be king!"

What's wrong with this picture? It denies one of the clearest themes in the whole Bible: God is the King of the universe; he alone is sovereign. Whatever Jesus meant by his teaching, he did not mean to overthrow the sovereignty of God in favor of the sovereignty of human beings who believe without doubting.

Secondly, problematic interpretations of this text often fail to take into account that sometimes Jesus spoke provocatively. He stated things in language aimed to catch us off guard, to grab our attention, to force us to take a deeper look at an issue. To do this, he didn't hesitate to use a common form of communication: exaggeration. For example, in teaching on sin, Jesus said, "If your right eye causes you to sin, gouge it out and throw it away. It is better for you to lose one part of your body than for your whole body to be thrown into hell" (Mt 5:29). Some people have taken his words literally, gouging out their eyes, only to discover that lust resides in the heart, not the eye. Jesus wasn't teaching on dismemberment in this text. He was making a point provocatively: that sin kills us, and we must be willing to do whatever is necessary to be free from it. Similarly, in Mark 11:24, Jesus is making a point about faith provocatively: faith in God is more important and more powerful than we ever imagined.

Finally, some charismatics simply fail to take human depravity seriously when applying Jesus' teaching on faith. "You do not have," James wrote, "because you do not ask God. When you ask, you do not receive, because you ask with wrong motives, that you may spend what you get on your pleasures" (James 4:2-3). We don't have a *little* problem with selfishness, one that occasionally colors our faith. We have a *big* problem with selfishness. Our hearts are desperately wicked—a condition that is not completely healed until the kingdom comes in fullness. And often we are blind to our own wrong motives. Jesus' statement "Ask whatever you will..." must be understood in the light of his revelation of the human heart, since "out of the fullness of the heart the mouth speaks."

Jesus is not giving us a blank check to be filled in by whatever happens to be in our heart, as long as we cash it by faith. He expects us to interpret his words in one place in the context of his whole message. "Ask whatever you will" is to be understood in light of our need to be found in him, to have our will conformed to his will. As John writes, "This is the confidence we have in approaching God: that if we ask anything according to his will, he hears us" (1 Jn 5:14). When we ask from that posture, our faith will move mountains.

"Receive your inheritance." Charismatics properly emphasize the wonderful privileges that belong to the children of God. The Spirit, after all, is the "Spirit of sonship" who confirms our new status as heirs (see Romans 8:15-17) so there is a great deal of encouragement among charismatics to "receive your inheritance." The concept of receiving is at the heart of the charismatic perspective: whether receiving Christ as Savior, or receiving the Spirit, tongues, prophecies, healing, or deliverance. All that comes to us is viewed as a dimension of our inheritance as the kids of the kingdom. Among some charismatics, there is the added emphasis on receiving physical health and material wealth as an aspect of our inheritance. If we are the children of a Great King, the reasoning goes, why shouldn't we "live as king's kids"?

This emphasis on our new standing in Christ—sons and daughters of God, and therefore heirs to the kingdom—is one of the strengths of the charismatic approach to God. Many evangelicals are quick to admit that in focusing on the new birth, the new life that follows birth has too often been neglected within their own tradition. The classic conservative evangelical testimony paints a detailed picture of darkness before conversion, drawing to a dramatic climax at the point of conversion, with only cursory treatment of what it means to live as a new creation. In that sense, the charismatic emphasis is a welcome development.

The danger in the charismatic emphasis is similar to the problem of the charismatic congregation in Corinth: the failure to recognize that the kingdom has both an "already" and a "not yet" dimension. Jesus death and resurrection brought a release of kingdom power into the world; but the kingdom still awaits fulfillment in the second coming of Christ. Until then, we live in a time when some of the blessings of the kingdom are realized, while others remain a future hope. (See chapter 3 for a more detailed treatment of this subject.)

This emphasis on receiving our inheritance remains balanced and healthy only when we understand that the kingdom has broken into this world through Jesus, but that the fulfillment of the kingdom (and our inheritance) awaits his coming in glory. Until then, we receive only the first fruits of our inheritance; out of his grace, God gives us a preview of coming attractions, whether through physical healing, financial blessing, or reconciled relationships—but the inheritance in its fullness (including new bodies) awaits the end of all things.

"If you ask for bread, would he give you a stone?" I once attended a conference where a speaker led the whole crowd in "receiving the Spirit." We were led in a prayer for the Holy Spirit that was similar to the sinner's prayer, followed by his assurance that we had indeed received the Spirit, simply because we had asked. While this was done by a conservative evangelical leader, it has become an increasingly popular approach among charismatics.

In the early days of the charismatic movement, "baptism in the Spirit" along with speaking in tongues was viewed as a discernible experience. Something really happened: The Spirit came, the person receiving felt something distinct (though feelings varied from person to person), and the person's tongue was loosed to speak in an unknown language. In fact, sometimes people couldn't stop speaking in tongues, for hours or days at a time.

As time progressed and more people prayed to receive the Holy Spirit, a new problem emerged: Some people felt frustrated if they didn't experience anything noticeable. Leaders naturally made various attempts to alleviate the frustration. Sometimes people were coached in "yielding" to the gift of tongues, occasionally to the point of being asked to repeat a phrase over and over to "prime the pump." Sometimes the "experience" of receiving the Holy Spirit was reduced to an act of faith that something happened though nothing was experienced. The following text is often cited in support of this approach:

> Which of you, if his son asks for bread, will give him a stone? Or if he asks for a fish, will give him a snake? If you, then, though you are evil, know how to give good gifts to your children, how much more will your Father in heaven give good gifts to those who ask him! **Matthew 7:9-11**

This approach to receiving the Spirit might be called "If you ask, assume that you have received." It places a high value on the goodness of God. God isn't a reluctant giver, but a lavish giver. He wants to give us gifts—more than we want to receive them—because he is good. Often this is just the assurance we need as we approach the throne of grace. We don't need to approach God with an expectation that he is reluctant to give. We need to shake off our fear, remembering his goodness.

But this approach, pressed too far, skates over two important realities. First of all, it fails to acknowledge that we cannot control God. There is an aspect of mystery to the business of asking and receiving that defies cut-and-dried formulas. Sometimes we ask but don't receive, at least not right away. Perhaps this is why Jesus said, "Ask and it will be given to you; seek and you will find; knock and the door will be opened to you." The tense for the Greek verbs (ask, seek and knock) is present imperative: keep on asking, keep on seeking, keep on knocking. It's an invitation to persistence and boldness in asking.

Secondly, the "If you ask, assume that you've received" approach to asking and receiving can become a form of sophistry, a mental game of "smoke and mirrors" that does violence to the ordinary meaning of words and defies common sense. If I'm blind and I ask for sight, I haven't been healed until I can see. Perhaps my prayer has been heard. Perhaps a decision has been made in heaven to confer healing. But as long as I can't see, I'm blind, not healed. It's a bit like the emperor in the fable: the reason he appears naked is because he has no clothes.

"If you ask, assume that you have received" is most troublesome when applied to issues such as physical healing, where we can apply objective criteria to determine whether we have actually received what we've asked for. But there is also a danger in pressing it too far with other issues, like receiving an infilling of the Spirit. While it may provide reassurance to the fearful, it may also reduce a biblical reality to a mere formula. If a person repeats the sinner's prayer but shows none of the biblical effects of conversion, has he or she been truly born again? If large numbers of people are led through a process by which they are "filled with the Spirit" without any of the subjective manifestations seen in the Bible when people are filled with the Spirit (a stirring of love, of praise to God, a vivid awareness of God's presence, sometimes to the point of feeling overwhelmed) or without evidence of the biblical effects of being filled with the Spirit, such as increased boldness, wouldn't we be wise to wonder if something is missing?

THE BEST OF BOTH WORLDS

When it comes to exercising faith, we need to learn from the best of the conservative evangelical and charismatic worlds. We need the witness of charismatics who remind us that it is the Father's good pleasure to give us the kingdom and that we have an active role in receiving the kingdom. And we need the reminder from evangelicals to keep first things first: to remember that God has always been, and ever will be, *God*, that we can only receive what he actually gives us, and that he is ultimately in control of the process. It is only as we learn from the experience of evangelicals and charismatics that we can approach God with an expectant faith that moves beyond fatalism, without falling into presumption.

FOR DISCUSSION

1. Have you been influenced by any of the slogans covered in this chapter? If so, which ones? What did you think of the authors' analysis for the slogans that influenced you?

2. Discuss what the authors mean by presumption and fatalism in prayer.

3. When it comes to your own approach to God in prayer, which side of the horse do you tend to fall off—presumption or fatalism?

WHEN SEEKING A CHURCH

1. When the church gathers to pray, do you recognize a biblically balanced approach to faith, or does the church consistently lean toward presumption on the one hand, or fatalism on the other? Which set of slogans, if any, seems to characterize the prayers of people in the church?

2. Is there a spirit of humility in the church? Specifically, is there an emphasis in the church on the sovereignty of God? Is there a recognition that our will and his are often different? Do people freely acknowledge when they are not sure of God's will or do they sound equally confident about everything? Is there an appreciation for the capacity of the human heart to be deceived?

3. Do you get the impression that people are encouraged to be active or passive in seeking spiritual gifts? Is there any opportunity for new Christians to learn about spiritual gifts?

4. What kind of expectation do people have of the power of God to break into our present experience? What do people expect God to do on a regular basis?

FOR PASTORS

1. Listen to the prayers of people in your church. Do they tend to lean in the direction of presumption or fatalism?

2. Prayer from the pulpit following a sermon provides an excellent opportunity to pray with conviction and faith rooted in God's Word. Do you pray publicly after preaching? Are you aware of the influence your prayers have as a model for the congregation?

3. Of the slogans treated in this chapter, which do you think have had the most influence on the spirituality of the people in your church?

SIX

Dusting off the Gospels

I'll admit it; I, Ken, am partial to the Gospels. My first exposure to the Bible was the Gospel according to Matthew. It was unlike any literature I'd ever read before. The Jesus of Matthew's Gospel wasn't merely an historical figure; he was a living presence who seemed to emerge from the pages of the text. Haskell Stone, a Messianic Jewish teacher from Detroit, once told me, "Never stray from the Gospels. Always return to the Gospels. And understand everything else that you read in the Bible in light of those four books."

I was surprised to find that, apart from my Jesus People friends in Detroit, Christians weren't nearly as excited about the Gospels. Evangelicals seemed to emphasize the letters of Paul, especially the Book of Romans, while charismatics spent a lot of time teaching from the Book of Acts and Paul's First Letter to the Corinthians. The Gospels, on the other hand, seemed to be something less than central in the teaching of many churches.

So in 1984, when I first heard John Wimber teach from the Gospels, I was intrigued. I knew that the Gospels were originally written to instruct the earliest Christian communities and that they must have provided much of the regular diet of teaching in the emerging churches. But I was accustomed to hearing teaching from the Gospels that emphasized one of three things: the miraculous signs attesting to the divinity of Christ, the ethical teaching of Jesus, or the account of the death and resurrection during the week before Easter. Wimber, however, saw in the Gospels a window into the supernatural realm and a picture of the conflict of the kingdoms. He also saw in them a model for engaging in the works of the kingdom such as healing the sick, proclaiming good news, freeing the demonized, caring for the poor. As it turns out, the Gospels are providing a place for evangelicals and charismatics to find fresh insights into the power of the Spirit.

THE DUST GATHERS

A number of factors exist for the relative neglect of the Gospels in the teaching ministry of the church. The defining doctrine of evangelicals is justification by faith. The book of the Bible that served as a catalyst for evangelical revival was Paul's Letter to the Romans.

For example, a worldly-wise young North African man named Augustine was led to the Book of Romans when he heard a boy randomly crying out, "Take and read!" Augustine's Bible was open to the Book of Romans (Romans 13:12-14), which spoke directly to his dissolute lifestyle. The experience triggered his conversion. Centuries later, Martin Luther, a monk in the order named after Augustine, experienced a similar conversion as he encountered Paul's teaching on "a righteousness that is by faith from first to last" (Rom 1:17) from the same book. Two hundred years later, the Great Awakening was sparked when an Anglican cleric named John Wesley listened to a reading from Luther's commentary on the Book of Romans. Wesley felt his "heart strangely warmed" as the power of God's grace dawned on him. Little wonder then that the letters of Paul, especially Romans, would have such a prominent place in the teaching of the churches which identify with the Protestant Reformers.

The Pentecostal emphasis on baptism in the Spirit with speaking in tongues brought a renewed emphasis on the Book of Acts, as well as Paul's teaching on spiritual gifts in 1 Corinthians 12-14. Much of the teaching in the Pentecostal and charismatic streams of the church are drawn from these portions of Scripture.

Modern-day evangelicals have been profoundly influenced by the teachings of modern dispensationalism. This theological system places a great deal of emphasis on the second coming of Christ, focusing on the Book of Daniel and the Book of Revelation. In this scheme, the emphasis in the Gospels on healing and deliverance (a substantial portion of these accounts) is emphasized as proof of his Lordship, but not as a model of ministry for the church today.

Within what are sometimes called the "mainline churches," both Protestant and Catholic, the Gospels have been neglected for other reasons. Many of the seminaries that supply the pastors for these churches teach that the Gospels tell us very little about "the historical Jesus" and a great deal about the faith of the early church. The supernatural events recorded in the Gospels (healings, resurrections, exorcism, and other miracles) are dismissed as the reflection of a superstitious view of the world. This makes teaching or preaching from the Gospels a complicated task that many pastors trained under this outlook simply avoid. For example, one noted biblical scholar has taught that the miracle of the feeding of the five thousand was not a miracle of multiplication, but a miracle of sharing. As the hungry crowd watched Jesus and his friends sharing their lunches with each other, they were all inspired to do the same. Most pastors trained in this view of the Gospels have felt understandably intimidated by the imagination such an approach entails!

DUSTING OFF THE GOSPELS

This neglect of the Gospels in the teaching of the church is being reversed as conservative evangelicals, in particular, have been dusting off the Gospels and allowing them to challenge their preconceptions about the supernatural world and the power of the Spirit. A leading evangelical theologian from Fuller Theological Seminary, the late George Eldon Ladd, has had a significant impact on this phenomenon. Ladd is primarily known for his teaching about the kingdom of God derived from the Gospels, especially Matthew, Mark, and Luke. Ladd points out that an understanding of the kingdom is the overarching theme of Christ's teaching.[1] Jesus' gospel is the "gospel of the kingdom" (Mt 24:14), the good news of God's influence breaking into this world through the arrival of the kingdom's King. The context of Christ's ministry is the conflict between the kingdom of God and the kingdom of Satan. The works of Jesus—preaching good news, healing the sick, raising the dead, casting out demons, gathering a new community of disciples— are all "works of the kingdom." These are the things that happen when God is having his way in our world—when his kingdom comes, when his will is done on earth as it is in heaven.

From Ladd's perspective, the Gospels are more than the historical record of Christ's earthly ministry culminating in his death and resurrection. They also provide—through their focus on the coming kingdom—a theological framework for understanding the meaning and power of the gospel. Throughout *The Best of Both Worlds*, we have attempted to show how this emphasis on the theology of the kingdom plays an important role in the empowered evangelical perspective.

Some of the key emphases of empowered evangelicals are derived from a renewed place for the Gospels in the teaching ministry of the church. Let's look at a few of these perspectives.

Christianity: a personal encounter with Christ. One of the occupational hazards of Bible-based churches is what some have called "bibliolatry." Daniel Wallace, assistant professor of New Testament Studies at Dallas Theological Seminary, has said that "while charismatics sometimes give a higher priority to experience than to relationship, rationalistic evangelicals give a higher priority to knowledge than to relationship. Both of these miss the mark."[2] Wallace goes on to speak of his own brush with bibliolatry.

> For me, as a New Testament professor, the text is my task—but I made it my God. The text became my idol.... The net effect of such bibliolatry is a depersonalization of God. Eventually, we no longer relate to him. God becomes the object of our investigation... the vitality of our religion gets sucked out. As God gets dissected, our stance changes from "I trust in...." to "I believe that...."[3]

Jesus once said to the Pharisees and teachers of the law, "You diligently study the Scriptures because you think that by them you possess eternal life. These are the Scriptures that testify about me, yet you refuse to come to me to have life" (Jn 5:39-40). That's bibliolatry. The religious leaders of Israel were doing what comes naturally to human beings: missing the forest for the trees. They had come to view the study of the Holy Scriptures as an end in itself, rather than as the inspired means to the end of a personal encounter with the living God. They reduced religion to a set of precepts and principles, but in the process missed the person.

As mentioned earlier, I began to read the Bible at the age of nineteen, beginning with the Gospel of Matthew. The experience was more than I had bargained for. As I read this first book in the New Testament, I was encountering a person I had heard much of but knew little about. Some of the things he said and did endeared him to me, but other things left me perplexed. However, the more I read, the more it became clear to me that this book was something more than a biography of a long-dead historical giant. The author was writing about someone who had a living presence. I wasn't just learning about Christianity; I was being introduced to Jesus Christ.

Of course, this experience of reading the Bible is not restricted to reading the Gospels. But it certainly is the main theme of the Gospels. Christianity, if it is anything, is a personal encounter between human beings and the "Word made flesh," Jesus of Nazareth, risen from the dead. The disciples were not following a program; they were following a person. As they came to know this person, they were encountering God; as they conformed their lives to his teaching, they were growing in godliness.

The Gospels: model for missions. Several years ago, just before leaving for a missionary assignment in a Muslim nation, a young Presbyterian couple attended a class at Fuller Seminary. There they learned a model of ministry that included praying for the sick and demonized, a model rooted in the ministry of Jesus as portrayed in the Gospels. They were open to new approaches to planting churches, since previous models had not generated much fruit.

Some time after they arrived, a young Muslim mother brought her infant daughter to them, asking for help. The child had been placed under a spell by some superstitious Muslims, and the mother didn't know how to handle the situation. As they prayed for deliverance in the name of Jesus, the baby was freed from her oppression. Soon word spread and Muslim mothers were bringing their children one by one for deliverance prayer. This ministry provided the spark which resulted in a new church planted among the people of that area.

Experiences like this have motivated Christians devoted to the missionary enterprise to view the Gospels as a model for spreading the good news of the kingdom in third world missions. In places like Asia, Africa, and Latin America, the gospel has been effectively introduced following the pattern of Christ's ministry in the gospels—speaking the words and doing the works of the kingdom.

A different angle on spiritual gifts. Within Pentecostal and charismatic churches, most teaching on the gifts of the Spirit is derived from 1 Corinthians 12-14. Here, Paul gives instructions regarding nine charismatic gifts: wisdom, knowledge, faith, healing, miracles, prophecy, discernment, tongues, and the interpretation of tongues. This treatment of spiritual gifts comes in the context of how the church should act when it gathers together. For example, chapters 10 and 11 deal with issues like the celebration of the Lord's Supper and the participation of women when the church gathers for worship. So the context for this particular treatment of spiritual gifts is the church meeting: how the gift of tongues should be handled in public worship, what to do when more than one prophet has a message to give to the congregation, and so on.

Within the charismatic movement of the 1970s and 1980s, one of the primary expressions of renewal was the "prayer meeting." A typical prayer meeting would have the participants meeting "in the round" to maximize the sense of participation. Elements of the meeting would include singing, interspersed with vocal praise and punctuated perhaps by a message in tongues, followed by an interpretation, a prophecy (in which the speaker would address the group in the first person, "The Lord says...") and "singing in the Spirit" (the assembly singing together in the same key, some in their native language, some in tongues). In the charismatic movement, a primary context for experiencing the spiritual gifts is the prayer meeting.

The ministry of Jesus portrayed in the Gospels provides another perspective on the exercise of spiritual gifts. Conservative evangelicals tend to view the supernatural elements of Jesus' ministry as an expression of his divinity. He could do these things, in short, because he was God. Certainly the miracles of Jesus are important evidence for his divinity. Yet a case can also be made that Jesus performed these works of power as a human being, led by the Holy Spirit. (Though this statement is not meant in any way to detract from his full divinity.) While fully human and fully God, Jesus relied on the promptings of the Spirit for his ministry. Jesus made a point to underline his dependence: "I tell you the truth, the Son can do nothing by himself; he can only do what he sees his Father doing, because whatever the Father does the Son also does" (Jn 5:19).

It is no accident that Jesus began his public ministry of preaching good news, healing the sick, raising the dead, and casting out demons after the Spirit descended on him in his baptism by John (see Matthew 3:13-17). Finally, if Jesus' supernatural ministry was simply an expression of his divinity, how could he command his disciples, mere human beings, to "heal the sick, raise the dead, cleanse those who have leprosy, drive out demons" (Mt 10:8)?

In other words, Jesus modeled for us what it means to be a human being led by the Spirit. From this perspective, when Jesus told the accusers of the woman caught in adultery, "If any one of you is without sin, let him be the first to throw a stone at her" (Jn 8:7), he may have been speaking what Paul later called a "message of wisdom" in his description of various gifts of revelation (see 1 Corinthians 12:8). Or when he told the Samaritan woman that she had five husbands, he spoke by a word of prophecy. His insights concerning the kingdom were what Paul called "the message of knowledge" (1 Cor 12:8).

This perspective on spiritual gifts has prompted empowered

evangelicals to seek to exercise gifts of the Spirit not only in the meetings of the church but also in the opportunities for ministry at work, in one's neighborhood, at school, and in the wider community. My friend David worked in an office with a woman who complained of severe shoulder pain whenever the weather was rainy. Though the woman wasn't a Christian, or perhaps because she wasn't a Christian, David asked if she would like him to pray for her. She was surprised but willing to humor his faith. David placed his hand on her shoulder and asked God to heal her. A brief period of time passed, with no results. David asked his coworker, "Do you mind if we try again?" She was still willing so he again asked for the presence of Jesus to come for healing. Within moments the atmosphere in the room changed noticeably. David felt it was the manifest presence of Jesus to heal, so he asked the woman: "Do you feel something different in the air?"

"I sure do!" she replied, full of wonder. As David continued to pray, the woman heard and felt a series of six popping sounds from deep inside her arm, moving from her upper arm, through her shoulder, and into her neck. The pain in her arm was gone. From that point on, it didn't return even with bad weather. This was a firsthand experience with the power of the kingdom, designed to reinforce David's explanation of the gospel.

Ministry to the least, the last, the lost. A few years ago I preached a set of sermons from the Gospel of Luke which emphasized (as Luke does) the ministry of Jesus to the poor. Someone raised in the Baptist tradition came forward with the concern that this sounded a lot like "the social gospel." In other words, ministry to the poor didn't seem like a good evangelical emphasis; instead it made him suspicious that his pastor was becoming "liberal" in his theology.

In the early part of the twentieth century, many conservative evangelicals were dismayed by the inroads of liberal theology, which often reduced the gospel to helping the poor. While some evangelicals have maintained a consistent focus on ministry to the poor without adopting the "social gospel," many others became wary.

As conservative evangelicals rediscover the power of the kingdom through a new look at the Gospels, they are placing a new emphasis on ministry to the poor. And little wonder. A person can't read the Gospels without being confronted with the fact that Jesus' ministry was largely aimed at the least, the last, and the lost: the people least valued by society, the poor, the socially outcast; those ranked last in the order of prestige and privilege, including two groups considered inferior in ancient society—women and children; and the lost, the sinners and prodigals.

In point of fact, much of the impetus for modern social reform has come through evangelical revivals of the past three centuries. The Great Awakening in the eighteenth century stemmed the tide of alcohol abuse in England. Many organizations that provide help for those in desperate need were launched by evangelical Christians, including Alcoholics Anonymous and the Salvation Army.

This renewed concern for social justice, combined with a firm adherence to the Bible, is a mark of many evangelicals involved in renewal. The emphasis of the Promise Keepers men's movement on racial reconciliation is one expression of this. Our church has developed a partnership with a church of African-Americans. We have exchanged pulpits, held joint Sunday evening services, and planned other activities to promote relationship between the two congregations. The fact that we have to make a special effort to interact with a "black church" is symptomatic of the pervasive influence of racial segregation in the body of Christ. But as our society becomes increasingly polarized along racial and ethnic lines, we've got to do something to bear witness to the reconciling power of the cross.

A concern for social justice is also evidenced in growing ministries to the poor in empowered evangelical churches. Rich's church in Columbus, Ohio, provides thousands of meals to those in need every year and sponsors a ministry to single moms. They also have a free medical clinic and a ministry to hundreds of AIDS patients and their families.

THE GOSPELS: POINT OF ENTRY FOR A NEW GENERATION?

Danny Harrell, a pastor working with young people at Park Street Church in Boston, has observed that college students raised in the postmodern mentality are more responsive to the teaching from Gospel accounts than to the theological teaching of Paul. The truths in Paul's writings are more direct doctrinal statements, while Jesus brings the same truths home through the use of parables, stories, and analogies. "Too often the church has used Paul to interpret Jesus, but I think we'll find it not only more effective but a better starting point to use Jesus to interpret Paul," according to Harrell.[4]

In other words, the Gospels provide a model for teaching that is especially effective for the baby-buster generation, called by some "Generation X." This generation's value on personal experience, their hunger for community, and their renewed interest in a spiritual realm beyond the material, make the Gospels especially effective tools for reaching them.

Of course, this doesn't mean the rest of the New Testament is any less important. The truths of justification by faith, for example, are as foundational now as they were during the time of the Reformation. But in order for these truths to be heard most effectively, the church would do well to accompany them with a compelling presentation of Christ and his kingdom revealed in the Gospels.

Paul's teaching on justification by faith, for example, can be illustrated by a parable such as the prodigal son, which deals with issues of sin, forgiveness, and reconciliation from a different perspective. Paul's teaching on sanctification can be brought home to this generation by taking a closer look at what Jesus taught about the need to "wash the inside of the cup" for an inner transformation, a change of heart.

NEEDED: A BALANCED DIET

If there is a heavenly purpose in this rediscovery of the Gospels on the part of conservative evangelicals, it is to help the church to receive a balanced diet of teaching. The truths of the New Testament come to us in different forms for a reason: we need them all to grasp the truth. We need to see Jesus as he was revealed during his earthly ministry. We need to know the history of the early church, which is a history of the risen Christ working in the church through the outpoured Spirit. We need the teaching of Paul, who interprets the meaning of these events. And we need the vision of Revelation to encourage us as the day of Christ's return draws near.

FOR DISCUSSION

1. Does the authors' discussion inspire you to "dust off the Gospels"? If so, what do you feel a need to emphasize more in your life?

2 What insights gained from the Gospels would the Pentecostal and charismatic wing of the church most benefit

from? What insights are needed to strengthen the ministry of other evangelicals?

3. What are your thoughts on the role of ministry to the poor through the church?

WHEN SEEKING A CHURCH

No local congregation of redeemed sinners is perfect, but the church that aims for a "pure and sincere devotion to Christ" makes up for many other deficiencies. When you're new to town and looking for a church home, what are some of the signs of a Christ-centered church?

1. Is Jesus prominent in the weekly messages? Do you come away with a deeper appreciation for Christ, a longing to know him better?

2. If the church has a particular emphasis (for example, building a sense of community, ministry to the poor, missions, praise), is this emphasis clearly related to Jesus, or does it seem to be displacing the congregation's focus on Jesus?

3. Is there an honest attempt to grow in Christlikeness? Is the power of Christ within stressed as the key to growth, or is the focus on willpower, determination, and human effort?

4. Does the congregation's statement of beliefs unapologetically uphold the centrality of Christ's work on the cross, his living presence, and the power of his teaching in the Bible?

5. Is the worship of the church personal? Does it seek to promote a sense of intimacy with the Father and his Son?

6. Are there signs of passion within the church for the mission of Christ to the poor and needy, to the lost? Is this expressed in the way the church spends time, money, and human resources? Is there a prevailing sense that everyone would be better off if they could know Jesus better?

FOR PASTORS

Consider including a series of sermons based on the Gospels at least once each year. Here are some ideas that may prove useful:

1. A series on Jesus' teaching about the Kingdom of God, using selections from Matthew, Mark, and Luke. Topics might include:
   - What is the Kingdom of God?
   - How does the Kingdom come?
   - What are the key works of the Kingdom?
   - The *already* and *not yet* of the Kingdom

2. A seven-week series on the seven miracles in the Gospel of John, stressing the role of miracles as signs pointing to the Son of God. Note the progressive power of each sign, and what the sign is meant to signify about Jesus and the kingdom he brings.

3. A series of sermons aimed at equipping the church to pray for the sick based on the healing ministry of Jesus. Based on his ministry, build a biblical model of praying for the sick and those tormented by the devil.

4. A series of sermons on "Jesus and Women" based on the Gospel of Luke. How was Jesus' ministry to women unique for his time? What do some of the key women in the Gospels model for all Christians? What was the response of women to the crucifixion and resurrection of Christ?

5. Spiritual warfare in the Gospels. Teach through a Gospel, focusing on what we can learn about spiritual warfare. What is the nature of spiritual conflict? How does Jesus engage the enemy? Relate the example of Jesus with the teaching of Paul in Ephesians 6.

FOR FURTHER STUDY

George Ladd, *The Gospel of the Kingdom* (Grand Rapids, Mich.: Eerdmans, 1974).

George Ladd, *A Theology of the New Testament* (Grand Rapids, Mich.: Eerdmans, 1974).

James Dunn, *Jesus and the Spirit* (London: SCM Press, 1975).

SEVEN

Worship and the Word

The year was 1741. Jonathan Edwards, a thirty-eight-year-old pastor of a country church in Northampton, Massachusetts, was invited to preach in Enfield, Connecticut. The text he chose for the occasion was Deuteronomy 32:35, "Their foot shall slide in due time."

Listen to Edwards expound:

That world of misery, that lake of burning brimstone, is extended abroad under you. There is the dreadful pit of glowing flames of the wrath of God; there is hell's wide gaping mouth open; and you have nothing to stand upon, nor anything to take hold of; there is nothing between you and hell but the air; it is only the power and mere pleasure of God that holds you up.

You probably are not sensible of this.... You find you are kept out of hell, but do not see the hand of God in it; but look at other things, as the good state of your bodily constitution, you are of your own life, and the means you use for your own preservation. But indeed these things are nothing; if God should withdraw his hand, they would avail no more to keep you from falling than the thin air to hold up a person suspended in it.

The effect of Edwards' sermon was overwhelming. Here is an account of someone in attendance:

> We went over to Enfield where we met dear Mr. Edwards of Northampton, who preached a most awakening sermon from the words Deuteronomy 32:35. And before the sermon was done, there was a great moaning and crying out through that whole house, "What shall I do to be saved? Oh, I am going to hell. Oh, what shall I do for Christ, etc.?" There was so much crying out, the minister was obliged to desist. The shrieks and cries were piercing and amazing. After some time of waiting, the congregation were still so that the prayer was made by Mr. Wheelock. And after that we descended from the pulpit and discoursed with the people, some in one place and some in another. And amazing and astonishing was the power of God. Several souls were hopefully wrought upon that night. And, oh, the cheerfulness and pleasantness of their countenances that received comfort. Oh, that God would strengthen and confirm. We sung a hymn and prayed. And then we dismissed the assembly.[1]

What was felt was the power of the Word of God preached under the anointing of the Holy Spirit.

RECOVERING THE CENTRALITY OF WORSHIP

For years, our conservative evangelical churches taught us to believe in the power of God's preached Word. What they didn't teach, either by practice or through the messages, was that biblical preaching needs to be complemented by biblical worship.

At about the time Edwards preached his awesome sermon,

another preacher, George Whitefield, recorded in his journal a night to remember. He wrote:

> Mr. Gilbert Tennent preached first and then I began to pray. In about six minutes someone cried out, "He is come! He is come!" and could scarce contain the manifestation of Jesus to his soul.
>
> But having heard the crying of others....I prayed over them as I saw their agonies and distress increase. At length we sang a hymn and then retired to the house, where the man that received Christ continued praising and speaking of Him until near midnight. My own soul was so full that I retired and wept before the Lord, and had a deep sense of my own likeness, and the sovereignty and greatness of God's everlasting love. Most of the people spent the remainder of the night in prayer and praising God. It was a night much to be remembered.[2]

Have you ever been in a meeting in which the planned speaking or praying was cut short by the awesome coming of God's presence? Have you ever been together with other believers and had the Holy Spirit suddenly seem so sensibly present that the only response was to worship, to sob, to pray, and to bow down before God?

The Bible describes many such meetings![3] They are fore-tastes of heaven on earth. Nothing in this world can compare to God's deciding to give his people a sense of his presence. Indeed, God's *presence* is what distinguishes his people from the rest of the world. The church is usually not better organized than many corporations. We do not always have better teachers than major universities. Nor is our music necessarily better than late-night TV bands. What we should have, that no one else can have, is the presence of God![4]

Each of the meetings where we have experienced God's

awesome presence had these elements in common: Anointed preaching of God's Word, a willingness on the part of the preacher not to entirely steer the meeting toward a humanly pre-designated end, and a central place for worship.

The goal of salvation. We must understand the purpose for God's dealings with us. *God is trying to make you and me into worshipers.* Of course, by saying this we are saying nothing new. In 1647 the Westminster Shorter Catechism answered its very first question, "What is the chief end of man?" this way: "Man's chief end is to glorify God, and to enjoy him forever."[5] Much of conservative evangelicalism is focused today on helping people make decisions for Jesus. We think that if we can just get people to make decisions for Jesus, they have reached their destinies. As we understand the Bible, making a decision for Jesus is not the last stop of God's train. The last stop on God's train is to take somebody who has made a decision for Jesus and turn him or her into a worshiper of Jesus. God has always sought people, in both the Old and New Testaments, who will become worshipers of him.

Toward what end were the children of Israel saved out of Egypt? They were saved for the purpose of worshiping God. Consider the way that the nation of Israel was commanded to set up camp as they traveled through the desert. God commanded the twelve tribes to camp with three tribes on the north, three tribes on the south, three tribes on the east, and three tribes on the west. But in the center of the camp, God commanded the nation of Israel to set up the tabernacle that contained the Ark of the Covenant and the Holy of Holies.

Why did God make this kind of arrangement for their camp? God was communicating a spiritual principle via this physical encampment. The spiritual principle was that no matter what individuals in the Israelite community were doing—from finding new ways to cook manna to getting married, transacting business, or having sex—God wanted them to know that the very center of their lives was worship. Life in the nation of Israel was to revolve around the worship of God.

People are saved to become worshipers! Peter said, "But you are a chosen people, a royal priesthood, a holy nation, a people belonging to God, that you may declare the praises of him who called you out of darkness into his wonderful light" (1 Pt 2:9).

Why are people brought into the church? People are brought into the church to praise God (see Ephesians 1:3, 6, 12). Indeed, even in the Old Testament the word "Jew" was taken from Jacob's son, Judah, whose name meant "praise." Jews were chosen primarily to bring praise to God. Worship is the last stop on the train of salvation. If you ride the train long enough, eventually you will get to God's end, which is that you learn to become a worshiper of him.

The end of history. Consider, further, history's termination point. At the end of history, after the dead are raised and judged, what will the redeemed be doing? The apostle John tells us:

> Then I looked and heard the voice of many angels, numbering thousands upon thousands, and ten thousand times ten thousand. They encircled the throne, and the living creatures and the elders. In a loud voice they sang, "Worthy is the Lamb, who was slain, to receive power and wealth and wisdom and strength and honor and glory and praise!" Then I heard every creature in heaven and on earth and under the earth and on the sea, and all that is in them, singing: "To him who sits on the throne and to the Lamb be praise and honor and glory and power for ever and ever!" The four living creatures said, "Amen" and the elders fell down and worshiped.   **Revelation 5:11-14**

The ultimate priority. History is moving toward the worship of God. But worship is not only the goal of history: *the worship of God ought to be the highest priority of the church.* Nothing else we do—teaching, Bible reading, evangelism, or ministry to the poor—should supplant worship as the ultimate priority of the Christian life.

For conservative evangelicals this may come as a startling thought. Bible study, which is hugely important to us, should not be an end in itself. Jesus challenged the Pharisees on precisely this point when he said: "You diligently study the Scriptures because you think by them you possess eternal life. These are the Scriptures that testify about me, yet you refuse to come to me to have life" (Jn 5:39-40). The reason to study the Bible is so that you might find Jesus through the Bible. And the reason why God wants us to find Jesus is so that we might worship him "in order that we, who were the first to hope in Christ, might be for the praise of his glory" (Eph 1:12).

And however important evangelism is (and we believe evangelism and world missions are a primary target of the church), evangelism in not an end in and of itself. Consider how Paul summed up his ministry of evangelism. He placed it in the context of worship. In Romans Paul wrote:

> God has given me the grace to be a minister of Christ Jesus to the Gentiles with the priestly duty of proclaiming the gospel of God, so that the Gentiles might become an offering acceptable to God, sanctified by the Holy Spirit.
>
> **Romans 15:15-16**

Paul saw his evangelistic ministry and his missionary activity as being his way of worshiping God. He pictured himself as a priest standing before God with empty hands. And he said to God, "God, I want to make you an offering that is worthy of you. God, what can I give you?" And then he said, "I know what you are calling me to give you, Lord. You want an offering of people who are being converted through the preaching of the gospel. I will offer you the Gentiles as a spiritual sacrifice to you."

To Paul, everything was an offering of worship to God: the fruit of his evangelism, money, even his life, which was ultimately poured out in martyrdom.

> But even if I am being poured out like a drink offering on the sacrifice and service coming from your faith, I am glad and rejoice with all of you.　　　　**Philippians 2:17**

> For I am already being poured out like a drink offering, and the time has come for my departure.　　　　**2 Timothy 4:6**

NEITHER ON THIS MOUNTAIN NOR IN JERUSALEM

You are probably already familiar with the story. Jesus was traveling back from Judea to Galilee and he passed through Samaria on his way. John recorded the conversation between Jesus and the Samaritan woman:

> "Sir," the woman said, "I can see that you are a prophet. Our fathers worshiped on this mountain, but you Jews claim that the place where we must worship is in Jerusalem." Jesus declared, "Believe me, woman, a time is coming when you will worship the Father neither on this mountain nor in Jerusalem. You Samaritans worship what you do not know; we worship what we do know, for salvation is from the Jews. Yet a time is coming and has now come when the true worshipers will worship the Father in spirit and truth, for they are the kind of worshipers the Father seeks. God is spirit, and his worshipers must worship in spirit and in truth."　　　　**John 4:19-24**

158 Empowered Evangelicals

Why did Jesus say, "A time is coming when you will worship the Father neither on this mountain nor in Jerusalem"? What did the "this mountain" and "Jerusalem" represent, in terms of worship, that was somehow defective?

The mountain Jesus referred to, and could have pointed to from where he stood, was Mount Gerizim. To understand the importance of Mount Gerizim, we must go back in history. Back in the eighth century B.C. the Assyrians deported most of the inhabitants of the Northern Kingdom of Israel (see 2 Kings 17:1-33). The Assyrians then resettled the land, now referred to as Samaria, with captives from many different nations (see 2 Kings 17:24ff). These captives brought with them the worship of their various gods and combined that with the worship of Yahweh into a syncretistic hodgepodge of truth and error. The writer of 2 Kings summed up the Samaritan mongrelized religion this way:

> They worshiped the Lord, but they also served their own gods in accordance with the customs of the nations from which they had been brought. To this day they persist in their former practices. They neither worship the Lord nor adhere to the decrees and ordinances, the laws and commands that the Lord gave the descendants of Jacob, whom he named Israel.   **2 Kings 17:33-34**

By the fifth century before Christ the Samaritan religion was purged of its polytheism and the Samaritans decided to build a temple for the worship of Yahweh alone. They chose to build their temple on Mount Gerizim, in Samaria, near where Abraham had built an altar to the Lord (see Genesis 12:7). It was also the place from where blessings for obedience were pronounced on the Jews (see Deuteronomy 11:29).

In the second century before Christ, Jews from the south

went up to Mount Gerizim and burned the Samaritan temple that was the chief rival to the Jewish temple in Jerusalem. Nevertheless, Mount Gerizim continued to be considered sacred by the Samaritans.

That brings us up to the time at the well when the conversation between Jesus and the Samaritan woman took place. Again, why did Jesus say that the Father would not be worshiped *on this mountain or in Jerusalem?* Certainly, he was saying that a time was coming when the presence of God would not be confined to a certain spatial location or temple. As a result of the Spirit's coming, people would be able to enter into God's presence any place on earth!

But as his later remarks indicate, Jesus was also pointing out the deficiencies of Gerizim-type worship on the one hand and Jerusalem-type worship on the other. The Samaritans, Jesus said, "worship what they do not know; we worship what we do know" (Jn 4:22). Additionally, Jesus said that God wants to be worshiped *in spirit and in truth* (see John 4:24). The deficiency of Samaritan worship was on the "truth" side of the balance, while the deficiency of Jewish worship was on the "spirit" side.

Examining Samaritan worship first, "they worshiped *what they did not know.*" What does that mean? At some point in their history the Samaritans had tossed out most of the Old Testament as authoritative Scripture, and held on to the Pentateuch alone. Thus, the fuller revelation of God in the prophets and the Psalms was completely cut out from the Samaritans' understanding of God. What happens when people cut themselves off from portions of the written Word of God? Among other things, three problems can arise: (1) idolatry substitutes for worship of Yahweh; (2) human authority substitutes for the authority of God; and (3) churches and movements lose their staying power.

The problem with idols. Let's tackle the three problems in turn. When a church loses its grip on God's written Word, the vacuum is often filled by idolatry—the worship of what is *not* God. In fact, failing to respect God's Word is repeatedly linked to people turning to idolatry. Idols can be anything that we are banking on, other than God, to grant us a secure future or to give us ultimate meaning in the present. Our careers, our grades, our marriages, our money, even our ministries can serve as idolatrous substitutes for God.

Regarding idolatry, we frankly do not see a particular difference between charismatics and conservative evangelicals. Both movements, at least in the United States, seem to be equally drawn toward God-substitutes. In the case of charismatics, it may be called the latest wave of God's Spirit, what God is doing through so-and-so's ministry, or being part of the cutting edge of God's work in the world today. In the case of conservative evangelicals, it may be called a church growth insight, a new technique to grow small groups, or *"A New Breakthrough In Evangelizing Your Community—6 cassettes—only $49.95! Study Guide Included!"* Technique and the power of managerial insights can be an idolatrous substitute for reliance on the power of God.

But whether charismatic or conservative evangelical—idols are idols! And human beings, even Christian human beings, have the seemingly infinite capacity to dress up our God-substitutes in spiritual language, especially when they help us reach a noble goal.

The substitution of human authority. There is a second and more subtle error that occurs as people lose their grip on the written Word of God. This second error is one that has been a continual problem for charismatics from the beginning of the Pentecostal movement. Simply stated, as people become enamored with charismatic prophecies and leadings from God, they can potentially be drawn away from God's written Word. If they succumb to that temptation, the authority of people can replace the authority of God for a person or a church!

The authority of men can be, and has been, a trap for conservative evangelicals as well. Certainly, many young seminarians do not follow the example of the Bereans by always searching out the Scriptures to see if their professor's theology is backed up by what the text actually says (see Acts 17:11). My tendency, especially early on in my Christian life, was to almost completely absorb my teachers' theology like a sponge. The line between God's Word and men's opinions was not a bright one for me. And it isn't particularly bright for many conservative evangelicals.

For now, it is sufficient to note that even though conservative evangelicals loudly claim 2 Timothy 3:16 as a rallying point, "All scripture is God-breathed and [all scripture] is useful for teaching, rebuking, correcting and training in righteousness," some rip out pages and verses from the New Testament by their theological systems and declare them to not be for today. This is the Samaritan error exactly!

We have been in close relationship with charismatic Christians for more than two decades now. Among many we see a firm grip on and a love for the written Word of God. This loving grip on the Scriptures serves as a sure anchor, giving my friends stability and consistency in their walks with Christ. But we must honestly confess to have met others who seemed to have lost their grip on the written Word. A particular "prophet" or church leader's words in a prayer meeting became more controlling in their lives than the words of Paul!

Although direct contradictions of Scripture occasionally occur, what is more common is the expansion of a "prophet's" authority in a person's life because of that "prophet's" revelatory gifting. In other words, because someone knew certain secrets about a Christian's past, the "prophet" was given presumptive authority to direct the Christian's future. I have met several very gifted individuals who have been able to tell people things that no one else knew, such as conversations held at the deathbed of a parent or vows made in prayer while alone with God. These gifted individuals were orthodox in their theology and sincerely believed and taught the historic creeds of the church. But their prophecies sometimes went to people who were not maturely grounded in God's written Word. As a result, because of the gifted person's amazing clarity about certain secret things, he or she became sought after by the recipient of the revelation.

Even among mature Christians, amazing accuracy about secret information will give a prophetically gifted person "instant credibility" about anything else the gifted person says. The gifted individual soon becomes a substitute for the seeking of God himself, and an almost quasi-mediator of God's will for a church or an individual. Gifted people with mature character, of course, resist and reject this overdependence. But the less mature can foster and be flattered by being sought out for "God's will for my future." The domination of churches, pastors, and church members by such individuals is too frequent an occurrence in the charismatic movement to be ignored. What are the correctives?

Many of these are listed in chapter eight, which is on hearing God's voice: individual believers must also seek counsel, have words confirmed by their own sanctified reason, and do nothing that contradicts God's written Word. Further, each of us must seek God for ourselves, and are responsible to listen for and discern God's will for our own lives. None of us will be able to "pass the buck" on the Judgement Day by claiming, "But, Lord, I was just doing what you told me through that prophetically gifted person!"

In addition, prophetically gifted people should never supplant the appointed government of the church. God appoints elders and pastors to care for and govern the church, not prophets![6] Prophets can strengthen, encourage, and comfort, but the leadership of a church is not given to prophets unless they also meet the scriptural requirements for elders or pastors and are appointed as such.

The loss of staying power. The third problem that occurs when a grip is lost on the written Word of God can be summed up by the phrase "no God and no grandchildren." If the loss of God's written Word causes churches to supplant God's authority with human authority, such loss also leads to the problem of "no grandchildren." A revival or renewal, even if it began as a genuine work of God, loses its staying power without the systematic study of the Scriptures and an appreciation for theological reflection. Like the days of the Judges of Israel, an earlier move of God can quickly become forgotten by the children and the grandchildren.

> After that whole generation had been gathered to their fathers, another generation grew up, who knew neither the Lord nor what he had done for Israel. Then the Israelites did evil in the eyes of the Lord and served the Baals. They forsook the Lord, the God of their fathers, who had brought them out of Egypt. They followed and worshiped various gods of the peoples around them. They provoked the Lord to anger. **Judges 2:10-12**

The charismatic movement has suffered the problem of "no grandchildren" often in its brief history. Early in Pentecostal history (about a year before the meetings at Azusa Street that spread Pentecostalism throughout North America), a significant revival took place in Wales. Between September 1904 and June 1905, it is estimated that over a hundred thousand Welsh were converted under the preaching of Evan

164 Empowered Evangelicals

Roberts and others. Chapels, barns, and every other conceivable meeting place were filled night after night as people worshiped, praised God ecstatically, and listened to testimonies by recent converts. Often the meetings were not scheduled in advance! People were simply drawn to the meeting places by the leading of God's Spirit.

Newspaper accounts of the Welsh revival reported enormous short-term results from the revival meetings. The crime rate dropped dramatically throughout Wales, as did gambling and alcohol consumption. Anecdotal stories are told of pit ponies at coal mines who had to be retrained to respond to new vocabularies, because they had been previously trained to respond to cursing and swearing!

Yet despite the many wonderful events of 1904 and 1905, Evan Roberts and other leaders of the revival neglected expository teaching of the Bible. They failed to encourage the study of the Scriptures in their meetings and treated theology as a "fleshly discipline." As a result, when World War I broke out just a decade after this extraordinary revival, there were a few pockets of believers remaining in the Welsh chapels. By the 1920s, visitors to Wales said that one could find virtually no evidence that a revival had ever taken place. How extraordinarily tragic! But experiencing the Spirit unsupported by teaching the full written Word of God is like water spilled on the ground. After a brief time, the ground dries up and no sign remains that water was ever poured there.

WHAT WAS WRONG WITH WORSHIP IN JERUSALEM?

Recall that Jesus not only condemned the Samaritans' *loss of truth*; he also rebuked the Jews in Jerusalem for their *loss of spirit*. Thus Jesus said to the Samaritan woman, "A time is coming when you will worship the Father neither on this mountain nor in Jerusalem.... God is Spirit, and his worshipers must worship in spirit and in truth."

What might Jesus have meant by "in spirit" worship? What was Jerusalem missing by way of "in spirit" worship? Certainly Jews may have lost the Holy Spirit in worship either by refusing the Holy Spirit's presence via his gifts and ministry or by squelching the Holy Spirit through some sinful practice such as legalism or self-righteousness. But we think, in addition to the absence of the Holy Spirit, Jesus was also referring to Jerusalem's loss of worshiping with the *human* spirit.

The human "spirit" is the God-related part of us—not the body that deals with this world, but that part of our humanity that connects us with spiritual things. Worship "in spirit" includes worship from the very core of our personalities and can be contrasted with worship that involves only our voices or our intellects.

The criticism of Jerusalem-type worship, then, may be the same criticism Jesus leveled at the Pharisees when he said, "These people honor me with their lips, but their hearts are far from me. They worship me in vain" (Mt 15:8-9).

It is easy for us as human beings to worship with our lips but keep our hearts far from God. We forget that God is not a man! He is not deceived as men are by outward appearances.

We conservative evangelicals, in particular, often get caught in the trap of believing that correct doctrine is the highest mark of spirituality. So long as we have accurate notions about God, we can think that we are spiritual. Without in any way demeaning the importance of sound doctrine, we need to realize that *doctrinal accuracy is not the high-water mark of the Christian life*. We may be able to "fathom all mysteries and all knowledge... but [without] love [we are] nothing" (1 Cor 13:2). Love involves our whole person—our hearts, not just our heads; our spirits, not just our mouths. It was this *whole-person* love of God that Jerusalem-worship, technically correct as it was, was lacking.[7]

THE WORD THAT PIERCES THE HEART

How can conservative evangelicals escape Jerusalem-type worship? By asking Jesus through the Holy Spirit to do to us what he did to the Samaritan woman—to shred our surface-only worship with a piercing revelatory word.

Understand that God wants people to worship him from the very depths of their personalities, from their hearts and from their spirits. The Samaritan woman in this story is a wonderful example of someone who vainly tried to fend God off from the depth of her being. She tried to change the subject, to raise objections, to ask questions—anything to insure Jesus didn't get too intimate. She had a line of defenses around her heart, guarding it from hurt, from disappointment, maybe from the pain of radical self-honesty.

Jesus said something that assaulted the fortresslike defenses built by the Samaritan woman. He said: "'Go, call your husband and come back.' 'I have no husband,' she replied.... 'You are right in saying you have no husband. The fact is, you have had five husbands, and the man you now have is not your husband. What you have just said is quite true'" (Jn 4:16-18).

Do you understand what Jesus did? At first blush, his statement may seem harsh, unkind, and out of character for the Jesus you have come to know. We must understand that the hardness of God is kinder than the softness of men and women. When God, the surgeon, takes out his knife and cuts into our hearts, he is being kinder by far than friends who flatter us while we are being eaten away by some moral cancer or self-deception.

Many people are in this woman's place today. If they are not yet Christians, they may use objections or unanswerable questions as an excuse for not accepting the gospel. Or if they are Christians, they may say to themselves, "I will attend church and listen to a sermon and sing some songs, but I will not let Jesus get too close to me. I am afraid of the choices he will make for my life. I am afraid that what Jesus will call me to may rob me of happiness or fun. Probably Jesus will call me to be a missionary or to break up with a girlfriend or boyfriend I like. Bottom line, if Jesus gets too close, if I really let him in, he will probably make me do something I really don't want to do. I will worship Jesus with my lips, but my heart will be kept safe and secure and under my control."

But Jesus doesn't permit people to keep him at arm's length forever. He came for a soul-penetrating relationship. He is a personal Savior who insists on a personal, intimate relationship with you and me.

Why then did Jesus speak to the Samaritan woman about her sex life? What he was doing was reaching under the lines of defense that this woman put up to God's touch and God's Spirit. Like many of us, the woman must have felt incredible guilt about her past and present sexual practices. She probably thought, "If God knew what I was like, he would surely reject me. I must keep my heart safe from God's rejection."

By speaking right to her hidden sin, Jesus pulled away the blanket of guilt and shame she hid under. In effect, Jesus was saying to her (and to us): "I know what you are like. I see you just as you are. I know what you have done. I see it all, yet I still love you with the Father's perfect love. I also know the plans I have for you—plans to prosper you and not to harm you, plans to give you a hope and a future.[8] You were not meant to be alone. You were made for relationship."

A prophetic revelation pierces the neatly constructed defenses we have built around our hearts. Such a word may come from the Holy Spirit illuminating a Bible text as we study it or meditate upon it. For years we may blandly read over a text such as "This is how my heavenly Father will treat each of you unless you forgive your brother from your heart" (Mt 18:35). Suddenly, because God's Spirit illuminates the text, we are forced to face our unforgiveness of someone who has sinned against us. A revelatory word may come through a prophecy or an unsettling dream we have or someone else has about us. It may come through anointed preaching. Or it may come as a direct word, without mediation, as Paul wrote: "The Holy Spirit, himself, testifies with our spirit that we are God's children" (Rom 8:15, 16).

Several years ago, I was in Russia on a short-term mission trip to St. Petersburg (formerly Leningrad). I got together with a small group of pastors and their spouses to pray. During our prayer time, the conversation turned to issues from our pasts that we felt God had never touched. When my turn for personal prayer came up, I briefly mentioned some of the pain I experienced as a child as a result of my parents' divorce. I said it matter-of-factly, without much feeling. Frankly, like the Samaritan woman with Jesus, I was not interested in becoming overly personal with this group of strangers.

One of the women looked me in the eye and said, "I believe God wants to say something to you." I said, "That's great. What do you think he wants to say?" She said, "I don't think it's going to come through us. I think what God wants to say will be spoken directly from his Spirit to your heart. That's what you need."

So I said, "OK, I will ask for that sometime." She said, "No, we are going to ask God to speak to you right now!"

Embarrassed, I was forced to pray right there for God to speak to my heart. Immediately, I felt the Lord speak a very personal, very reassuring word to me about his love for me and my sonship. As I was pondering what I sensed God saying to me, the pastor's wife said, "OK, now tell us what God said to you."

I replied, "Well, it is kind of personal."

She responded, "I think you need to share it."

Knowing she wasn't about to let up, I began to speak. I got

five words out, "I feel the Lord said..." and then I broke down in deep, profound sobbing. I didn't know that there was still so much pain in my heart that hadn't been touched by God. Somehow when I chose to say what I felt God spoke to me, I was opening my heart to the touch of his Spirit. When that happened, my defenses fell and God marched in and took my heart.

Revelation through prophecy, through the secret work of the Spirit in the heart, or through expository preaching of the Scriptures, often reaches under people's defenses and touches the heart. It did so in the case of Jesus' word to the woman at the well. It did so with me in Russia. And in numerous worship services, I have seen revelation—a simple word shared during our ministry times about some need that God wishes to meet or someone God wishes to touch—convert someone from an arm's length, mouth-only worshiper to a fuller "in spirit" worshiper. Paul wrote: "But if an unbeliever or someone who does not understand comes in while everybody is prophesying, he will be convinced by all that he is a sinner and will be judged by all, and the secrets of his heart will be laid bare. So he will fall down and worship God, exclaiming, 'God is really among you!'" (1 Cor 14:24-25).

If we conservative evangelicals in our small groups simply left room in our worship services and in our personal prayer for God's fresh word—"God, we ask you to speak through a read Scripture, through a spontaneous prayer, through a secret stirring by your Spirit, or through a prophecy"—many of our people would be changed.

Nice, well-scrubbed, theologically correct evangelicals might really begin to do business with Holy God. Secret sins might come to light. Hidden abuse, past or present, might be revealed. Fears, hurt, and doubt might all come to the surface. Wouldn't you like to be among people who were changed not only on the outside but on the inside as well? Wouldn't you like to be in a church full of "true worshipers"—who worship God in the truth of the Scriptures and also from the deep recesses of their souls? Does that excite you? It should!

WORSHIP THAT IS INTIMATE

Let us pull together the various threads of this chapter. Biblical worship must be worship "in truth." Thus, for people to worship biblically, they must have a true knowledge of God and not confuse God with any idol or imagination of their own minds. We also must have a true view of ourselves as creatures, as sinners, and as God's redeemed children.

But biblical worship goes beyond simply having a true view of God and ourselves. Biblical worship must be worship "in spirit" from the deepest part of our beings. A wonderful word to describe "in spirit" worship is *intimate* worship. Intimate worship draws the inner part of the worshiper close to God. Intimate worship involves our hearts, not just our mouths. Intimate worship should sound romantic at times and be directed to God. In other words, intimate worship involves songs and praise communicated *to* God, not simply the declaration of truths *about* God. We can preach the gospel, serve and minister in Christ's name, but those are activities directed to others, not to God. Intimate worship is directed to God.

Some people have found the language of the Jewish theologian Martin Buber to be helpful here. Instead of speaking *about* God as an object, an "It," we speak *to* God as a "Thou." Thus intimate worship is I-Thou worship, often involving a personal encounter between the Holy Spirit and the deepest part of our beings.

Finally, intimate worship includes an invitation to God to draw near and enter the sanctuary of our hearts. It is God's desire to draw near, to see into us, to penetrate our defenses, to be intimate with his children. Nowhere will intimacy with God happen as fully as in worship.

WHAT GOD HAS JOINED TOGETHER: WORSHIP AND THE WORD

For charismatics, the prescription of this chapter would be an emphasis on the written Word of God as the chief gift of the Holy Spirit to the church. Richard Lovelace wonderfully describes the balance of Word and Spirit when he says,

We may conclude, therefore, the key to live orthodoxy offered by the Puritan and Pietist traditions is the proper balance between the Spirit and the Word with appropriate attention given to the role of each. What this really means is that to proclaim Christ in living power, it is necessary for us to depend on him in a double way. On the one hand, for accurate knowledge of the Incarnate Word, we must look back in dependence of the written Word which he inspired through the Spirit and which is the continuing instrument through which his mind is present among believers. On the other hand, for illuminated understanding of the written Word and power to transmit it to others, we must look up in dependence on the risen Word, who alone is able to enliven the dead conceptual knowledge of the fallen human mind through the sanctifying operation of the Holy Spirit, and to focus existentially so that it will be wisdom in the biblical sense and not mere knowledge.[9]

For conservative evangelicals, the prescription lies in recovering the centrality of heartfelt, whole-person worship involving not only truth in the mind but intimacy with our spirits. It also involves leaving room in our personal worship and in our worship services for God to surprise us through the spontaneous expression of spiritual gifts, through prophecy, and through corporate prayers. After we have gone through all our calculations and our time allocations and our planning about what will happen and what won't happen in our worship services, it is appropriate for us to ask, "Have we left room for God to break in, in any way that he sees fit?"

We are not suggesting that we should only look for God in a certain way or with a certain kind of emotion. But we should *look for God.* How God chooses to manifest his presence is up to him. But very often, if we simply permit it, God would come in a way that would be memorable, perhaps extraordinary, and, at times, even awesome!

FOR DISCUSSION

1. What insights do the authors offer on the need to maintain a strong grip on the written Word of God? What could you add to the authors' list?

2. What is the authors' understanding of "in spirit" worship? What dimension does this add to worship "in truth"?

3. Have you ever had a word from God pierce your defenses? If so, describe the occasion. If not, do you regularly ask God to speak to you or draw near to you?

4. What benefits can you envision from developing a more intimate relationship with God?

WHEN SEEKING A CHURCH

1. Did solid Bible teaching have a prominent place in the Sunday worship time?

2. Was the worship time mainly participatory, involving the congregation, or did it turn the congregation into an audience?

3. Did you sense the presence of the Holy Spirit in the church? Was his presence obviously valued and welcomed by the leaders and the pastor?

4. Was the worship intimate, whole person, "I-Thou" worship? Was there any room for something to happen that was not pre-planned?

FOR PASTORS

1. Consider teaching a series of sermons on the subject of worship. Consider making worship (more than a token ten minutes) a part of virtually all of your church's activities including board meetings, small group Bible studies, training events, Sunday school classes, etc.

2. Are your worship services completely pre-engineered? Is there any room for God to do something unplanned? Within your particular church setting, how can you leave room for some spontaneity?

3. As you look out at your church on Sunday mornings, ask yourself the following questions: Do a significant number of

people seem to be engaged in "in spirit" worship with their whole persons? Are the songs or hymns your church sings mostly "I-it" hymns or "I-Thou" hymns? Do they merely talk about God or do they engage in intimate conversation with God? Do they create intimacy between God and the worshiper? Are you satisfied with what you observe in your church's worship? If not, what can you do with your dissatisfaction?

4. As a stretching exercise, consider attending a conference or seminar on contemporary worship with several key leaders, including your music minister or worship leader. Gradually apply some of the relevant lessons.

5. Are people in your church sufficiently grounded, to your satisfaction, in the written Word of God? Consider opportunities for other leaders and teachers, both inside and outside the church, to support the goal of Bible learning. For example, if you have small groups, how can they do a better job of encouraging Bible learning? Consider hosting or leading a seminar on personal Bible study.

EIGHT

Hearing God's Voice

Mike woke up in the middle of the night, nudged his wife awake, and asked, "Honey, do you know a place called Clifton?"

Too sleepy to protest, she mumbled, "You mean Clifton, New Jersey?"

"That sounds right."

"But, Mike, it's three o'clock in the morning!"

"I had this dream about a black man named Leonard T. Olden, Jr. [pseudonym]. I was telling him about the Lord. He lived in a place called Clifton."

"Do you know a Leonard T. Olden, Jr. in Clifton?"

"Never heard the name before. Besides, I've never been to Clifton!"

"Well, what are you going to do about it?"

"I don't know."

Two days later, at his wife's urging, Mike reluctantly called information for Clifton, New Jersey, asking for the number of a "Leonard T. Olden, Jr." Sure enough, he was listed. Mike called the number and spoke with Mrs. Olden.

Feeling a little sheepish, Mike introduced himself and told her that he didn't know Leonard but had a dream about him the other night. Mrs. Olden confirmed that her husband was black and that she had been praying for him because she was concerned about him. She told Mike that her daughter had recently become a Christian. They were both concerned about him.

Mike said, "Well, all I know is that God must be concerned about your husband, too. Concerned enough to give a total stranger in Michigan a dream about him."

Since Leonard wasn't home at the time, Mike left his phone number. Later that evening, Mr. Olden himself called. Again, Mike recounted his dream, to Mr. Olden's amazement. They had a good conversation about God's love, and Mike prayed with him.

Mike is the owner of a small business and the father of three young children. He's not a psychic and wouldn't describe himself as a prophet. But he does believe in the validity of what a theologian would call "subjective revelation"—impressions given by the Spirit through dreams, visions, and inward promptings.

CHILDREN OF DIVORCE

For too long, Christians have been divided into two camps over the issue of subjective revelation. One camp views the Bible as the sole means of revelation. God speaks through the Bible and there is no need for any other direction from God. Dreams, visions, and inner promptings are all highly suspect.

In the other camp are those who view a rich diet of subjective revelation as a must for the truly spiritual believer. Their favorite stories are stories of God speaking through visions, dreams, and prophecies. They gladly recount conversations with God as though telling of a phone conversation with a friend. "I said, 'God, what do you mean?' And he said, 'Bob....'"

Like a husband and wife in marriage, God has joined these two together—the objective revelation of the Bible and the subjective revelation of dreams, visions, and inner promptings. The two must be clearly distinguished, and it must be clear that subjective revelation must always be subordinate to the infallible revelation of Scripture. But the enemy has tried to divide them. As members of the church in history, we are all, in a sense, the children of this divorce. We've inherited a divided testimony over what it means to hear God's voice.

The confusion dates back to the Reformation. Martin Luther observed that many of the extra-biblical traditions of the Roman Catholic church—the very reasons for the reform he sought—were supported by various forms of subjective revelation: visions of Mary, angelic messengers, and the like. So Luther was highly suspicious of miracles and promptings reported from the Spirit.

The conservative evangelical tradition has been profoundly influenced by a book written in 1918 by Benjamin Warfield, *Counterfeit Miracles,* advancing the theory that miracles and gifts of the Spirit (including gifts of revelation) were limited to the apostolic era. Once the canon of Scripture was complete, these charismatic phenomena ceased. The holy words of Scripture were contrasted with virtually all forms of subjective revelation, including forms described in Scripture. Some modern-day critics of the Pentecostal and charismatic movements keep the battle alive by citing the abuses of subjective revelation as typical and dismissing any valid place for visions, dreams, and inner promptings.

The modern era has also witnessed a great assault on the reliability of the Bible. Once widely accepted as the very words of God by the whole church, the words of Scripture are now the subject of fierce dispute. Is the Bible uniquely inspired, or is it a compilation of history and myth to be sifted and sorted like any other great work of literature?

Meanwhile, as this controversy drags on within the modern church, society's view of the inner working of the human being has undergone a revolution. Sigmund Freud replaced the notion of the soul—a fundamentally religious concept—with that of the unconscious. In effect, the modern world divorces its old mate, the soul, and remarries another, the unconscious. This removes dreams, impressions, and inner promptings from the realm of spirituality and places them under the expert interpretation of psychiatry. Only those trained in the technology of the social sciences are equipped to make any sense of these things. (The techniques of the New Age movement—handbooks on dream interpretation and the like—are a religious equivalent to the techniques of psycho-analysis.) Freud's currency in the modern world is greatly diminished, but the effects of his philosophy of the human psyche exert considerable influence. Is it any wonder that the children of these divorces feel bothered, bewildered, tentative, and confused about what it means to hear God's voice?

EARS TO HEAR

Of the various healings Jesus performed, there was something especially vivid about the way he restored a person's hearing.

> Some people brought to him a man who was deaf and could hardly talk, and they begged him to place his hand on the man. After he took him aside, away from the crowd, Jesus put his fingers into the man's ears. Then he spit and touched the man's tongue. He looked up to heaven and with a deep sigh said to him "Ephphatha!" (which means, "Be opened!") At this, the man's ears were opened, his tongue was loosened and he began to speak plainly.
>
> **Mark 7:32-35**

How do you describe the style of this healing? Jesus puts his fingers into the man's ears, spits and touches the man's tongue, lifts his head, and sighs deeply. This was not a dispassionate exercise. Jesus was *involved* in this healing—perhaps because Jesus wants us to hear, not just the sounds of this world, but his voice.

A lengthy allegory in the Gospel of John concerns the shepherd and his sheep. The chief characteristic of the sheep is that they hear the shepherd's voice. Everything, it seems, hinges on hearing his voice. Indeed, the Jewish people historically understood the importance of "hearing" by making the *Shema* the central prayer of Judaism: "Hear, O Israel, the Lord our God, the Lord is one" (Dt 6:4).

Jesus had a favorite expression to accentuate his message, sometimes crying out in a loud voice after an especially important discourse: "He who has ears, let him hear!" The first and most extensive parable in Mark's Gospel is the parable of the sower. It's a story about hearing God's word. Three times, the phrase is repeated, "He who has ears, let him hear!"

As the children of a church divided over what it means to hear God's voice, how do we hold together what God has joined together: the utterly trustworthy words of Holy Scripture and the various forms of subjective revelation (dreams, visions, and inner promptings) that the Bible portrays as part of the package of hearing God's voice?

THE WITNESS OF PHILIP

Philip was one of the seven individuals chosen by the church in Jerusalem to oversee the distribution of funds to the poor Impelled beyond Jerusalem by the wave of persecution led by Saul of Tarsus, Philip had a wonderful encounter with an Ethiopian official. The account is especially helpful because it illustrates the interaction between subjective and objective revelation.

> Now an angel of the Lord said to Philip, "Go south to the road—the desert road—that goes down from Jerusalem to Gaza." So he started out, and on his way he met an Ethiopian eunuch, an important official in charge of all the treasury of Candace, queen of the Ethiopians. This man had gone to Jerusalem to worship, and on his way home was sitting in his chariot reading the book of Isaiah the prophet. The Spirit told Philip, "Go to that chariot and stay near it." Then Philip ran up to the chariot and heard the man reading Isaiah the prophet. "Do you understand what you are reading?" Philip asked. "How can I," he said, "unless someone explains it to me?" So he invited Philip to come up and sit with him. The eunuch was reading this passage of Scripture:
>
> He was led like a sheep to the slaughter, and as a lamb before the shearer is silent, so he did not open his mouth. In his humiliation he was deprived of justice. Who can speak of his descendants? For his life was taken from the earth.
>
> The eunuch asked Philip, "Tell me, please, who is the prophet talking about, himself or someone else?" Then Philip began with that very passage of Scripture and told him the good news about Jesus. **Acts 8:26-35**

The account concludes with the baptism of the Ethiopian official.

Without question, the centerpiece of revelation in this account is the biblical text. The words of the prophet Isaiah have already begun their work on the Ethiopian well before Philip arrives. And the text provides the most significant revelation in the episode: the revelation of Jesus to one who knew nothing of the good news before. Nevertheless, subjective revelation is an important preparation and support for the encounter with God's Word in the prophet's writings.

And now a word from the angels. The Book of Acts is full of angelic visitations. Cornelius, the God-fearing Gentile, Peter the apostle, Paul and Silas in prison are all introduced to angels. The increased angelic activity seen in the New Testament is a sign that with the coming of Jesus, heaven is open as never before. A new level of communication between heaven and earth is possible. As Jesus told Nathaniel, "You shall see heaven open, and the angels of God ascending and descending on the Son of Man" (Jn 1:51).

There's more to this world than meets the eye. There is an intersection between heaven and earth through the coming of Jesus, and angels are frequently found at the intersection. To this day, angels appear to ordinary people. Sometimes they speak a message. Sometimes their mere presence conveys the message that the kingdom is near.

My (Ken's) own grandmother—we called her Gammy—was a stern, no-nonsense woman. She had reason to take life seriously. Born in England, she wanted to immigrate to North America at the age of nineteen. She tried to purchase a one-way ticket on a new ocean liner called the Titanic, the ship even God couldn't sink. Bad luck: the ship's maiden voyage was sold out! She purchased a ticket on another vessel. Imagine sailing the lonely Atlantic as a young woman, knowing that the ship "even God couldn't sink" was somewhere two miles below on the ocean floor.

Several decades later, Gammy lay dying in the house I grew up in—in my bed, as a matter of fact. Toward the end of a difficult evening, she looked up at my father with a sense of wonder in her eyes.

"Do you see them, Glen?"

"See what, Mother Meyers?"

"Over there," she replied, with a note of mild irritation (a common note in Gammy's voice).

"Yes, over there by the closet," she continued. "The angels." These were the last words anyone remembers hearing from Gammy Meyers.

It was a remarkable report because my grandmother was not one to wear her religion on her sleeve. No, that was a private affair, nobody's business but her own. She was a proper Baptist, who worshiped in the nearby Episcopal church. This was not a woman subject to charismatic enthusiasms.

The vision of angels that Gammy reported was a message from heaven (a form of subjective revelation) to her, and to her grieving family, that the kingdom of heaven is nearer than we think.

The idea of angelic visitation is understandably troubling to some conservative evangelicals. After all, Satan can disguise himself as an angel of light. Some of the most peculiar heresies (for example, the teachings of Mormonism revealed to its founder, Joseph Smith) are based on messages from angels.

Yet Philip's encounter with an angel is typical of the valid appearances of angels in the New Testament and in the church throughout history. The angelic encounter served two important but limited functions. First, it got Philip's attention. Second, it led Philip to the road where the Ethiopian was pondering the words of the prophet Isaiah. The angel was not the source of any doctrine (indeed, angels purporting to reveal doctrine should be met with grave suspicion); it was simply an agent of God's providence.

The Spirit's prompting. Having been directed by an angel to travel a particular road, Philip was led by yet another form of subjective revelation, an inner prompting of the Spirit. In the Bible, the actual process of the Spirit prompting someone is never analyzed or described in detail. It is simply reported in a matter-of-fact, if frustratingly succinct, fashion: *"The Spirit told Philip."*

These promptings of the Spirit come in various ways, with varying levels of intensity. If it is any comfort, the biblical figures to whom they are given typically respond with uncertainty. When young Samuel heard a voice calling his name, he assumed it was the voice of Eli the priest. It took three tries and consultation with Eli to discover that the voice was the voice of the Lord. That's one reason this form of revelation is called subjective revelation. It's not cut and dried, not subject to unmistakable outside verification or replication in a laboratory.

Say what? In describing the promptings of the Spirit, we are always reduced to the language of metaphor. Like wine connoisseurs describing the taste of a fine wine: "dry, delicately balanced, with a floral bouquet—assertive yet not over-bearing." Fair enough, but what does it *taste* like?

In Jesus' allegory of the shepherd and his flock (see Jn 10:1-18), he speaks of the sheep who *"know his* [the Shepherd's] *voice."* But even this is not precise, scientific language. Jesus acknowledges as much in his telling of the parable: "'They will run away from [the stranger] because they do not recognize a stranger's voice.' Jesus used this *figure of speech,* but they did not understand what he was telling them" (Jn 10:5-6, italics added).

The very phrase "hearing God's voice" employs a figure of speech. After all, what does it mean for God, who is Spirit, to speak with a "voice"? Surely it is something different from a conversation between mortals.

Perhaps we can take some comfort in the difficulty the disciples had with the whole concept. Here it is, the classic description of the disciple's relationship with his Lord—the sheep who recognize the shepherd's voice—and Jesus' closest disciples don't get it. Shepherd? Sheep? Hear his voice? What are you talking about? Jesus understands that when he's dealing with the likes of us, he's not teaching the accelerated class. When it comes to hearing God's voice, we are all in need of special education.

And yet, as a figure of speech, the idea of hearing God's voice is helpful. After all, voice recognition is a subjective process. Words can convey a precise meaning, but voices are another matter. How do you recognize a person's voice? Difficult to describe, isn't it? High pitched, soft, gravelly, whiny—we do have words to describe the sound, but the words don't do justice to the actual sound.

Voice recognition is a subjective process, but it is nevertheless very real. And it can be quite reliable. A household pet doesn't recognize many words, but it knows its owner's voice. A small baby has a limited vocabulary, yet she knows her mother's voice.

And so we are simply told that the Spirit "told Philip" to approach the Ethiopian official's chariot. We don't know how Philip received this message: did he hear a voice like thunder from a cloud, or was it the "still small voice" that Elijah heard (see 1 Kings 19:12)? Did he hear it in the form of words, or did he simply have an inner urge to go to the chariot? We just don't know.

Subjective revelation: we've all had it happen. In all likelihood, Philip experienced this message from God as an inner prompting, rather than an audible voice. While conservative evangelicals and charismatics have a different language to describe this phenomenon (fruits of their isolation from one another), nearly every Christian has experienced a "prompting of the Spirit"—including those who bristle at the concept of subjective revelation.

The act of placing our faith in Jesus for salvation comes at the prompting of the Spirit. "No one can come to me unless the Father who sent me draws him," said Jesus (Jn 6:44). And, "No one can say, 'Jesus is Lord,' except by the Holy Spirit," according to Paul (1 Cor 12:3). When you placed saving faith in Jesus, you did so at the prompting of the Spirit. How did you experience the prompting? Hard to say. You felt drawn. You saw something with a new and convincing clarity.

Perhaps you are familiar with the difference between simply reading the words of the Bible (or hearing biblical preaching) and having an internal witness to something you read or hear. The one is simple exposure to God's Word—valuable in its own right and reason enough to read the Bible or listen to preaching. But the other is a more personal and powerful form of communication from heaven to your heart. Something "grabs you" or "strikes you" or "leaps off the page." These are all crude attempts to describe a process that defies description.

I was once listening to an older speaker ramble on about intimacy with Jesus. I began by listening to his message like an editor reading a manuscript. (The editor's motto: "Never met a sentence I couldn't improve.") But after a few minutes of critical analysis of the sermon's organizational strengths and weaknesses, I found myself exerting enormous energy to muffle my own sobbing. I felt that Jesus himself was standing next to the speaker. I knew for a certainty that intimacy with Jesus is possible and that I wanted it more than anything. That was an inner witness of the Spirit.

John described the inner witness when he wrote, "As for you, the anointing you received from him remains in you, and you do not need anyone to teach you" (1 Jn 2:27). What happens when you experience the inner prompting of the Spirit in one of these well-known ways? You learn to recognize the phenomenon. You come to expect it. Your faith for hearing God in that particular way increases. And as your faith increases, you tend to hear more clearly.

Hearing God's voice is not some mystical business reserved for the super-spiritual. Chances are, you've heard his voice already. And there is the wonderful opportunity to hear his voice more.

According to biblical testimony, the Spirit's prompting can come to us in several forms.

The Spirit's prompting: dreams. Most dreams are the meanderings of our minds when our alert self is off duty. But occasionally a dream contains a divine deposit from heaven. Joseph, the paternal guardian of Jesus, received significant subjective revelation through dreams: first to abandon his plan to divorce Mary, then to take Mary and Jesus to Egypt, and finally to return to Nazareth (see Matthew 1-2).

A few years ago my wife Nancy had a dream in which Jesus came to her and said, "Tell Maja she has a choice." A cryptic message, but full of meaning for a mother and dad struggling with the pain of letting go that occurs as children move into the teen years. The Lord himself was sending a message to our daughter that the power to choose is a holy thing; it was a message that affirmed her journey into adult responsibility. And for Nancy and me, it was reassurance that Jesus is Lord of the process of growing up. If Jesus respected our daughter's power to choose, then we could more joyfully do the same.

Some time ago I had a vivid dream of heaven. I was with a large group of men and women assembled in a small auditorium. We were waiting for Jesus to appear (in what resembled a press conference format), after which time we would all enter heaven. Like a crowd of eager reporters, we were all bursting with questions to ask Jesus once he arrived. I had my own list of questions: compelling questions, perplexing questions, all the "Why God?" questions we accumulate over the years. Finally, like the President arriving in the White House press conference room, Jesus took the podium and said,

"I'll take your questions now." And just like so many press conferences I've seen, we all raised our hands, clamoring for him to call on us. It seemed that nothing was more important than the questions we each had. But then a curious thing happened. As soon as Jesus recognized the first person to speak, the lucky questioner found himself pausing, then stammering, then finally saying, "I've forgotten all my questions!" We had all forgotten all our questions! Suddenly, simply being in his presence was enough. We all knew it together: He was the answer to our most troubling questions. Jesus simply smiled, as if he expected as much, and with a wave of his hand pointed to the exit (which was really the entrance) and said, "What are we waiting for? Let's go!"

I've never been a vivid dreamer. I rarely recall my dreams and if I do, only vague shadows of the dream remain. But this dream was different. Clear. Unforgettable. I not only have my own "Why God" questions, but as a pastor, I also accumulate the toughest questions of many others. This dream has provided immense comfort to bear all those questions and to keep them in perspective.

Later on, we'll consider some biblical guidelines for sorting through various forms of subjective revelation, an obvious concern in discerning God's voice in dreams. But those guidelines are superfluous if our dreams are only a kind of psychological snapshot, providing a glimpse into the deep waters of our subconscious. Dreams may well be that, but they can be more, because there is more to us than Freud postulated. We may have something like Freud's id, ego, and superego. But we also have a soul. There's more to us than meets the psychologist's eye. The biblical testimony and the experience of ordinary Christians throughout church history suggests that God can and does speak to us in our dreams.

The Spirit's prompting: visual images. In Scripture, when God speaks to people through visual images, these images (at least the most vivid) are called visions. Peter had a vision of a sheet coming down from heaven filled with ritually clean and unclean animals. Paul had a vision of a man from Macedonia calling him to come and tell the good news. The writings of the prophets are filled with the description of visual images: Ezekiel's wheel, Jeremiah's boiling pot, Daniel's man dressed in linen. When the disciples returned from a mission trip, Jesus responded by reporting a vision of Satan falling like lightning from heaven.

Once while praying for healing for a woman with chronic migraines, a picture formed in my mind of a young girl alone in a dark room. After I reported the picture to the woman, she seemed to open her heart to God's love for healing an internal wound. She wept. A year later, the woman told me that from that point on, she had no recurrence of migraine headaches.

The Spirit's prompting: a knowing beyond natural means. When Jesus conversed with the Samaritan woman at the well, it was clear that he knew things about her that he could not have known by natural means. Charismatics have sometimes referred to this as a "word of knowledge."

This seems to be one of the favorite "gifts" of some television ministers where the exercise seems to be just another part of the show. "There's a woman listening now who has female problems. You're to call our number now with your financial pledge and God will heal you." These "words" seem designed to impress only those who willingly suspend all critical judgment. What television audience doesn't include a woman with gynecological problems?

But God does give Christians knowledge of other people or situations as an opportunity to extend his favor. Rich had such an experience:

He was praying with a woman in another state—someone

he did not know. She was thinking of ending her involvement in the choir at her Congregational church, but this was obviously a troubling issue. Rich had the distinct impression that the problem in the choir involved a man named Ralph. He had no natural means of having this information. When he asked, "Does the problem with the choir involve your relationship with a person named Ralph?" the woman began to sob, revealing that Ralph, a member of the choir, had been making sexual advances toward her. Rich counseled the woman to speak immediately with her pastor about the problem. Ralph was confronted, and the problem was resolved.

Sometimes this knowledge is extraordinarily specific, as it was in this case. But the Spirit may prompt you to reach out to someone by giving less detailed information. The details are not the issue; the Spirit's leading is the ultimate question.

I HEAR, SO NOW WHAT?

As soon as we engage in a serious consideration of subjective revelation, two questions become paramount: first, how do we know if it's God? Second, once we decide a prompting may well be from the Spirit, what do we do with it?

How do we know it's God? The first question is perhaps the most troubling. In fact, one of the chief reasons we shy away from subjective revelation is the possibility of getting it wrong. For every story of a prompting of the Spirit releasing the grace of Christ, we can easily muster a hair-raising tale of spiritual deception: The Volkswagen full of disrobed believers who were directed to take off their clothes through a "revelation"; the small band of religious enthusiasts who quit their jobs and sold their homes in preparation for the final showdown between God and Satan somewhere in Idaho.

Philip's interaction with the Ethiopian official provides important clues to both of these questions.

The priority of objective revelation. While Philip's experience with subjective revelation (the angel's direction to go down the desert road, the Spirit's prompting to stand near the Ethiopian official) is intriguing, it's the objective revelation of Scripture which is most prominent in the story.

Once Philip approaches the Ethiopian official, he finds him reading aloud from Isaiah, chapter fifty-three. The official asks Philip about the passage, "Then Philip began with that very passage of Scripture and told him the good news about Jesus" (Acts 8:35).

The Spirit's promptings merely set the stage for the main event: telling the good news through a Bible study. No doubt Philip was well-versed in the presence of Christ in the Old Testament Scriptures. This was a major theme of Jesus' teaching after his resurrection and before his ascension into heaven (see Luke 24:27). The writings of Moses, of the prophets, and the psalms were all springboards for telling the good news about Jesus. In the case of the Ethiopian eunuch, the springboard was Isaiah's depiction of the suffering servant. Philip knew his Bible. His understanding of the good news about Jesus was rooted in the Bible.

The subjective revelation that Philip received was wonderful and fascinating, but the revelation did not get the Ethiopian official saved. In the ancient world, the concept of revelations from the spirit world were a staple of religious life. But the objective revelation of the One True God of the Hebrew Scriptures coming to save us in the person of the God-Man Christ Jesus—*that* was truly revolutionary. It was this message—the promises of the Hebrew Scriptures fulfilled in the gospel of the risen Christ—that had the power to bring the Ethiopian eunuch into the waters of baptism.

The power of this good news contained in the Bible is well attested throughout history. Gladys Aylward, a missionary from England, was on a mission trip in a remote section of China, well beyond the scope of the existing Christian missions. She came upon a group of Buddhist monks who welcomed her into their lamasery as a visiting speaker. Gladys Aylward was stunned by the receptivity of these monks to her telling of the good news. Through the night they visited her one by one to inquire further about the things she told them.

Eventually Miss Aylward went to the head of the Buddhist monastery and asked him why his fellow monks were so open to the gospel. He showed her a frame containing a torn piece of paper. The paper was the fragment of a gospel tract that the monks had found several years earlier, containing little more than the text, "For God so loved the world that he gave his... only Son" (Jn 3:16). Then the Buddhist monk told her, "We have revered this sacred message for many years. And we have longed to learn of a God who loves the world. So when you came, we knew that this God must have sent you."[1]

This is the unique power of the word "which can save you" when humbly accepted (see James 1:21). This is the word Philip preached, beginning "with that very passage of Scripture" (Acts 8:35). The point is plain: The subjective revelation of visions, dreams, and inner promptings attested to in the Bible are meant to be subordinate to the objective revelation of the Scriptures.

The clarity of biblical revelation. One of the hallmarks of an evangelical view of Scripture is the idea that the message of the Bible is plain to the honest reader. Without denying the considerable challenges of correct interpretation, or the presence of obscure or difficult passages of Scripture, this perspective asserts that the things we need to hear from God through the Bible can be heard, loud and clear.

Throughout the history of the church, there have been intense debates over the issue of biblical interpretation. How do we know what God is actually saying through the Bible? In the early centuries of the church, there were two competing schools of interpretation. One emphasized the need for an allegorical interpretation of the text. This view asserts that the true "spiritual" meaning of a passage of Scripture is buried beneath the literal meaning of the text. The six wings of the seraph in Isaiah's heavenly vision represent the six attributes of the Christian leader, or the six centers of Christendom, or the six keys to true worship. You can see the objection to the allegorical method: it seems to remove any objective basis for determining the meaning of a text.

When a speaker tells us that "the Spirit has shown me the meaning of the pomegranates on Aaron's robes," chances are he's dabbling in the allegorical method of interpretation. Allegory itself isn't forbidden. The biblical writers themselves sometimes interpret Scripture allegorically. (See Paul's treatment of Hagar and Sarah in Galatians 4.) But allegory can only be used on a limited basis, and always in deference to the plain sense of the text.

The other main school of interpretation was the literal school. A text could be understood by applying the basic rules of reading any historical book: understanding the rules of grammatical construction, and the meaning of words within their literary and historical context. The primary meaning of the text was the literal meaning: what the original author intended to say within his original context. Other levels of meaning might be derived, but they were subject to this "literal" meaning.

Here's a favorite text of charismatics:

This is what we speak, not in words taught us by human wisdom but in words taught by the Spirit, expressing spiritual truths in spiritual words. The man without the Spirit does not accept the things that come from the Spirit of God, for they are foolishness to him, and he cannot understand them, because they are spiritually discerned.

1 Corinthians 2:13-14

Sometimes a charismatic speaker will use this text to introduce a "Spirit-led interpretation" of Scripture that abandons the primacy of the literary-historical method, with its concern for the actual meaning of words in their literary-historical context, and replaces it with a new allegorical model. This is by no means a typical charismatic approach to Scripture, but it does occur where charismatics are playing fast and loose with the Bible. To say that "subjective revelation" must give way to the "objective revelation of Scripture" implies a firm grounding in the evangelical view of Scripture, the literary-historical method of interpretation.

Having a firm anchor in the objectivity of Scripture also involves an appreciation for the rules of sound biblical interpretation. Any serious teacher of the Scriptures should be well-grounded in the biblical discipline called "hermeneutics," or interpretation. While beyond the scope of this book, the rules of interpretation include items such as the importance of context, understanding the progressive nature of biblical revelation, interpreting obscure passages from the basis of clear passages (not vice versa), interpreting the parts of Scripture in light of the whole of Scripture, and so on.[2]

The Spirit's prompting and wisdom. Philip also models the interaction between subjective revelation and godly wisdom. Just because he has been remarkably led of the Spirit, Philip does not stop using his brain. The angel's message gets him on the right road, the Spirit's prompting brings him to the right chariot, but then with wisdom and understanding Philip converses with the Ethiopian official. Though heaven-sent, he doesn't barge in on the official, claiming that God has sent him by special arrangement. In fact, Philip treats the official with respect, beginning with a simple and appropriate question ("Do you understand what you are reading?"), and only speaking further once the official asks him for help (see Acts 8:30-31).

With these considerations as background, five simple rules for handling subjective revelation emerge.

1. Test every revelation by the certain words of Scripture. Paul confirms the secondary status of subjective revelation by his exhortations to test prophetic revelations. "Do not treat prophecies with contempt. Test everything. Hold on to the good. Avoid every kind of evil" (1 Thes 5:20-21). He affirms that "we know in part and we prophesy in part" (1 Cor 13:9). The spiritual gifts, including gifts of revelation, are limited, partial, and in need of testing and discernment.

By contrast, there is no corresponding exhortation to test the veracity of Holy Scripture. The Word of God is reliable, trustworthy, pure, in need of no further refinement. "All scripture," according to Paul, "is God breathed and is useful for teaching, rebuking, correcting and training in righteousness" (2 Tm 3:16). This affirms the testimony of Jesus, who declared that "the Scripture cannot be broken" (Jn 10:35).

It follows that no revelation, no matter how vivid, dramatic, compelling, or supernatural, can be accepted if it violates the written Word of God. As Paul said, "If we or an angel from heaven should preach a gospel other than the one we preached to you, let him be eternally condemned" (Gal 1:8). It's not enough for Paul to know that an angel is a holy angel from heaven rather than a demon from the pit of hell. If the angel's message contradicts the gospel, the good news reliably transmitted in the Scriptures, it has no place. What could be more plain?

2. Test every subjective revelation by the measure of Christ. The Scriptures do not stand apart from the person of Jesus. They are the God-breathed witness to Jesus. Any form of subjective revelation that contradicts the character of Christ, that does not pass the test question, "Does this sound like something Jesus would say or do?" should not be accepted.

3. Don't discern subjective revelations in isolation, but in the context of honest, loving relationships in the church. Some of the most foolish mistakes made in responding to revelation are made in isolation. Jesus contrasts the voice of the good shepherd with the voice of the stranger (see John 10:4-5). Satan is the ultimate stranger. Hell is a strange place, an alien nation. There is no true relationship in hell—it's every person for him or herself. A sure sign of a phony revelation is one that comes with the postscript, "By the way, don't tell anyone about this; you're the only one spiritual enough to understand these things."

Jesus calls us into authentic relationship with each other under his lordship. The body of Christ, therefore, provides a context for us to discern God's voice. We should take counsel with one another when we are unsure if what we are hearing is from God. That doesn't mean the church is an infallible guide. Whole groups of Christians can slide into error. But the counsel of wise and trusted believers is a considerable safeguard.

4. Don't do anything unwise or drastic simply on the basis of a subjective revelation. The angel's message to Philip to take a certain road, and the Spirit's prompting to draw near to a certain chariot did not demand a high level of cautious discernment. If Philip was the victim of an overheated imagination, the only thing he had to lose was time. Revelations which involve greater risk should be subject to a higher standard of discernment.

In some circles, however, whatever is outlandish, high-risk, awkward, or odd is considered more likely to be from God. Granted, God has required some strange things from his servants. Hosea was called to marry a harlot. Isaiah was told to remove his clothing. But these were the exception, not the rule. There is no indication that these prophets had a predisposition to treat revelations of this sort as though, "If it's odd, it must be God."

5. Make room for mistakes in the adventure of hearing God's voice. If your highest value is never making a mistake, you may never risk stepping onto the playing field. If your criteria for adopting a particular practice or resource is imperviousness to abuse, then you will adopt no practices, make use of no resources. Jesus has decided to bring his kingdom into the messiness of our world. He knows that means that his Holy Word will be misused and abused, as will the precious gifts of his Spirit. Indeed, every good and perfect gift can be tarnished by a fallen race.

As a pastor called to a pulpit ministry, I am painfully aware that at times I have not perfectly communicated the truth of the Scriptures. I've misunderstood the truth at times and misapplied it. I've lessened the impact of the truth, emphasized one aspect at the expense of another. I'm a vessel of holy things all right, but I'm made of clay, and the pot has a few cracks. But that knowledge doesn't keep me from preaching God's word as faithfully as I know how. It does require that I go about the task with a healthy dose of humility and a willingness to admit mistakes.

The same applies to our attempts to hear God's voice and respond to the promptings we sense from the Spirit.

What do you DO with subjective revelation? A great deal of evangelical concern over subjective revelation is rooted in the actions of those who claim to be moved by the Spirit. If God does speak to us, what is the purpose of prompting?

1. A prompting is often an invitation to reach out. When the Spirit prompted Philip to go to the official's chariot, he was positioning Philip to reach out to a fellow human being. The explicit directions were simply to go to the chariot, but we can imagine that Philip strongly suspected that he was to be an ambassador of the kingdom to the treasurer of Candace.

After all, this is what God is *doing* on the earth. The Spirit of Jesus is seeking out and saving the lost, telling good news to the poor and the spiritually impoverished, releasing prisoners from captivity. So many of the promptings of the Spirit are simply the commander-in-chief directing the rescue operation. His is not an abstract campaign waged in generalities. Person by person he is extending the influence of the kingdom. Philip knew this full well. So when the prompting came to go to a specific road, near a particular chariot, he was ready to reach out.

If you sense the Spirit drawing your attention to a particular person through a dream or an inner voice, or a knowledge that goes beyond natural means, be alert to the possibility that you are being prompted to reach out to that person. Strike up a conversation, make a phone call, send a note of encouragement, inquire as to the person's well-being.

2. A prompting is often an invitation to intercede. "We do not know what we ought to pray for, but the Spirit himself intercedes for us with groans that words cannot express. And he who searches our hearts knows the mind of the Spirit, because the Spirit intercedes for the saints in accordance with God's will" (Rom 8:26-27).

The Spirit is an intercessor. Is it any wonder, then, that the Spirit's promptings would frequently be an invitation to intercession? Not just a general encouragement to pray, but a specific prompting to pray for someone, here and now, or in a certain way.

This morning the alarm woke me up and I realized I was dreaming about Dale, a man in our church. He was trying to tell me that he was at the end of his rope, but it was taking me a while to realize what he meant. The dream was striking because I wouldn't by natural observation expect Dale to be feeling this way. I took the dream as an invitation to pray for Dale. Later in the day, I called him. In fact, he was feeling overwhelmed. His wife and children had gotten over a severe flu and now Dale had come down with it. He had to miss work and some key deadlines were looming. I told him that, in my dream, he said he was at the end of his rope. "Is that right?" he said. "Well, that's exactly how I feel." That led to an open conversation about the things Dale was struggling with. As Dale's pastor, I gave him some counsel and encouragement. At the very least, Dale knew that God was concerned for his situation and that grace was near.

The "communion of saints" referred to in the apostle's creed is a fellowship of the Spirit. The Spirit himself binds us together with cords of love and concern for one another. Through prompting us to pray for each other, and for those he's seeking to save, Jesus is asserting his leadership of the church.

THE CHURCH THAT DRAWS FROM
THE BEST OF BOTH WORDS

So how does a local church seek to hear God's voice, drawing from the best of the conservative evangelical and charismatic traditions?

1. First, the church upholds the priority of the objective revelation of the Bible. The genuine move of the Spirit will never replace or deemphasize the prominence of the biblical word. The Word of God is the definitive revelation from heaven. This Word endures forever.

To maintain this priority, the church must live on a regular diet of biblical exposition. The Bible must be taught and preached and mined for all it's worth. By exposition, we mean that the biblical texts themselves determine the content of the messages, rather than simply including biblical references to illustrate a point. If a theme or topic is the focus of pulpit ministry, the primary aim is to communicate what the Bible teaches about the particular issue at hand. And there should be opportunities to teach through a particular book of the Bible to guard against the tendency to focus on favorite topics of the speaker or the listeners. Believers should be encouraged and equipped to read and study the Bible for themselves. In a church drawing from the best of both worlds, an emphasis on subjective revelation would not be allowed to detract from the priority of objective revelation.

2. Subjective revelation is taught, practiced, and reported as clearly subordinate to the Bible. In many charismatic circles, prophetic revelations are often given using the formula, "The Lord says," followed by a message given in the first person. (The speaker gives the message as if God were speaking, where the personal pronouns "I" and "me" refer to

God.) Dr. Wayne Grudem of Trinity Evangelical Seminary, in his study on the gift of prophecy, has wisely discouraged this way of reporting prophecies on the grounds that it encourages listeners to value the words of the prophecy on a level with the Bible. While this form of prophecy is clearly the predominant form in churches that allow a place for prophecy, it's time to learn other ways of reporting prophetic senses—ways that leave no doubt about the nature of such revelations as secondary to God's revealed Word.

When people in the church share various senses and impressions from the Spirit, it should be explicitly understood that these senses must be tested, sifted, discerned. It should be understood that subjective revelation is never foolproof. These senses should always be offered with humility and not with the level of confidence that should be reserved for biblical truth. This applies when someone addresses the church in public or in personal ministry where senses are reported.

Those reporting senses should be careful not to assert more authority than such impressions—even those received with the greatest clarity and conviction—can bear. There's nothing wrong with saying something like, "This is what I sense the Spirit saying to us today..." or "I had this dream, and I believe there may be something in it from the Lord." Encouragement for the listeners to test what is being offered should not be a rare occurrence. Messages given by inspiration of the Spirit should not be treated as if they come with word-for-word accuracy.

3. A biblical approach to subjective revelation is taught.

In a church where the Bible is the unambiguous rule of faith and practice, the biblical means of subjective revelation can be safely taught, modeled, and encouraged. Openness to subjective revelation is not a blank check for any and every approach to subjective revelation. There are a great deal of occultic, New Age, or merely odd approaches to subjective revelation. Some forms of subjective revelation are explicitly forbidden in the Scripture, and these must be kept out of the church. When churches don't insist on a biblical approach to hearing God's voice, there may well be an increase in subjective revelations, but people may well be attending to many other voices than the voice of God.

But the cautions provide biblical boundaries; within these boundaries subjective revelation can thrive. In fact, what other approach does justice to the good news of the kingdom? Joel's prophecy about the Spirit poured on all people is being fulfilled (see Acts 2:16-21). What was formerly the privilege of the few—hearing God's voice—is becoming the privilege of the many. The Bible itself is no longer simply the sacred Scripture of a tiny nation. God is speaking through the Bible to men and women and children in every nation. And the experience of the relative few in the Bible is becoming the experience of the many. He is speaking by his Spirit in dreams, visions, inner promptings.

After years of controversy between the conservative evangelical and charismatic camps, isn't it time to recognize that there is really only one camp? Why should we be satisfied to choose between the biblical emphasis of the conservative evangelical tradition and the spiritual vitality of the charismatic tradition? After years of construction, the walls between these two camps are falling down. When it comes to hearing God's voice, why shouldn't the church incorporate the best of both worlds?

FOR DISCUSSION

1. After reflecting on the various ways of hearing God's voice, can you identify any ways that you may be hearing God's voice?

2. Discuss different approaches to reporting visions, dreams, or prophetic revelations. What are the strengths and weaknesses of the various approaches?

3. Share any occasions when you have observed subjective revelation working in a positive way.

WHEN SEEKING A CHURCH

1. Is the approach to hearing God's voice balanced? Is the Bible held up as the infallible rule of faith and practice? Is subjective revelation considered secondary to biblical revelation?

2. When people report subjective revelations, is there a healthy humility or are these things reported in a way that seems manipulative? Is hearing God's voice presented as the privilege of all believers, or are these certain individuals held up as the only ones who can receive guidance from God?

3. Does the leadership of the church seem willing to discern messages purported to be from the Spirit? How do leaders handle occasions when something that seems off-base is shared?

FOR PASTORS

1. Select a passage from the Bible that demonstrates the way Scripture and subjective revelation go hand-in-hand and teach from it.

2. In a Sunday school class or small group setting, ask the participants to share any experiences they have had in hearing God's voice through dreams, visions, or inner promptings.

3. When teaching or preaching, give examples of hearing God's voice from your own life and the lives of those you know. Include examples of subjective and objective revelation. Model the appropriate humility and caution when speaking of subjective revelation. Be sure to include examples from those that are not perceived by the church as "especially spiritual."

4. During a Sunday evening meeting, or a more informal gathering of the church, follow a time of worship or intercession by asking if anyone felt the Lord giving them a particular sense or impression, or bringing a particular passage of Scripture to mind. Allow people to report these briefly.

FOR FURTHER STUDY

Gordon D. Fee and Douglas Stuart, *How to Read the Bible for All It's Worth* (Grand Rapids, Mich.: Zondervan, 1982).

Wayne Grudem, *The Gift of Prophecy in the New Testament and Today* (Westchester, Ill.: Crossway, 1988).

NINE

Receiving the Spirit: an Empowered Evangelical View

Jenny came to church with her roommate. While overseas Jenny was attracted to the Baha'i faith, which incorporates aspects of Islam, Hinduism, and Christianity. Now, back in the United States, she was still trying to discover what she believed. Jenny enjoyed the singing, the worship, and the focus on Jesus that she found at her roommate's church, but she was not prepared for what happened to her during the first Sunday evening service.

Sometime during the worship, Jenny felt what seemed to be a surge of electricity through her body. Soon she felt what she described as an electric current dancing over her face and around her eyes. Jenny then became conscious of the fact that she was in the presence of holiness; she felt compelled to lie prostrate on the floor, even though she felt slightly self-conscious. "This God required complete submission and I knew it," she said.

When the experience, which lasted about thirty minutes, subsided, Jenny realized that she could see better. Months earlier she had contracted a virus that had nearly blinded her.

There had been some improvement, but the doctor's prognosis wasn't encouraging: she needed permanent prosthetic contact lenses, which could only be worn for part of the day and would still leave her with a substantial vision deficit. At first Jenny ascribed her improved vision to the healing of her eye muscles, which stopped hurting through the prayer. But at her next visit with the eye doctor, tests confirmed that the corneal scarring was gone—an unusual development the physician couldn't explain.

What was the result of this encounter? Jenny was now intensely interested in finding out about Jesus, a figure she only knew about in a peripheral sense. She realized that she had experienced an encounter with the living God and that Jesus was a central part of what happened to her. She began to read the New Testament for the first time in an effort to find out what it meant to be a Christian and to follow Jesus.

What do you call what happened to Jenny? It wasn't conversion, because at the time she didn't know enough about the gospel to commit her life to Christ. Pentecostals wouldn't call this "the baptism in the Spirit" since it wasn't subsequent to conversion and Jenny didn't speak in tongues. It was an introductory power encounter with the living God in which she felt herself bathed in his love and presence. File it under "How God Got the Attention of Someone He Loved."

Jenny's experience raises an important issue. What does it mean to be filled with the Spirit? How does this correspond with the new birth or conversion? Does the transition from the kingdom of darkness to the kingdom of light always follow a similar pattern? Is it a crisis event or events, or is it a process, or both?

WHAT HAPPENS WHEN?

Shortly after my conversion in 1971, I (Ken) naively inquired about this business of receiving the Holy Spirit. Without realizing it, I had become party to a family squabble over how spiritual babies are born. Phrases like "born again," "conversion," "Spirit baptism," and "Spirit-filled" were loaded with a long history of controversy.

After talking with friends from different church backgrounds, I realized that there were at least three main viewpoints. Mary, a classical Pentecostal from India, referred to a "baptism in the Spirit" subsequent to conversion and signified by speaking in an unknown language called "tongues." Mary spoke of a crisis experience (something that occurred at a specific point in time, often suddenly) that the believer was to both actively seek and patiently wait for. She called this process of seeking and waiting "tarrying." In her church there were even special meetings set aside for this purpose. Mary's devout mother, a lifelong Pentecostal, was still waiting after thirty years.

John, a participant in the Jesus movement in Detroit, encouraged me to "seek the giver, not the gifts" when asked about this Spirit baptism. Speaking in tongues was viewed with suspicion; as the "least of the gifts" according to the Apostle Paul, it was certainly not something to seek.

Meanwhile, Roman Catholic charismatic friends from Ann Arbor found themselves in the middle of a renewal in which "being baptized with the Spirit" and "speaking in tongues" played a major role. In contrast to Mary's admonition to "tarry" until the Spirit comes with power, they encouraged me to sign up for a seminar that seemed almost guaranteed to produce the experience. From their point of view, this was explained as a fulfillment of my infant baptism and later confirmation in the Episcopal church—events that Mary and

John viewed as little more than empty rituals.

Maybe you've heard a similar range of answers to the same questions. And maybe you came away from a similar inquiry convinced of the same things I was. First, that all three friends were drinking from the same Spirit, even if they described the process differently. Second, that each perspective did justice to a different set of biblical texts. Third, that a merciful God might be more concerned with the actual impartation of the Spirit to humans than with the correct articulation of the process.

And yet, in spite of these irenic conclusions, the theological task is unavoidable. Sooner or later someone—a new Christian, a son, a daughter, a friend—asks the question again. Only this time it's up to you to give a reasonable, biblically accurate answer. What does it mean to receive the Holy Spirit? What relationship does this have to being born again? Does the phenomenon involve an experiential dimension? If so, what? To answer these questions as best we can, we would do well to consider two important issues: the interplay between crisis and process in the Christian life, and the place of subjective experience in any personal encounter.

A LOOK AT THE PENTECOSTAL VIEW OF SPIRIT BAPTISM

When Agnes Ozman asked Charles Parham to pray for her to receive the Holy Spirit on the first New Year's Eve of the twentieth century, he placed his hands on her head and she began to speak in a form of the Chinese language (unknown to her by natural means). She spoke in this language for three days straight, unable to speak in English. Before this experience, Agnes Ozman, along with the earliest participants in the Pentecostal movement, was a dedicated believer in Jesus.

She had already experienced conversion as a crisis event, what we might call getting saved or being born again. In addition, she held to the holiness doctrine of a "complete sanctification" which also came as a crisis event, a second blessing, subsequent to conversion.[1] People from what was called the "Holiness Movement" who had these experiences would describe them in testimonies organized in "before and after" terms. It was only natural, then, for Agnes Ozman and others to describe baptism in the Spirit in the same terms: as a sudden event marked by speaking in tongues.

Since that time, Pentecostals and charismatics have understood that sometime after a person comes to saving faith in Christ (conversion, the new birth), he or she should seek to be baptized with the Holy Spirit. The sign of Spirit baptism, in this view, is speaking with other tongues. (Charismatics, especially those within the Catholic, Presbyterian, Anglican, and Lutheran traditions, don't necessarily insist on tongues as *the* sign of baptism in the Spirit, but speaking in tongues is usually viewed as the normal sign of this experience.)

The biblical support for this position is drawn primarily from the Book of Acts, where speaking with tongues seems to be presented as a normal—or at least common—occurrence when people are initially filled with the Spirit. Conservative evangelicals will often point out an accepted rule of biblical interpretation: that doctrinal positions should not be reached by narrative portions of the Scripture alone. The Book of Acts, in other words, recounts the experiences of the early church, but there is not a clear statement in Scripture that says that speaking in tongues is necessary in order to receive or be baptized with the Spirit. If this were such a pivotal issue, why doesn't the apostle Paul identify tongues as the initial evidence of Spirit-baptism? When Paul does refer to tongues in 1 Corinthians, the context is the church meeting. Though Paul reports that he speaks in tongues "more than anyone," the account of his conversion and baptism doesn't include anything about speaking in tongues.

Conservative evangelicals point out that the experience of the church on the day of Pentecost was in some sense, at least, a nonrepeatable experience. There can only be one first outpouring of the Spirit in the history of the church. They point out that the form and function of tongues (speaking known languages that could be understood by observers from various nations) at this first Pentecost was different from subsequent experiences. Other phenomena from that first Pentecost were not repeated, such as the flames of fire or the wind blowing through the room.

These are valid criticisms of the Pentecostal (and to a lesser degree, charismatic) view of Spirit baptism as an experience *necessarily* subsequent to conversion, marked by speaking in tongues. While this gives us good reason to look for a different view of what it means to receive the Spirit, it doesn't refute the charismatic's experience of the Spirit. This is precisely where conservative evangelicals would do well to listen to their charismatic brothers' and sisters' experience of the Spirit's power.

RECEIVING THE SPIRIT:
IT'S WHAT HAPPENS WHEN WE'RE BORN AGAIN

The work of God to transfer us from the kingdom of darkness to the kingdom of light is first and foremost a work of the Holy Spirit. And it's a work of the Spirit from first to last. All the initial inclinations that we have to consider the gospel, to investigate the claims of Christ, the tug that we feel to go to church after years of staying away, to pray when we've not been in the habit of prayer, are all manifestations of the Spirit drawing us to the Father, through his beloved Son.

Similarly, the process which leads us to accept Jesus as Savior and Lord, the yielding of our will to his will, the offering of our lives to him, is a work of the Spirit.

> I tell you the truth, no one can enter the kingdom of God unless he is born of water and the Spirit. Flesh gives birth to flesh, but the Spirit gives birth to spirit. You should not be surprised at my saying, "You must be born again." The wind blows wherever it pleases. You hear its sound, but you cannot tell where it comes from or where it is going. So it is with everyone born of the Spirit. **John 3:5-8**

As Paul testified, "No one can say 'Jesus is Lord,' except by the Holy Spirit" (1 Cor 12:3). Later in the same chapter Paul adds, "We were all baptized by one Spirit into one body" (12:13). The new birth, signified in water baptism, is a new birth into a new family, the body of Christ. As conservative evangelicals we believe that when we are born again, we are all baptized by one Spirit into one body.

From a conservative evangelical perspective, then, receiving the Spirit is what happens when we're born anew. In the original language of the New Testament, the word for "spirit" is the same word as "breath." The process of receiving new life is the process of receiving the Spirit—just as human birth is not complete until the newborn begins to breathe.

When charismatics either imply or explicitly state that a person who is born again may not have received the Holy Spirit, many evangelicals naturally bristle. And rightly so. We wouldn't be alive in Christ if we hadn't received the Spirit. Language like this doesn't educate the evangelical; it alienates him or her.

So what is a conservative evangelical to do with the testimony of charismatics to the Spirit's presence and power? Rather than be offended by the misplaced inferences, we would do well to consider the reality to which Pentecostals and charismatics bear witness. That reality is simply this: there's more. Not a "Second Blessing," a baptism in the Spirit necessarily distinct from the new birth, necessarily signified by speaking in tongues; but a lifetime of subsequent and ongoing fillings with the Spirit. What does the experience of the early church recorded in the Book of Acts lead us to expect? What does the experience of people like D.L. Moody, Charles Finney, A.B. Simpson, and others lead us to expect? The same thing that the experience (not necessarily the explanation) of charismatics leads us to expect: when it comes to receiving the Spirit, there's more. Through the new birth, we've been launched on a journey in which we can expect personal visitations of the Spirit's power.

AN EVENT WITH MANY DIMENSIONS

Thomas Oden, a respected evangelical scholar, in his book *Life in the Spirit,* describes conversion as a multidimensional event including regeneration (the impartation of new life), incorporation into Christ, conversion from the economy of law to the economy of grace, and the impartation of power from on high, all signified in the ordinance of water baptism.[2] Appropriating a new birth of such magnitude requires a lifelong process, just as it takes a lifetime to live up to the potential contained in a newborn child. We are born anew into a journey that is marked by progressive, at times imperceptible growth, as well as "watershed experiences" that amount to quantum leaps forward.

The charismatic understanding of "baptism in the Spirit" as a distinct event could also be viewed as yet another dimension of the new birth, if in fact the new birth is a multidimensional event. This way of looking at the process of entering the kingdom allows room for a variety of personal experiences. For example, I gave my life to Christ one evening in May 1971, after reading the Gospels and C.S. Lewis' *Mere Christianity*. But it wasn't until months later that I gained any real understanding that I was a sinner in desperate need of the grace that comes through the blood of Jesus. At the time I gave my life to Christ, I did so because I was convinced that Jesus was who he claimed to be, that he was risen from the dead; but I had little awareness of being a sinner. When was I saved? The night I gave my life to Christ, or later, when it dawned on me how much I needed the Atonement in order to be saved from God's wrath? The recounting of one's conversion experience often gets condensed and simplified—the "three minute testimony" in some evangelism programs. In reality, even the most dramatic conversions often take place in fits and starts.

As a multidimensional event that may occur over a period of time, the new birth is similar to natural birth, which can be described as both an event and a process, depending on your point of view. If you ask the attending physician when a child was born, he might look at the birth record and say "3:03 A.M., November 27, 1972." Yet from the mother's perspective, the birth of the child was a process that spanned several hours.

The experience of charismatics can teach conservative evangelicals to make room in their theology and their expectation for various experiences of being filled with the Spirit. It has already been noted that conservative evangelical leaders like D.L. Moody and Charles Finney experienced a form of baptism in the Spirit that they viewed as a significant empowering for ministry. The fact is, the witness of the saints through the ages (charismatic and noncharismatic) and the witness of Scripture lead us to expect multiple fillings with the Spirit. In addition to the initial impartation of the Spirit described in the Book of Acts for new believers, the Spirit came

214 Empowered Evangelicals

with power on the church on many occasions, often to invigorate her for a particular task (see, for example, Acts 4:8, 4:31; 7:55; 13:9).

EMPOWERED FOR MINISTRY

R.A. Torrey, who participated in the evangelistic ministry of D.L. Moody and served as superintendent of the Moody Bible Institute, wrote of a "baptism in the Spirit" in 1898, before the Pentecostal movement began. In Torrey's view, baptism in the Spirit was a definite experience which occurred after conversion, though it was not signified by speaking in tongues, as Pentecostals (and to a lesser extent, charismatics) define the experience of Spirit baptism. It was first and foremost an empowering for ministry. This "baptism with the Spirit," according to Torrey, "always imparts power in service" and "boldness in testimony."[3]

This corresponds to D.L. Moody's experience of being filled with the Spirit years after his conversion, referred to in an earlier chapter of this book. "I had such an experience of His love," Moody recalled later, "that I had to ask Him to stay His hand. I went to preaching again. The sermons were not different; I did not present new truths, and yet hundreds were converted. I would not now be placed back where I was before that experience if you should give me all the world."[4] Moody was already actively involved in preaching the gospel, but his experience provided new power for ministry.

Whether we call it a "baptism in the Spirit" or an experience of being "filled with the Spirit," the point is the same: we need the power of the Spirit for ministry. We need the power of the Spirit for the ministry of worship to God. It's no accident that those who were filled with the Spirit often burst out in praise of God, as we see in Acts 10:44-46. We need the power of the

Spirit for the ministry of building up the body of Christ, through gifts of teaching, revelation, wisdom, service, and hospitality. And we need the power of the Spirit for ministry to a hungry world.

As conservative evangelicals, convinced of the world's need for good news, we should be the first in line to be filled with the Spirit's power. The closer we are to a needy world, the more we will feel our desperate need for power to minister in Christ's name. We will be like the person awakened at midnight by a neighbor in need of bread. We don't have any ourselves, so we go to someone who does, knocking on the door, until the door is opened and we receive what we need to give away (see Luke 11:5-13).

I first became aware of my need for the Holy Spirit when, as a new believer, I worked for a local community mental health center as an after-hours suicide prevention worker. I would sleep in my living room, next to the telephone. Calls from a crisis phone line would be forwarded to me. Some nights there wouldn't be any calls. Other nights, especially around the holidays, there might be half a dozen. Often people simply needed a listening ear. But sometimes they were as desperate for hope as people ever get.

I remember one call from a man in a phone booth. His speech was already slurred from an overdose of barbiturates. He told me that he just wanted to tell another human being why he decided to kill himself. He refused to give me his location so I could send help, and the longer he talked, the more slurred his speech became. Finally, when it was clear that he wouldn't reveal his location and time was running out, I said, "Listen to me carefully. There's something I need to tell you, even though it goes beyond my professional responsibilities." I then shared the gospel with him as clearly and succinctly as I knew how. Eventually he stopped talking and I don't know what happened to him. But the experience left me shaken. I realized that we have been given a precious gift in the gospel. And I also realized my need for God's power to share this good news.

After that experience, I did two things. First, I went to my supervisor and told him that there were times when I might feel a moral obligation to share my faith with a client in similar circumstances, even though this was not part of my job description. Secondly, I went to a Lutheran pastor, whom I knew had power to preach the gospel, and I asked him to pray with me to be filled with the Spirit to do the same.

We're all in similar circumstances. There are people all around us who need to hear the gospel. There are some who will hear the gospel for the last time from our lips. We don't simply need to understand the gospel clearly enough to share it with another person, though we do need that. We also need boldness to speak when the opportunity is given and power to speak as those who have been given the very words of life. How we refer to the experience of being empowered by the Spirit for ministry (as a baptism in the Spirit, or being filled with the Spirit) is quite secondary. What we need is the glorious gospel message coupled with the Spirit's power on our preaching of it.

WHAT ABOUT THE GIFT OF TONGUES?

While a conservative evangelical view of the Spirit doesn't accept the charismatic teaching of tongues as the sign of Spirit baptism, the experience of charismatics should open conservative evangelicals to the possibility and the value of this, "the least of" the gifts.

The New Testament seems to indicate three possible functions for the gift of tongues. First, and perhaps of most interest to conservative evangelicals, is the missionary function of tongues as it was given on the day of Pentecost (see Acts 2). Members of the church were empowered to speak God's word in languages they didn't understand themselves, but others did. Second, Paul refers to a devotional use of tongues, as an aid in personal prayer (see 1 Corinthians 14, especially verses 18-19). Third, a message in tongues, when followed by interpretation, can function as a form of Spirit-inspired prayer or worship to God that would encourage corporate worship (see 1 Corinthians 14:2, 13-17). Charismatics also see a fourth use of tongues as an expression of corporate worship; this may be expressed through "singing in the Spirit" or through many participants praying aloud in tongues simultaneously in a form of corporate praise. As we'll discuss later, this fourth use of tongues seems to have the least biblical grounding.

While we like to have things neatly organized, we know of at least one case where someone used tongues as he would in private prayer, only to discover that it was having a powerful missionary effect. Rob is an elder of his local Lutheran church and a volunteer at the critical care family waiting room at a local hospital. A family from the Middle East was gathered to be with their mother who was dying. They asked for a visit from the local chaplain but when the female chaplain arrived, the family asked to see someone else. Rob, who was nearby, saw what was going on, and offered to pray with them.

Rob is a charismatic Lutheran who makes liberal use of the gift of tongues. So when he came into this rather intimidating situation, not knowing how to pray, he began as he often did, by praying quietly (though audibly) in tongues. As he prayed, the patient mumbled her own prayer in her native language. When Rob was finished praying, one of the family members asked him where he learned to speak Farsi. The conversation went something like this:

"I don't speak Farsi," Rob told them.

"But you were just praying with our mother in our

language," a family member replied.

"What was I saying?" Rob asked, incredulously.

"You were saying that my mother still had time to accept Jesus and that he was willing to accept her."

"I did?"

"Yes. And that's what my mother was doing when she prayed."

Of course, everyone was stunned, Rob no less than the family. They asked him to speak to them further about Jesus. When he gave a simple outline of the gospel, three other family members joined him in praying the sinner's prayer. Now, *that's* a use of the gift of tongues that bridges the gap between a charismatic's use of tongues (primarily an aid to prayer) and an evangelical's concern to spread the gospel through every means possible!

AN EVANGELICAL APPROACH TO TONGUES

The conservative evangelical concern over some charismatic uses of tongues is understandable. But wouldn't it be a shame if these concerns kept evangelicals from exercising a gift that has potential use in a missionary context? Perhaps God is renewing the gift of tongues in the church precisely because he wants us to be more aware than ever of our role in bringing the gospel to every tribe and tongue and nation. Perhaps it's time for an empowered evangelical approach to this controversial gift.

First of all, conservative evangelicals would be wise to discourage the use of tongues without interpretation in public worship (a common charismatic practice). Paul discouraged the use of uninterpreted tongues in public worship and so should we.

For this reason, anyone who speaks in a tongue should pray that he may interpret what he says.... I thank God that I speak in tongues more than all of you. But in the church I would rather speak five intelligible words to instruct others than ten thousand words in a tongue.... If the whole church comes together and everyone speaks in tongues, and some who do not understand or some unbelievers come in, will they not say that you are out of your mind?

1 Corinthians 14:13, 18-19, 23

Charismatics justify the use of uninterpreted tongues as a form of praise in public worship on the grounds that those who speak in tongues are not addressing the whole church. But the fact remains that those in the vicinity of the person speaking in tongues do hear this form of prayer and they don't understand what the person is saying. Often charismatics pray quite loudly in tongues in a public worship setting, magnifying even further the effect Paul wanted to avoid. In the absence of any biblical encouragement for the use of uninterpreted tongues in public worship, Paul's counsel against this practice should prevail.

But this leaves us with other uses for the gift of tongues which are sanctioned by Paul. Paul apparently made liberal use of a devotional gift of tongues (see 1 Corinthians 14:18). He also allowed for the use of tongues with interpretation as a form of inspired prayer in the church (though it is not clear that he encouraged it). Finally, the narrative portions of the Book of Acts refer to new believers speaking in tongues as they are filled with the Spirit. While this is not adequate biblical testimony to establish the Pentecostal doctrine of Spirit baptism signified by tongues, it does suggest that people may well speak in tongues as they are filled with the Spirit. The original appearance of tongues on the day of Pentecost also suggests that there may be a missionary use of tongues which involves preaching the gospel in a language unknown to the speaker.

An empowered evangelical approach to tongues would certainly not give this gift of the Spirit the same prominence that it receives in the charismatic wing of the church,[5] but neither would it discourage the use of tongues within biblical parameters. It's time we made room for the gift of tongues as an accepted (though not necessary) experience of new Christians, as well as an accepted (though not necessary) form of devotional prayer. It is the least of the gifts, but it's one that Paul himself thanked God for, and so should we. Conservative evangelicals who do speak in tongues should not feel the need to hide their experience as aberrant or take it with them to the local Pentecostal or charismatic church. Leaders should be free to encourage the use of tongues within biblical parameters.

With an approach like this, the conservative evangelical controversy with charismatics over baptism in the Spirit with tongues would lose much of its acrimony. Tongues would not need to be the linchpin experience for a whole stream of Christianity, defining the boundary between two camps of Christians, which seems too great a load for the least of the gifts to carry. After all, why shouldn't it be possible for conservative evangelicals to learn from the charismatic experience of power without having to adopt all the charismatic practices and perspectives associated with these issues?

RECEIVING THE SPIRIT: A PERSONAL ENCOUNTER

Conservative evangelicals have another lesson to learn from the experience of charismatics. In an age when power is viewed primarily in impersonal terms—nuclear power, electrical power, computer power—we need more than ever to hear the witness of the Bible to the Holy Spirit as *personal* in nature. Christians, especially those who downplay a personal experience of the Spirit, often fall into an impersonal view of the Holy Spirit. It's an understandable error, since so much of our understanding of what it means to be a person is connected with having a body. When we picture a person, we picture a physical body. Since the Holy Spirit does not share this dimension of being a person with us, it's easy for us to misunderstand him. The Spirit is viewed as an invisible force, much like electricity; sometimes the Spirit is spoken of as the "energy of God," again conjuring up impersonal images.

Yet Jesus bears powerful witness to the Holy Spirit as a person, not an "it," an impersonal force. For example, Jesus, referring to the Holy Spirit, said, "But when he, the Spirit of truth, comes, he will guide you into all truth" (Jn 16:13). The Greek used by John makes the point even sharper by breaking a fundamental rule of grammar. As you may know, Greek nouns are assigned a gender—either feminine, masculine, or neuter. The same is true with other languages, such as French. When referring to a noun in the feminine gender, one uses the pronoun "she"; when referring to a word in the masculine gender, one uses the pronoun "he"; when referring to a noun in the neuter gender, the pronoun is "it." If a Greek sentence mixed up the gender on its nouns and pronouns, it would be like saying "Have you met my mother? He's a wonderful woman." It would make you sit up and take notice.

That's exactly what happened when John translated Jesus' words the way he did: *"When he* [masculine pronoun], *the Spirit* [neuter noun] *of truth, comes, he* [masculine pronoun] *will guide you into all the truth."* The sentence, according to the rules of grammar, should be, "When it, the Spirit of truth, comes, it will guide you into all the truth." But John was forced to break the grammatical rule because the Spirit is a *person,* requiring the personal "he," not the impersonal "it." (Since the Spirit has no physical body, he has no gender either;

the point is not that the Spirit is a "he" rather than a "she" but a person rather than a thing.)

Excuse the grammar lesson, but the point is of crucial importance: the Spirit is a person! This is confirmed in many ways. The activity of the Spirit is the activity of a person, not a thing. The Spirit speaks, is spoken to, teaches, convicts, intercedes, and calls. The Spirit can be grieved and lied to. Even though the Spirit doesn't have a physical body, the Spirit is a Someone, not a Something.

In other words, when we receive the Spirit we are engaged in a personal encounter. The encounter involves us as a whole person: intellectually, socially, emotionally, even at times physically. There's no getting around the fact that when we encounter the Spirit, we shouldn't be surprised if there is a subjective dimension to the encounter. This is just what the Bible bears witness to: people sometimes experience the Spirit's presence intellectually, emotionally, even physically. That's what charismatics have been trying to tell us.

While some charismatic explanations don't do justice to the nature of the new birth as a multidimensional event, the charismatic theology does do more justice to the encounter with the Spirit as a personal encounter, which includes a subjective element. We often associate an emphasis on subjective experience with the charismatic tradition, but there are strong voices within noncharismatic evangelicalism for the subjective experience of God. Jonathan Edwards, who did not endorse the use of charismatic gifts, did emphasize the role of emotion in religion.[6] In the view of Edwards, for example, love is not merely an act of the will, but an affection of the whole person toward the object loved. To speak of joy apart from feelings of joy would be, according to Edwards, to speak of something other than joy. And joy, of course, is one of the chief fruits (or effects) of the Holy Spirit.

In other words, while the Spirit is invisible, an encounter with him is not necessarily indiscernible. Among other things, his presence can be *felt*—through an experience of joy, for example, or a sense of profound inner calm, of peace. Similarly, the Spirit can produce deep feelings of sorrow—not merely the intellectual knowledge that sin is wrong, but an emotional response that corresponds to that knowledge. What evangelicals have long referred to as "gaining a heart for the lost" includes an emotional response to the presence of the Spirit, a response designed to move us to action.

Edwards also defended the validity of physical responses to the work of the Holy Spirit in a person's heart. Consider this observation, which though it uses antiquated terminology, demonstrates profound insight into the connection between our emotions and our bodies.

> Such seems to be our nature, and such the laws of the union of soul and body, that there never is any case whatsoever, any lively and vigorous exercise of the will or inclination of the soul without some effect upon the body, in some alteration of the motion of its fluids, and especially of the animal spirits. And on the other hand, from the same laws of the union of the soul and body, the constitution of the body and the motion of its fluids may promote the exercise of the affections. But yet it is not the body, but the mind only, that is the proper seat of the affections."[7]

Presumably, by the phrase "the motion of its [the body's] fluids" Edwards had in mind phenomena such as tears in the eyes, weeping, dryness of mouth, changes in blood pressure, increased heart rate, and so on. (What he meant by "animal spirits," however, is beyond us!)

One of the weaknesses in many conservative evangelicals' understanding of the Holy Spirit is the tendency to underestimate or even dismiss the place of emotions and the response of the body to the encounter with the Spirit. Surely this fuels a great deal of the conservative evangelical reaction against phenomena experienced by charismatics. Within conservative evangelicalism, warnings abound against "emotionalism" but little is said about the appropriate place of feelings or the corresponding physical effects that attend an encounter with the person of the Holy Spirit.

If the Spirit is a person, is it odd to think that as the Spirit comes to us, we might respond at the emotional or physical level? Profound encounters between persons are marked by a human response at this level. When I stood at the altar to marry my wife, my knees were shaking. When I watched her give birth to our first child, I hyperventilated. When I had an opportunity to shake hands with a man running for the presidency of the United States, my heart began to thump. Why would we ever think an encounter with God wouldn't sometimes produce these effects?

Look around the room sometime when people are engaged in a profound experience of worship. Some will have tears in their eyes. Others will be flushed in their faces. Others may look entirely relaxed, while still others may be experiencing a mild tremor in their uplifted hands. One couple visiting our church began to weep inexplicably during the first song of worship. They cried throughout the service and all the way home in their car.

Of course, it is a mistake to view these human responses as the presence of the Spirit himself. It's not always clear whether a given response is prompted by the Spirit or something else. The best tests, of course, of any phenomena is whether they are scriptural, and whether any fruit is borne as a result of any experience.

These responses shouldn't be viewed either with automatic suspicion or as the sure sign of the Spirit's presence. They are simply the kinds of things that often occur in the presence of God. Sorrow for sin is at times accompanied by tears. The fear of the Lord may be manifested in knocking knees, even fainting (or "losing one's bodily strength," as the Great Awakening observers called falling over). The joy given by the Holy Spirit may be expressed in laughter. A friend of mine laughed for an hour and a half after he gave his life to Christ on a Christian retreat, long before anyone had heard the phrase "holy laughter." No one else was laughing at the time, and the people on the retreat were completely perplexed by his response. While I don't believe God made my friend laugh, it was simply his response to a very significant encounter with God. He was happy beyond belief to be saved.

NEEDED: THE BEST OF BOTH WORLDS

The church needs an understanding of the work of the Holy Spirit that does justice both to the evangelical view of the new birth as a multidimensional event and to the Spirit's power experienced and valued by charismatics. This empowered evangelical understanding of the Spirit requires an appreciation of both the crisis and process aspects of being incorporated into Christ. The new birth is an event of such magnitude that it requires a lifelong journey to incorporate, a journey marked by numerous watershed experiences of the Spirit's power, given for the purpose of revealing God's love to us personally and empowering us to share his love with others.

We also need an understanding of the Spirit that goes beyond warning against the dangers of unbridled emotionalism to articulate a positive, biblical view of the subjective response to the presence of the Spirit in the believer. The effect of this understanding would not simply discourage emotionalism, but would also provide a hospitable environment for a truly personal response to the Spirit, including at the emotional and physical dimensions of being human. This would both respect our creation as human beings and honor the reality that the impartation of the Spirit is at its core a personal encounter. This understanding of the Spirit's work depends on conservative evangelicals and charismatics learning from each other. What we need, in short, is the best of both worlds.

FOR FURTHER DISCUSSION

1. What do you think of the authors' recommendations for an evangelical approach to the gift of tongues?

2. What do you think of the authors' statement, "We are born anew into a journey that is marked by imperceptible growth as well as watershed experiences that amount to quantum leaps forward"?

3. Compare the experiences of those who grew up believing with those who came to Christ as adults. How does the authors' view of receiving the Spirit fit in with these two pathways to faith?

4. Where do you feel a need to grow in your experience of the Spirit's work in your life?

WHEN SEEKING A CHURCH

1. Read the official doctrinal statements of the church regarding the new birth and the impartation of the Spirit. What influence do these statements seem to have on the approach to these issues in the church today?

2. What is the pastor's understanding of receiving the Spirit? How does the pastor communicate his or her understanding to the church?

3. Ask a few respected lay leaders or other active members of the church to share their personal experience of finding Jesus and learning to serve him.

4. If you brought a new Christian or a sincere seeker to church, what opportunities would he or she have to meet God in a personal way?

FOR PASTORS

1. Review the official statements of your church body regarding the Holy Spirit. What historical forces shaped these views? How do you integrate your perspective with these statements?

2. Interview several members of your church to assess how they understand what it means to receive the Holy Spirit. Ask them to describe their personal experience as well as their understanding of the Bible's teaching. Is there a coherent view or a hodgepodge of varying perspectives? Where have people gained their understanding?

3. What if a person came to you with no church background or prior opinions on what it means to receive Jesus and be filled with his Spirit; how would you explain the process to him or her?

4. Prepare a series of teachings on receiving the Spirit aimed at giving the people in your church a better understanding, as

well as providing instruction to those with no prior opinions on these topics.

FOR FURTHER STUDY

D.L. Moody, *Secret Power* (Ventura, Calif.: Regal, 1988, originally published 1881).

Martyn Lloyd-Jones, *Joy Unspeakable* (Wheaton, Ill.: Harold Shaw, 1984).

John White, *When the Spirit Comes with Power* (Downers Grove, Ill.: InterVarsity, 1988).

TEN

Mind and Emotion: Room for Both

C hurch shouldn't be a place where you have to leave your emotions in the parking lot or your head on the hat rack. But sometimes that's the choice we face. Or so it seems.

In my (Ken's) hometown a local charismatic church announces with feeling that "The New Wine Is Flowing!" Whatever that means, it doesn't sound like a Bible study. Meanwhile the Baptist church near campus reassures the public that here is a place where "Thoughtful, Biblical Christianity" can be found. In other words, no funny business.

The charismatic tradition is well-known for its emphasis on heartfelt Christianity. A charismatic church is a place where faith is expressed with feeling. Tears, laughter, and outbursts of praise are warmly welcomed. The typical Bible church, on the other hand, places a premium on the mind. The centerpiece of the service is a thoughtful, tightly reasoned exposition of the Word. Are these two emphases mutually exclusive? Isn't there room for a thoughtful but also deeply felt (and expressed) biblical Christianity?

HEAD VS. HEART: THE FALSE DILEMMA

We in the western world are fond of cubicles and boxes. We like to organize the world into neat and tidy categories. So we naturally compartmentalize ourselves into distinct spheres.

For example, as new Christians, many of us learned that if we put our faith in the facts (through an active choice, a decision of the will) our feelings would follow, just as the caboose follows the coal car and the engine of a train. Our feelings, in other words, were a separate compartment, distinct from and clearly subordinate to our capacity to reason intelligently and choose. When working properly, feelings simply tag along.

Perhaps you've heard one speaker after another contrast the "head" with the "heart." The head represents the mind while the heart is the center of true feeling. It's a striking image since the head is anatomically some distance from the heart. Separate compartments again.

Charismatics have typically emphasized the place of feelings, while evangelicals have stressed the importance of a well-reasoned faith. Charismatics have often been suspicious of the mind, while evangelicals have been suspicious of emotions. Below is a list of these distinctive tendencies:

Charismatic Distinctive	Conservative Evangelical Distinctive
• gift of tongues (nonrational speech)	• gift of teaching (rational speech)
• warning against intellectualism	• warning against emotionalism
• emotionally expressive worship	• emotionally controlled worship
• spontaneous words of prophecy	• well-prepared preaching

Please keep in mind that we are speaking of tendencies. In some settings the distinctions don't hold up well. African-American churches often integrate feeling and intellect much more effectively than Euro-American groups. The sermons of Dr. Martin Luther King, Jr., and E.V. Hill exemplify a rich tradition of preaching that combines scholarship, erudition, and a message aimed to stir the emotions of the congregation. A white person walking into a conservative evangelical black church might easily mistake it for a Pentecostal church. While the best of the charismatic and conservative evangelical traditions integrate the mind and the emotions in matters of faith, there is a tendency for charismatic churches to emphasize emotion at the expense of intellect and a tendency for conservative evangelical churches to emphasize intellect at the expense of emotion.

Rather than emphasize the role of feeling at the expense of the intellect, why not emphasize the importance of both? Christianity is something we are meant to feel deeply and think clearly about. Our reason should be filled with the warmth of emotion and our emotion filled with the light of reason.

TOUCHING THE WHOLE HEART

The biblical view of the human personality is not nearly as compartmentalized as our western view. The biblical term "heart" for example, includes the feelings, the reasoning capacities, and the will.[1] Sharp distinctions are not drawn between these faculties; instead they are viewed as an integrated whole. One biblical scholar writes, "In particular, the widely held distinction between mind as seat of thinking and heart as seat of feeling (especially tender feeling) is alien from the meaning these terms carry in the Bible."[2] In other words, a "wholehearted" response to God is one that involves the emotions, the mind, and the will.

The writings of Jonathan Edwards reflect this perspective. According to Edwards, the affections (his word for feelings that incline us toward or away from a given object) are a faculty of the will.[3] The emotions are meant to move us, just as the will moves us, toward or away from God. Similarly, Edwards didn't place human reason above the emotions, but alongside them. Edwards felt that the religious person is one whose "reason is passionate and whose affection is intellectual."[4] In many respects, this reflects the biblical view of the heart as an integrated whole that includes what we would call the emotions, the mind, and the will functioning as a unity.

The writings of Jonathan Edwards on the proper role of feeling and reason in religion provide a model for integrating the best of the charismatic emphasis on the emotions and the conservative evangelical emphasis on the mind. Besides the fact that Edwards articulated what we might call a "holistic" view of human personality (in keeping with the biblical view), his perspective is especially helpful for two other reasons. First, Edwards is perhaps the finest evangelical philosopher ever to write extensively on the topic of emotions in religious experience. Secondly, Edwards wrote in the context of the evangelical revival known as the Great Awakening, when the church was engaged in a significant controversy over the role of emotions and reason in revival.

One of the most controversial aspects of the Great Awakening was the appearance of public expressions of deep emotion, manifested in weeping, crying out, trembling with fear, and sometimes falling over. Many observers were shocked and scandalized by all this. The pejorative term used to describe it was "enthusiasm," akin to what we would probably call "emotionalism." Picture the response of a conservative Baptist pastor to the carryings on of a Pentecostal meeting with people raising their arms in the air, weeping, a few people "falling under the power," and a preacher stoking the flames of all this intense feeling with his impassioned preaching. His response might mirror the eighteenth-century critics of revival who claimed the revival was nothing more than "religious enthusiasm." Remember, the controversy sparked by the Great Awakening wasn't over the role of charismatic gifts, but over the role of emotion in Christianity.

THE ROLE OF EMOTION IN
RELIGIOUS EXPERIENCE

If we didn't know better, we would think that a Puritan scholar like Jonathan Edwards, a man who served as president of Princeton University, would want nothing to do with these emotional displays. In fact, Edwards' writings provided a potent defense for the role of feeling, or what he called "the religious affections." Edwards vigorously asserted that what he called "true religion" has very much to do with the affections, or feelings. (Ironically, his writings are viewed by many as dry, dull, and overly academic.) Edwards argued that the most important figures in the Bible were people who expressed deep feeling.[5]

King David, for example, was a songwriter whose lyrics were filled with passion and deep longing. David didn't simply pray, he cried out to the Lord (see Psalm 3:4). He didn't bottle up his frustration or distress but spoke of it freely to his God. His songs are filled with expressions of deep longings, love, anger, and sorrow (see Psalms 43, 63, 69).

The writings of Paul are also filled with deep emotion. He spoke of his feelings of affection for the saints, his consternation at the work of false teachers, and his disappointment when his actions were misinterpreted (see 2 Corinthians 2:4;

12:14-21; Galatians 5:7-12). The tone of his writings is passionate—not reserved, emotionally detached, or cool.

The Lord Jesus himself—the ultimate example of true humanity and true divinity—was a person moved by strong feelings. On several occasions, Jesus performed a miracle of healing after he was "moved by compassion" (see Mark 1:40-42). Similarly, Jesus experienced and expressed feelings of frustration and anger. He expressed something like irritation when his disciples were slow to believe (see Mark 9:19). When the religious leadership resisted his efforts to show mercy to those in need, he was "deeply angered" (see Mark 3:1-5). It is evident from the accounts of the crucifixion that Jesus did not cope with the pain of the cross by detaching emotionally. He clearly felt the full weight of the physical, emotional, and spiritual pain of crucifixion.

Jesus was a man marked by joy. Luke records that Jesus was "full of joy through the Holy Spirit" (Lk 10:21). The word for joy in the original language means "jubilant exaltation," a vivid and expressive form of intense joy. He spoke of his own joy and his desire to impart it to his friends (see John 15:11).[6]

What we call the emotions plays a very prominent role in the biblical view of religion. Edwards identified the hard or stony heart referred to in Scripture as a heart incapable of feeling, inert, not moved by the things that ought to move it. Commenting on Ezekiel's promise to "remove the heart of stone" and replace it with a "heart of flesh" (see Ezekiel 11:19 and 36:26), Edwards wrote:

> Now by a hard heart is plainly meant an unaffected heart, or a heart not easy to be moved with virtuous affections, like a stone, insensible, stupid, unmoved, and hard to be impressed. Hence a hard heart is called a "stony heart" and is opposed to a heart of flesh, that has feeling, and is sensibly touched and moved.[7]

Some time ago I, came across this account of the hard heart and realized that it described my own heart. Sometimes pastors learn how to detach emotionally in order to survive, which only reinforced my family's reserved approach. But that detachment also made it difficult for me to feel the reality of the things I believed. For example, while I believed that sinners were lost without Christ, I never really felt the impact of this conviction. So I began to pray for a softened heart.

Over a period of months, some new things began to happen. A friend of mine suggested that we intercede together on Friday mornings for revival. After half an hour of unremarkable prayer during the first session, I began to pray for those now in their teens and twenties. Suddenly, I began to sob uncontrollably for an extended period of time. It was an experience of intercession like Paul alluded to, where the Spirit intercedes with "sighs and groans too deep for words" (Rom 8:26).

In subsequent weeks, as I meditated on various biblical texts during this time of intercession, I began to feel the impact of truths I had long believed, but rarely felt the impact of. Meditations on the sovereignty of God were accompanied by vivid feelings of relief. Texts that spoke of our future hope provoked feelings of joy, accompanied at times with laughter.

After overhearing the commotion of a particularly expressive time of prayer, my wife Nancy asked me what was going on. "It's hard to put into words," I replied.

"Whatever it is sounds pretty emotional," Nancy observed. Of course, given my lifelong tendency to view emotion with suspicion (especially in a religious context), this was not something that tickled my ears. Though not intended as a put-down, it sure sounded like one to me! But as I thought about it, I realized that worse things could be said about a person's prayers, than that they were deeply felt.

EMOTIONS THAT MOVE

What Edwards called "religious affections" are meant to move us—either toward God or away from sin. The point of receiving a "heart of flesh" (which includes the idea of a heart that can feel deeply) is not simply to experience feeling for feeling's sake.

> I will give you a new heart and put a new spirit in you; I will remove from you your heart of stone and give you a heart of flesh. And I will put my Spirit in you and *move you* to follow my decrees and be careful to keep my laws.
>
> **Ezekiel 36:26-27**

A heart that feels is a heart that motivates. Jesus provides the model, as we illustrated in the previous section. What a far cry from so much of our experience of emotion in the modern world—where feeling is often detached from action. The commercials on television are the ones that get me. Within the space of thirty to sixty seconds, a good commercial can elicit feelings of desire, nostalgia, and a noble sense of identification with humankind. The advertisement for cotton products generates this feeling of profound pathos in the face of the human condition: emotionally charged scenes of childhood, early adult romance, and old age all dance before the viewer, with cotton the common thread. But then the commercial is over and it's on to another image, designed to elicit another set of feelings. But to what end?

The more we feel outrage over the latest newsmagazine exposé of government corruption, or compassion over the poignant feature story on the local news, without ever being moved to some response by these feelings, the less our emotions mean. Feelings are meant to move us rather than simply entertain us.

THE ROLE OF THE MIND
IN RELIGIOUS EXPERIENCE

While emotion, as an expression of the heart, has a critical role to play in a wholehearted response to God, so does the mind. Remember, the biblical "heart" includes our thinking as well as our feeling capacities. We're to love the Lord our God "with all [our] mind" (Mk 12:30). We're to "take captive every thought and make it obedient to Christ" (2 Cor 10:5). When Paul describes the pagan version of the hardened heart, he describes their "futile thinking," their "darkened understanding," and their "lack of all sensitivity," the absence of feeling (see Ephesians 4:17-19). A mind that's missing the mark reflects the hardening of the heart as much as the loss of all feeling.

During the Great Awakening in the American Colonies, some people became so enamored of emotional responses to the Spirit's presence that they made these emotional displays the primary measure of God's activity. But Jonathan Edwards insisted that everything, including intense displays of religious affections, be tested by a thoughtful and balanced reading of Scripture. He was as concerned about "heat without light" (emotional stirring without understanding) as he was "light without heat" (a mental apprehension of the truth that did not stir the affections.)[8]

Our approach to Christianity must appeal to a thinking person. We should be able to explain what we do and why we do it by a thoughtful appeal to Scripture that respects accepted rules of sound interpretation. The fact that someone is "deeply moved," "feels a great anointing," and so on, is no excuse to cast reason to the wind. Too often, within some segments of the charismatic (and conservative evangelical) tradition, the reasoning capacity of our hearts is viewed with suspicion. It's true that our thoughts may not always be his thoughts, but we are still meant to think!

In fact, Edwards believed that religious affections (feelings) were normally stimulated by a work of the Spirit to enlighten the mind. His own experience of prayer reflected this. Often Edwards would enjoy moments of intense feeling (a sense of joy, sorrow, or peace, for example) after mulling over the meaning of a particular biblical text. The light of the truth would shine in his mind, and his feelings would be stirred.'

The lack of regard for clear thinking in some Christian circles is simple laziness. It takes time and effort to think things through clearly. If you are a leader and you have an idea to present, it's easy to announce: "God told me to have our church do this—end of discussion." It's more difficult to handle sincere objections intelligently, even to change your thinking if your discernment is shown to be faulty. When reading the Bible, it's easy to impose one of your inner impressions on the text because it feels inspired, but it takes time and effort to study the text thoughtfully, to understand the meaning of the actual words in context, to consider the teaching of the Bible as a whole, and so on.

EMOTIONS AND SANCTIFICATION

Part of our confusion over the place of feeling in the Christian life is the powerful tendency of our feelings to lead us astray. Much of what we think of as "crucifying the flesh" involves saying no to the urgings of a diseased heart. "For the grace of God that brings salvation has appeared to all men. It teaches us to say 'No' to ungodliness and worldly passions" (Ti 2:11-12). We may feel like doing all sorts of things that fly in the face of God's will. Obedience to Christ calls us to say no to some feelings. But the answer isn't simply to live out of our will, ignoring our feelings. The Stoic philosophers recommended as much, but their approach didn't produce holiness.

Jesus wants to give us a new heart, able to feel as he feels. We need to crucify the flesh, but our hearts need to be aroused, awakened, stimulated to love. In the Book of Romans, Paul speaks of our need to be "dead to sin but alive to God in Christ Jesus" (Rom 6:11). Christ Jesus himself demonstrates that part of what it means to be alive is to feel.

One of the wonderful effects of what we sometimes call our "first love"—the honeymoon period that often follows the new birth—is that we feel like pleasing God. Our motivation to obey him is high. The thought of disobeying him turns our stomachs. Our hearts are aroused to love, awakened to righteousness. People in the throes of their first love stay up late at night to read their Bibles, look for opportunities to give away their faith, allow bad habits to fall off with relative ease, and are eager to worship. There's nothing magical about this state, nor is it meant to be a once-in-a-lifetime experience. It's simply a foretaste of something Jesus wants us to have with increasing measure: a heart of flesh that feels good about God and righteousness and bad about the devil and sin.

A number of longtime Christians in our church have been in a season where the Spirit of Christ is awakening their hearts to love. Take Carol, the mother of three young children, for example. She called me the other day saying, "Ken, what do I *do* with this experience? I've never felt God's love as powerfully as I have in the past two weeks. I feel like I have to give it away!" When Carol prays these days, she's moved to tears more often than not. She gets a little frustrated when the church service is filled with too much "talk"—announcements, overlong introductions, and so on. All she wants to do is worship. She read the four Gospels in a week's time, without a lot of leisure time in her day.

Of course, the wizened veteran of spiritual renewal will remind us that these times of intense feeling don't last forever. Spiritual experiences fade. Some things we must learn to do because, like eating oatmeal, "It's the right thing to do." Of course. But let's not miss the obvious point: it's better to be filled with the Spirit than not. It's good for our feelings to be stimulated toward righteousness. If our hearts are cold, it's not a sign to give up, but a sign to seek a fresh filling with the Spirit, arousing our hearts to love.

In other words, sanctification is more than the process of developing the disciplines of prayer, Bible reading, and regular giving, although these are important. Sanctification is not simply growing through making godly choices and decisions. Sanctification includes the progressive influence of the Holy Spirit in the emotional expressions of our hearts, as well as the grace to obey God when our feelings aren't cooperating.

THE RENEWAL OF OUR MINDS

Do not conform any longer to the pattern of this world, but be transformed by the renewing of your mind. Then you will be able to test and approve what God's will is—his good, pleasing and perfect will.   **Romans 12:2**

Several years ago, a new Christian came to my wife and me for prayer. She found that every time she began to feel the presence of God in a time of worship, she felt pain in her abdomen. She also desired to feel God's presence more. She mentioned that she had had an elective abortion a few years ago, but didn't think it was wrong. As we prayed with her, we felt that the pain in her abdomen may have been related to the abortion. This may or may not have been an accurate assessment. We didn't share this thought with her, but my wife suggested that it might be helpful for her to speak with others who have experienced the pain of abortion and worked through the issue from a biblical perspective. We arranged to have the woman attend a post-abortion Bible study, sponsored by a pregnancy counseling center in her hometown. We felt that before this new Christian could experience the freedom of an emotional healing, she had to grapple with God's Word. In other words, her mind needed renewal for her feelings to be touched.

Our minds are an essential part of our inner person. The Spirit enlightens or renews our minds so that we "understand what God's will is." Those who claim that the Spirit seeks to bypass the mind, as if the mind is of little value in spiritual matters, are sadly mistaken. Our minds don't need to be bypassed, but renewed.

New Christians especially need to be encouraged to deal honestly and straightforwardly with their questions about what it means to live as Christians. Positions on a host of issues need to be thought through. Raising children in today's society makes it even more important to teach them to "have a mind of their own." Children must learn to examine the world they live in and test popular assumptions in order to understand what the will of the Lord is. In other words, they need to learn how to think, if they are to live for Christ in this world.

WORSHIP: THOUGHTFUL AND HEARTFELT

The return of the ark of the covenant to Jerusalem provides one of the most dramatic and disturbing worship experiences recorded in the Bible. It provides timely warnings to both charismatics and conservative evangelicals about the need to worship thoughtfully and with feeling. The first leg of the journey emphasizes the need for thoughtful worship.

A warning for charismatics? The story begins, as you may recall, with David and his friends transporting the ark (which represented, and in a sense contained, the holy presence of God with his people) from the house of Abinadab.

> David and the whole house of Israel were celebrating with all their might before the Lord, with songs and with harps, lyres, tambourines, sistrums and symbols. When they came to the threshing floor of Nacon, Uzzah reached out and took hold of the ark of God, because the oxen stumbled. The Lord's anger burned against Uzzah because of his irreverent act; therefore God struck him down and he died there beside the ark of God.   **2 Samuel 6:5-7**

The scene involves singing and dancing and celebration. Everyone is having a wonderful time worshiping God. It's the kind of expressive worship that a charismatic would gladly participate in. Suddenly the oxen stumble and Uzzah reaches out his hand to steady the ark—at which point he is struck down on the spot.

It is interesting how theological problems change over the centuries. In the Middle Ages, the main problem for people was how a just and holy God could save wretched human beings. Today, the problem is how God could ever judge any of us—least of all a person like Uzzah for simply lending a hand.

We tend to forget that God took great pains to communicate the reality of holiness, specifically the idea that fallen human beings must be careful in the presence of a holy God. Approaching a holy God is not something we can take casually in light of our own sin. Provision must be made to atone for sin, and it is an awful and costly proposition—fulfilled ultimately in the death and resurrection of Jesus. Without a vivid understanding of God's holiness and the danger of approaching God apart from his provision, the cross is meaningless.

Uzzah, who was a priest, would have understood this concept. The Law of Moses was filled with instructions about how the priests (and only the priests) were to handle the objects associated with the worship of a holy God. The priests were instructed to transport the ark much as an oriental monarch would be carried, on poles. No one was permitted to touch the ark or go near it. Just once each year, on the Day of Atonement, one person, the high priest, was permitted to touch the ark, and then only with the sprinkled blood of sacrificial animals.

But Uzzah wasn't thoughtful. He felt he could play fast and loose with God's commands. He discovered (and this is the warning for all of us) that God treats his Word with deadly seriousness.

How might Uzzah's judgment apply to worship in our churches today? Sometimes, when we are having a great time of celebration, and everyone is singing and the music is exciting, it is possible to forget that we are worshiping a God of utter holiness. That's when we may forget to take seriously the words of Scripture concerning worship. For example, Jesus told us to be reconciled with our brothers and sisters. If we are bringing our gift to the altar we should leave it to be reconciled first (see Matthew 5:23-24). When we harbor bitterness and do nothing to reconcile broken relationships within the church, we are not treating his holiness with proper reverence.

As we stated earlier, we think the writings of Paul discourage speaking in tongues without interpretation in the context of public worship.

For this reason the man who speaks in a tongue [in the church] should pray that he may interpret what he says.... I thank God that I speak in tongues more than all of you, but in the church I would rather speak five intelligible words to instruct others than ten thousand words in a tongue.

1 Corinthians 14:13, 18-19

In the course of joyful worship, Paul's instructions may seem a little restrictive. If the Spirit is moving people to speak in tongues, how could we ever discourage that? But the experience of Uzzah warns us to take the things God says seriously. We understand that Pentecostal and charismatic scholars interpret Paul's instructions in a way that allows for uninterpreted tongues speaking in public worship; we don't mean to say that people who pray in tongues without interpretation are in danger of being struck down as Uzzah was. The point is, we have to be thoughtful about God's commands regarding worship. The text has to be taken seriously; it can't simply be dismissed.

We may be tempted to believe that simply because we are worshiping God enthusiastically, God stops caring whether we follow biblical directives about worship or whether our lives are clean. But if we do, we are sadly mistaken. How could anything that feels so good be anything but pleasing to God? Uzzah's experience stands as a clear warning.

Warning for conservative evangelicals? Sometime after Uzzah's death, David decided to take the ark of the covenant back to Jerusalem. But he made sure God's wrath was placated, lest what happened to Uzzah should happen to him. So, it is recorded,

David went down and brought up the ark of God... with rejoicing. When those who were carrying the ark of the Lord had taken six steps, he sacrificed a bull and a fattened calf. David, wearing a linen ephod, danced before the Lord with all his might, while he and the entire house of Israel brought up the ark of the Lord with shouts and the sounds of trumpets. As the ark of the Lord was entering the City of David, Michal, daughter of Saul, watched from the window. And when she saw King David leaping and dancing before the Lord, she despised him in her heart. **2 Samuel 6:12-16**

Michal was uncomfortable with her husband's emotionally expressive worship. She despised it, in fact. And so do many of us in the conservative evangelical tradition. We prefer the spirituality of Mr. Spock, the character in *Star Trek* who advocated the removal of all emotion in favor of pure reason and logic. Of course, this places us squarely at odds with the biblical tradition of worship.

Indeed, no one handling the Bible fairly could deny that biblical forms of worship are emotionally expressive— involving, at times, extravagant use of the body and voice. Hebrew words for worship often refer to the body. One word means literally "to lie prostrate." Another, "to kneel down." A third, "stretch out the hand." In the New Testament, the most common word for worship means, "to draw near so as to kiss."

How can we see these emotionally and physically expressive words for worship and yet feel so uncomfortable if people raise their hands or kneel down in the aisle during worship? How is it that we despise these expressions of worship when the biblical culture for worship is so expressive—when worshipers cry aloud, clap their hands, lie prostrate, dance, weep, and rejoice aloud in God's presence? Those in the Bible who despise these worship forms certainly don't make good company: people like Michal, the Pharisees who were upset with the worship of the crowds on Palm Sunday, or those who despised Mary of Bethany when she wept over the feet of Jesus and wiped them with her hair.

What's our problem? In part, it may be the social class of many modern-day conservative evangelicals. Consider again Michal's response:

> When David returned home to bless his household, Michal daughter of Saul came out to meet him and said, "How the king of Israel has distinguished himself today, disrobing in the sight of the slave girls of his servants as any vulgar fellow would."
>
> **2 Samuel 6:20**

Twice, Michal is referred to as the "daughter of King Saul." Perhaps the author was trying to make it plain that *Michal is a little princess, well aware of her higher social standing.* Culture, particularly class and education but ethnicity as well, can lead to emotional inhibition. Have you ever noticed that the better-educated, wealthier churches tend to be more restrained in worship style? And churches that include more people with less money and education tend to be more expressive. Why?

We are taught to believe that education and wealth necessarily liberate. But one wonders, when it comes to emotional expressiveness, if quite the opposite takes place. Perhaps people feel that the higher they get on the social ladder, the more dignity they have to lose.

In addition, many conservative evangelicals in North America come from Northern European backgrounds, where emotion is not easily shown. Rich's wife Marlene, for example, was raised in a German family. Rich and his mother-in-law of twenty years still shake hands when they meet. Marlene, on the other hand, gets squarely kissed on the mouth by Rich's Jewish relatives.

Our church has occasional joint services with the Bible Church, a largely African-American congregation led by Rev. Levon Yuille. The first time Rev. Yuille preached at our church, he broke into a dance mid-sermon, which was a tightly reasoned exposition on the glory of God. Of course, the sight of the dignified Rev. Yuille dancing before the Lord did as much to communicate the glory of God—and the joyful response to that glory—as the word-study portions of the sermon.

Several years ago, a man approached Rich after a time of worship, red-faced and obviously upset. He said, "Pastor Nathan, when that woman on your worship team plays her tambourine, it reminds me of [here he paused, groping for the words to express his disgust]... it reminds me of a cabaret! It's undignified!"

Whose dignity, we wonder, was he concerned about? Certainly not God's. The woman playing the tambourine was doing nothing inappropriate. It's hard to play the tambourine without moving. I suppose you could have called her tambourine playing expressive, even enthusiastic. She may have even, at times, appeared to be having a good time. But none of that seemed much of a threat to God's dignity.

So whose dignity is on the line when we get a little expressive physically or emotionally in worship? While we protest that we are only trying to guard God's dignity by refraining from raising our hands or shedding a few tears, we are almost entirely concerned about preserving our own dignity. Perhaps we need to consider who is the object of our focus in worship.

David's response to Michal's complaint makes it plain:

It was before the Lord, who chose me rather than your father or anyone from his house when he appointed me ruler over the Lord's people Israel—I will celebrate before the Lord. I will become even more undignified than this, and I will be humiliated in my own eyes. But by these slave girls you spoke of, I will be held in honor.

2 Samuel 6:21-22

Michal was struggling with one of the great inhibitors of spiritual life—how we appear in the eyes of others. We rarely do anything—give a teaching, lead a small group, sing a song, or bake a cake—without immediately wondering how the reviews will read. What will the audience think?

David rebuked Michal (and us) by saying, in effect, "Perhaps you are reading the wrong reviews." The only review that matters is the one written by God! God, after all, is the only audience that really counts.

You'll notice that David even refers to the review that he gives himself. Often this is an even more inhibiting factor in our worship than our fear of the opinion of others. We continually hold up mirrors to ourselves regarding how we look in our own eyes. It is one thing to hold the opinions (real or imagined) of others at arm's length; it is quite another to hold our severest critic—ourselves—at bay.

This is an especially powerful obstacle to heartfelt worship, if we have been critical of the worship style of others. Jesus warned us not to judge others, lest we too should be judged (see Luke 6:37). He promised that the measure we use to judge others will be measured against us. If you, like me, have a tendency to observe people through critical eyes, finding fault rather than favor, you will no doubt reflect this in your view of yourself as you worship. Like me, you may need to repent of a judgmental view of others in worship in order to get yourself off your own back! And take a lesson from King David, who was willing to be humiliated in his own eyes in order to worship for the only audience that counts.

WHOLEHEARTED DEVOTION: THE BEST OF BOTH WORLDS

Fortunately, we don't need to choose between an intellectually satisfying faith and heartfelt religion. Turning off our minds won't make us more open to the Spirit. Nor will turning off our emotions make us more levelheaded. We were created to think clearly and feel deeply. Our thoughts and our emotions must be fully engaged if we are to respond to God with our whole heart. The emphasis in the charismatic tradition on feeling and in the conservative evangelical tradition on a well thought-out faith are both needed, but not in isolation from each other. We need the best of both worlds.

FOR DISCUSSION

1. What do you think of the authors' understanding of the heart as an integrated whole, including intellect, emotion, and will?

2. Do you feel more comfortable dealing with the intellect or the emotions in spiritual matters? What factors do you think contribute to this?

3. Discuss various worship styles that you have experienced and consider their strengths and weaknesses from a biblical perspective.

WHEN SEEKING A CHURCH

1. Is there a value in the church on thoughtfulness? Are explanations that appeal to a thoughtful person generally offered? How does the leadership respond to questions? Is there an atmosphere that supports intellectual activity or does the culture of the church tend to dismiss the value of intellectual activity?

2. Is there room in the culture of the church for feelings? Is there generally a positive view of human emotion, or a negative view?

3. If there seems to be an imbalance, does the church leadership seem to be aware of it and open to growth in areas that are undervalued?

FOR PASTORS

1. How would people in your church respond to emotionally expressive worship? Are there any settings in which people see emotions freely expressed?

2. Is intellectual activity honored in your church, or does it tend to be dismissed as "unspiritual"?

3. Do your sermons appeal to the feelings, the mind, or both? How did the teaching styles of Jesus and Paul appeal to both?

4. Consider teaching a sermon (or series of sermons) on the emotional life of Jesus as portrayed in the Gospels, covering compassion, joy, grief, and anger.

5. Study Ephesians 4:17-5:20 with an eye on what Paul teaches about the place of feeling and thinking, the nature of a "hardened heart," and the impact of the Spirit on these things.

FOR FURTHER STUDY

Jonathan Edwards, "The Religious Affections," from *The Works of Jonathan Edwards*, Vol. 1 (Edinburgh: The Banner of Truth Trust, 1992).

Harry Blamires, *The Christian Mind* (Ann Arbor, Mich.: Servant, 1978).

ELEVEN

The Future of Empowered Evangelicalism

G ene Veith, in his excellent book *Postmodern Times,* suggests that the modern age symbolically ended on July 15, 1972, at 3:32 P.M. That was the moment that the Pruitt-Igoe housing project in St. Louis, Missouri, a prime example of modern architecture, was demolished. Despite its modern aesthetics, high technology, and functional design, the development was so crime-infested, impersonal, and depressing that housing officials polled the residents asking for their suggestions. The residents' solution was simple: Blow up the buildings![1]

The destruction of the housing project provides a wonderful illustration of what has happened to the modern age. In spite of all its high technology, high hopes, and unbounded confidence in humanity's ability to conquer all its problems without reference to God, the modern age has come crashing to the ground. Modernity may be high-tech, but people have found that it is depressingly impersonal and does not answer our relational or spiritual needs. Further, the last century, filled as it has been with concentration camps and gulags, has convincingly demonstrated the absurdity of the modern age's trust in human goodness.

Where do we go from here?

CULTURAL OPPORTUNITIES FOR EMPOWERED EVANGELICALISM

As the new millennium draws near, we foresee unprecedented opportunities for the kind of Christianity advocated in this book, a Christianity that brings together the best of the conservative evangelical and charismatic worlds. As empowered evangelicals, where should we look to see the opportunities to bear witness to Christ in our day?

To think strategically, we should consider: (1) the rise of postmodernism; (2) the renewal of interest in spiritual experiences; and (3) the real pain and brokenness of the young.

The rise of postmodernism. The collapse of the modern age and the rise of what has been called postmodernism do provide causes for celebration among empowered evangelicals. For example, during the modern age, science dismissed supernatural healings, prophetic revelations, and even such fundamental doctrines as the Incarnation and Redemption as inconsistent with a closed natural universe. Modern science required that everything be explained in terms of a cause within the system. Thus under modern science, God was marginalized to the position of a stop-gap God, necessary for those decreasing numbers of issues such as "first causes" that couldn't otherwise be explained.

But postmodern physics has opened up the universe. Scientists no longer believe in mechanistic, orderly natural laws. Matter and even time itself are now understood to operate in a mind-stretching, disorderly way. A hot new area in mathematics, for example, is called "chaos theory"; it studies random happenings ranging from the movement of subatomic particles to the movement of financial markets.

What does all this mean for empowered evangelicalism? It means we do not have to be ashamed to assert the reality of divine healings, as if to do so renders us cave-dwelling Neanderthals. Christians who believe in contemporary miracles may have been at odds with modern science, but we are not at odds with *postmodern* science. Indeed, conservative evangelicals (who sometimes have accommodated their theology to Enlightenment rationalism) may raise their eyebrows at empowered evangelicals for their belief in contemporary miracles, but faith in the occurrence of healings from causes outside the system should not raise an eyebrow from a consistent, postmodern physicist.

On the other hand, we have our work cut out for us, since postmodernism not only rejects Enlightenment science but also rejects the existence of absolute truth. According to postmodernist thought, *the only absolute is that there are no absolutes*. Yet even here, we must remember that empowered evangelicals punch with both fists. We not only approach the world with a claim of miraculous healings or deliverances, but we also approach the world with "the word of our God [that] stands forever" (Is 40:8). If charismatics, in their emphasis on experience, have been slightly weak in affirming biblical truth and biblical morality, empowered evangelicals can fill the void by reemphasizing the priority of preaching the eternal Word of God.

The renewed interest in spiritual experience. The explosion of interest, in near-death experiences, "angelic" visitations, Native American spirituality, goddess worship, yoga, Tibetan meditation, and New Age basics such as channeling and crystals may strike a Christian observer as an unmitigated disaster for western societies. Yet empowered evangelicals can find here a powerful opportunity for evangelism and renewed cultural influence.

There is a legitimate thirst for spiritual experience that empowered evangelicalism affirms in New Age seekers. We reject the New Age's nonbiblical experiences, but we respond to this thirst, not by reasserting rationalistic Christianity, but rather by calling for *biblical* spiritual experiences. Instead of criticizing *all* experience as suspect, we prefer to push for biblical spiritual experiences such as prophetic revelations, divine healings, fillings with the Holy Spirit, and deliverances. We see in Jesus' words a powerfully relevant invitation to experience the power of the Spirit: "'If [anyone] is thirsty, let him come to me and drink. Whoever believes in me, as the Scripture has said, streams of living water will flow from within him.' By this, he meant the Spirit, whom those who believed in him were later to receive" (Jn 7:37-39).

At the same time, New Age spiritualities cannot be confronted by biblical experiences alone. This approach can lead to the relativizing of experiences, that is, "You have your experience that makes you happy; and I have mine." Biblical experiences must be undergirded by clear biblical exposition. As has been noted throughout this book, the *works* of Jesus must be coupled with the *words* of Jesus. The empowered evangelical's twin emphases on "the Scriptures and the power of God" aptly addresses the challenge presented by the Western world's renewed interest in (nonbiblical) spiritual experiences.

The pain and the brokenness of the young. Listen to the music of the group Nirvana and ask yourself why so many million young people have identified with their songs' angst-filled lyrics or felt such overwhelming remorse over the suicide of the group's lead singer, Kurt Cobain. Cobain's wife,

Courtney Love, said: "Every kid in America who has been abused loves Kurt Cobain's music" (and presumably identifies with his despair).[2]

Statistics support the overwhelming experience of pain felt by the young. If the divorce of his or her parents is one of the most traumatic experiences a child can go through, it is a trauma felt by one million American children each year. Since 1960, the rate at which teenagers are taking their own lives has more than tripled. Suicide is now the second leading cause of death among all adolescents. Homicide is now far and away the leading cause of death among African-American teenagers. In fact, a young black man living in Harlem, New York, is less likely to live till the age of forty than a young man growing up in Bangladesh![3]

How will the very real experience of pain in our youth be addressed by Christians in the next few decades? Certainly, we must have churches that function as families, not institutions, to combat adolescents' feelings of aloneness and alienation. Certainly, too, the young need spiritual fathers and mothers who will simply "be there" for them to replace parents who often are consumed by their own problems and issues. Nevertheless, simply creating a sense of family and just "being there" as spiritual fathers and mothers is not enough. We also must believe in and practice the healing of past hurts. Must the young limp through life as brutalized survivors of incest, drug abuse, adolescent sexual activity, abortion, and crime? We don't think so, and we trust that you don't think so either.

Christian community is precious, but we need to add opportunities for young people to *experience the Father's love personally*. Such experiences of the Father's love may occur through intimate, moving worship times. Others may occur though the practice of "laying on of hands" as prayer is offered to heal past hurts. Prophetic revelations may further reach under the self-protective walls and defenses surrounding a young person's heart and powerfully address hidden shame and hurt.

On occasion, a deliverance may be in order, particularly for a young person whose past involves participation in the occult, drug abuse, or sexual abuse. We have seen that wounds left by past abuse can get "infected" by the demonic. After ministering to the source of the wound—self-abuse or perhaps abuse by another—and leading a young person through prayers of repentance or forgiveness, we occasionally need to pray for deliverance.

Our point in even raising the issue of the demonic is to underline the need for ministries to the young that include a heavy dose of the supernatural—ministries of healing, deliverance, and prophetic revelation. And because the younger generation tends to be less interested in abstract truth taught classroom-style, and more interested in truth that is delivered just in time to meet a ministry need, we have found tremendous receptivity to biblical teaching that is offered as young people are themselves engaged in ministry.

Thus, supernatural ministry has two important influences on the young. The first is the healing of the young person's own soul. The second is to provide a "hothouse environment" in which a young person becomes thirsty for and open to learning biblical truth—truth that assists in his or her own ministry to other young people. We see this just-in-time delivery system of truth in Jesus' teaching of his young disciples. It was the stretching experience of difficult ministry situations that made the disciples thirsty for answers from Jesus. "Why couldn't we drive the demon out?" (see Mark 9:28). "Where could we get enough bread in this remote place to feed such a crowd?" (Mt 15:33).

If we want to move young people from blasé youth-group boredom to passionate interest in spiritual things, we would be wise to stretch them with hands-on ministry opportunities.

Such opportunities would include prayer for the sick, deliverance of the demonized, preaching the gospel in nonchurch settings, short-term missions, and ministry to the poor.

A CALL TO KINDNESS

In order to make the most of the opportunities facing us, conservative evangelicals and charismatics need each other. If we are to learn from each other, we must lay our guns down long enough to listen to and appreciate the strengths of each respective movement. Four rules ought to govern our relationship with each other.

1. Let's stop using negative labels. Charismatics have been called immoral, "keen but clueless," "anti-intellectual," and "perilously close to neo-baalism."[4] They have been lumped together with followers of Sun Myung Moon, Joseph Smith, and Edgar Cayce. Conservative evangelicals have been characterized as dead, dry as bones, and occasionally needing to be gunned down by a Holy Spirit machine gun.

This level of discourse in the body of Christ ought to stop. Christians within the bounds of orthodoxy have disagreed with each other since the days of Paul and Barnabas. Let's resolve to avoid lumping sincere differences in theological perspective or practice together with rank heresies. Let's further resolve, as much as is possible, to avoid using harsh, pejorative, or unnecessarily negative labels in our writing and our speaking when referring to the position or person of a Christian brother or sister.

2. Let's follow the example of D.L. Moody and Billy Graham. We love the story, told by Henry Drummond, of the warmhearted affection practiced by D.L. Moody toward Roman Catholics in his town.

> With everything in his special career, in his habitual environment, and in the traditions of his special work, to make him intolerant, Mr. Moody's sympathies have only broadened with time. Some years ago the Roman Catholics of Northfield determined to build a church. They went around the township collecting subscriptions, and by-and-by approached Moody's door. How did he receive them? The narrower evangelical would have shut the door in their faces, or opened it only to give them a lecture on the blasphemies of the Pope, or the iniquities of the Scarlet Woman. Mr. Moody gave them one of the handsomest subscriptions on their list. Not content with that, when their little chapel was finished, he presented them with an organ. "Why," he exclaimed, "if they are Roman Catholics, it is better that they should be good Roman Catholics than bad. It is surely better to have a Catholic church than none; and as for the organ, if they are to have music in their church, it is better to have good music."
>
> "Besides," he added, "these are my own townspeople."[5]

Shouldn't Moody's ecumenical spirit be a more compelling example when applied to fellow evangelicals—charismatic or noncharismatic—with whom we share a common history (in the great Reformation and Evangelical Revivals), common commitments (including the authority of Scripture, the need for personal conversion, and the Lordship of Jesus Christ), and a common goal (the preaching of the gospel to all the nations on earth)?

Perhaps Billy Graham has exhibited this ecumenical spirit best in our day by choosing to emphasize the common cause of evangelism and by deemphasizing matters that divide the

church. Graham has pulled believers together from every
denominational stripe and from every continent for half a
century.

3. Let's be open to reconsider traditional positions. Just as
we have not yet arrived at complete "unity in the faith,"
neither has any particular camp arrived at the perfect
"knowledge of the Son of God" (Eph 4:13). We do not need
to reconsider the fundamentals of faith; those are fixed for all
time. But we all, this side of the second coming, see in a mirror
dimly; we all have partial knowledge, especially regarding
secondary matters. As we listen with humility to each other,
perhaps we will find that it is time to reconsider traditional
positions.

From the charismatic side, it may be time to reopen consideration of such long-held positions as the necessity of a
second baptism in the Holy Spirit accompanied by speaking in
tongues, or the view that healing is guaranteed in this life by
the Atonement. With so many voices inside and outside the
charismatic camp calling for just such a theological reevaluation, perhaps charismatics can find a better way to express the
importance of empowering experiences in light of the past
century of theological reflection on these long-neglected
topics.

Likewise, certain charismatic styles of doing ministry may
need some rethinking. Do all of our traditions (yes, charismatics have traditions too!) best reflect Jesus' style of doing
ministry in the Gospels? Do certain of our styles unnecessarily
draw attention to the ministers? Are styles that were adopted
for a different era still relevant for the post-World War II
generations?

From the conservative evangelical side, perhaps it is time to
face the issue of the absence of prophetic revelations, healings,
deliverances, and intimate worship in many of our churches

and ask if we must continue to be so impoverished. In looking at a century of the best of charismatic and Pentecostal practice, can we say we have nothing at all to learn or to add to our repertoire from this enormous segment of the church?

Perhaps, too, it is time to honestly acknowledge our history, our actual practices, and our fears. Too much of evangelical history has been rewritten in reaction to the charismatic movement. Many conservative evangelical laypersons simply do not know that their heroes such as D.L. Moody, A.B. Simpson, Charles Finney, and Billy Graham certainly have believed in and have experienced empowering fillings of the Holy Spirit that changed their ministries forever. If our heroes experienced these things, why are they off limits to the man or woman in the pew? Further, many evangelicals taught and practiced divine healing before the Pentecostal movement made divine healing suspect for some. And if anecdotal information is to be believed, many missionaries are simply not fully informing their denominations of their actual practices on the mission field regarding deliverances, healings, prophetic revelations, and other spiritual gifts. Things that are taught against at home seem to be widely practiced on the mission field.

What prevents an honest acknowledgment of our own history and mission practice? Pride, perhaps—the demand that we publicly confess that some of our reactions to charismatics may have been overreactions. Pride, too, in that we may need to confess that we conservative evangelicals are not as all-sufficient and knowledgeable and powerful as we have sometimes claimed. Perhaps we also struggle with fear—fear of emotions, fear of losing control, fear of the unknown. It is easier and more comfortable to "do church" when we are experts and when we always know what to expect. But when did Jesus ever promise that church should always be risk-free or comfortable?

4. Let's stop fighting against straw men. We say this in love, but a visit to any Christian bookstore would quickly reveal a host of best-selling books by evangelicals that employ tabloid-style journalistic tactics. Thus, one prominent author, in rejecting modern-day miracles, begins his book with the bizarre story of Maria Rubio of Lake Arthur, New Mexico, who was frying tortillas in her kitchen when she noticed one of them seemed to have the likeness of a face etched in burn marks. She concluded that it was Jesus and even built a shrine for the tortilla.[6] The implication of this example (sadly, such examples can be multiplied by the bushel in this particular book) is that charismatics are as foolish in their belief in miracles as this woman who built a shrine to a tortilla.

When we Christians interact with each other, let's stop fighting against straw men (or burned tortillas). Instead, let's resolve to let the best proponents of the opposite position speak, or let's at least deal with positions that are held by a significant percentage of mainstream conservative evangelical or mainstream charismatic representatives, as we hope we have done in this book. We can always find the aberrant and the weird if that is our intention; let's try to love each other enough to deal with the best or the mainstream.

THE EVANGELICAL TARGET AND PENTECOSTAL POWER

Given the cultural opportunities presented to us as evangelical Christians, whether conservative evangelical or charismatic, and given the high degree of commonness that we share, including our common history and our common commitments, let's work together toward the ends to which the New Testament directs us: These ends include *the ends of the earth* and *the end of history.*[7] "The gospel must be preached to all nations and then the end will come" (Mt 24:14).

But aren't the obstacles facing Christians insurmountable? Some countries are legally closed. Others are spiritually dead. Still others are militantly anti-Christian. But when faced with closed doors we remember the promises of Jesus. "This gospel of the kingdom *will be preached* in the whole world as a testimony to all nations, and then the end will come" And further, "This is what is written: The Christ will suffer and rise from the dead on the third day, and repentance and forgiveness of sins *will be preached* in his name to all nations beginning at Jerusalem" (Mt 24:14; Lk 24:46-47).

We are not only *commanded* to bring the gospel to the ends of the earth, but when faced with seemingly insurmountable obstacles, let's remember that the Lord Jesus Christ *promised it will happen!* Indeed, the great promise of the Old Testament was that "the earth will be filled with the knowledge of the glory of the Lord, as the waters cover the sea" (Hb 2:14). Moreover, in some mysterious way, reaching the ends of the earth and bringing about the end of history is tied to our gospel preaching. Peter tells us to look forward to the day of the Lord and to "*speed* its coming!" (2 Pt 3:12).

We may be seeing the promise of Jesus being fulfilled in our lifetimes. Right now, Christianity is growing at over three times the rate of the world's population growth. Whereas Bible-believing Christians amounted to about one out of every twenty-four people in 1960, and one out of every sixteen people in 1980, in 1995 they comprise one out of seven or eight people![8]

Ralph Winter, from the United States Center for World Missions, has stated that the global statistics regarding the growth of Christianity represent a virtually irrefutable case concerning the opportunity for Christian missions in our day. In other words, despite the obstacles facing us, preaching the gospel to all the nations and reaching the ends of the earth *is an achievable task!*

But who is doing the preaching and how will the task be accomplished? It is a fact that the gospel is most rapidly advancing through Pentecostal, charismatic, and empowered evangelical churches. Again, the statistics are irrefutable. About fifty-five thousand people come to know Christ every day through the collective witness of these groups. And Pentecostal, charismatic, and empowered evangelicals are now tallied as the vast majority of all Bible-believing Christians worldwide, up from about one-third in 1970. But most interestingly, *the fastest growing segment of all is the empowered evangelical portion.* Their numbers are predicted by the premier church demographer David B. Barrett to double in the 1990s from thirty-three million to sixty-five million.[9]

Why is such rapid church growth occurring among Pente-costals and charismatics in general, and empowered evangeli-cals in particular? We believe it is because empowered evan-gelicals have embraced the two great sources of divine power to destroy strongholds: the gospel and the power of the Holy Spirit. The message of repentance and forgiveness itself has power! But the disciples were regularly instructed to preach the message with the provision of power from on high (see Luke 24:49). This is the biblical formula for success—the gospel message preached in the power of the Spirit.

Finally, there is a third end that we are called to remind ourselves of repeatedly in the Scriptures: *the end of our lives,* of course! Paul said to the Ephesian elders that "I consider my life worth nothing to me, if only I may finish the race and complete the task the Lord Jesus has given me—the task of testifying to the gospel of God's grace" (Acts 20:24). He further said, at the end of his life, "I have finished the race!" (2 Tm 4:7). Will we be able to say the same?

It is with these three ends in mind—the ends of the earth,

the end of history, and the end of our own lives—that we pray: "Now, Lord, enable your servants to speak your word with great boldness. Stretch out your hand to heal and perform miraculous signs and wonders through the name of your holy servant Jesus."

Perhaps God will answer as he did in the days of the apostles: "After [we] prayed, the place where [we] were meeting was shaken. And [we] were all filled with the Holy Spirit and spoke the word of God boldly" (Acts 4:31).

Appendix

The Healing Prayer Model

John Wimber has developed a helpful five-step healing model to assist people in following God's direction regarding how to pray for a person. This five-step model is not a technique or a secret formula that makes healing happen. We must always keep . in mind that God does the healing and that his sovereign will is determinative regarding whether someone gets healed. This model simply enables people to look for God's sovereign will when faced with someone who needs healing.

Step 1: The Interview. During the interview we ask the person, "What do you want me to pray for? An interview is not a medical interview, since unless we are medical practitioners, detailed medical information will typically be meaningless to us, at best. At worst, it will discourage us because we will realize how complicated the person's condition is, and it will feel unlikely to us that the person will ever be healed.

During the interview, we are listening not only to the sick person but also to God for any additional information that God may wish to show us regarding the person's need.

Step 2: The Diagnostic Decision. As we are interviewing the person, we are asking God for insight regarding the ultimate cause of the condition. We have heard from the individual regarding what the need is; now we are asking God about the cause. Again, this is not a medical diagnosis, since most of those who pray for the sick are not trained to diagnose illnesses.

Step 3: The Prayer Selection. This step answers the question, "What kind of prayer is needed to help this person?" The ultimate issue regarding prayer selection is what God wants to do at that particular time. So we are asking God how we should intercede for this person. Typically, we will simply pray a prayer regarding the person's announced need. For example, "Dear Father, please heal Joe's headache."

On occasion, however, God may instruct us to command a headache to leave, just as Jesus commanded blind eyes to be opened. Thus, our prayer may sound more authoritative.

At other times, God may direct us toward the underlying reason for the headache and we may pray accordingly. For example, "Father, please relieve the stress that Joe is experiencing from his job and fill Joe with peace"; or, "Father, please heal Joe's eyes that may be causing his headache."

Step 4: Prayer Engagement. After laying on hands, we pray that the Holy Spirit will come and minister to the person. Again, we must remind the reader that the Holy Spirit is present in the sense that he is omnipresent. By saying, "We invite the Holy Spirit's presence," we mean his beneficent presence, his presence to bless and to do good for the person we are praying for. Thus our prayer may sound like this: "Holy Spirit, I invite you to come to Mary and release your healing power." During the prayer engagement we are determining *how effective* our prayers have been. We may ask if the person feels any relief. Does he or she have any physical sensations that often accompany healing, such as unusual heat or tingling? The absence of physical sensations does not mean that healing is not occurring, but if such sensations are present, they possibly indicate the activity of God. During prayer engagement we often will interview the person further to see if we have missed any significant issues. We also may inquire if God is speaking to him or her about anything and if he or she feels free to share that with us.

Step 5: Post-Prayer Direction. After we pray for an individual, we often must give post-prayer direction. For example, if Bill has confessed the sin of pornography, we may encourage him to avoid certain situations of temptation, such as certain streets or stores that sell pornography. Or if Sally has not been healed, we may speak a word of encouragement to her regarding God's love for her and invite her to be prayed for at another time. If, during the prayer time, we have had the opportunity to lead someone to Christ, we would direct him or her to take certain steps to grow as a new Christian.

NOTES

1. Alister McGrath, *Evangelicalism and the Future of Christianity* (London: Hodder & Stoughton, 1994), 51.
2. In our book, unless we distinguish the terms, we have adopted the popular nontechnical usage of "charismatic" and "Pentecostal" and treat them as interchangeable terms.
3. David B. Barrett projected that by 1990 there would be thirty-three million doctrinally conservative evangelical practitioners of charismatic spiritual gifts. See "Global Statistics" in Stanley M. Burgess and Gary B. McGee, eds., *The Dictionary of Pentecostal and Charismatic Movements* (Grand Rapids, Mich.: Zondervan, 1988), 812, 813.

ONE
Looking for the Best of Both Worlds

1. I fundamentally believe, along with the theologian Jonathan Edwards, that dramatic experiences prove very little. What is crucial is *the fruit* borne from an experience. If someone claims to have had an encounter with the Holy Spirit, then we should expect, among other things, that the person will love God more, be more servantlike in relationship to other Christians, and be more interested in sharing his or her faith with nonbelievers. An experience without the fruit of biblical activity ought not to be credited to the Holy Spirit.

TWO
Evangelicals and Charismatics:
Children of Revival

1. Richard M. Riss, *A Survey of 20th Century Revival Movements in North America* (Peabody, Mass.: Hendrickson, 1988), 10-11.
2. Arnold A. Dallimore, *George Whitefield* (Westchester, Ill.: Crossway, 1990), 40.

3. Bernard A. Weisberger, *They Gathered at the River* (Boston: Little, Brown & Co., 1958), 92.

4. Dwight L. Moody, *Secret Power* (Ventura, Calif.: Regal, 1987, originally published 1881), 17.

5. Riss, 23-24.

6. Riss, 23-24.

7. David B. Barrett, "A Survey of the 20th Century Pentecostal/Charismatic Renewal in the Holy Spirit," *Dictionary of Pentecostal and Charismatic Movements,* Table 1.

8. David B. Barrett, "Global Statistics," *Dictionary of Pentecostal and Charismatic Movements,* 810.

9. J.R. Goff, Jr., "Parham, Charles Fox," *Dictionary of Pentecostal and Charismatic Movements,* 660-61.

10. John Thomas Nichol, *The Pentecostals* (Plainfield, N.J.: Logos International, 1966), 28.

11. Nichol, 28-29.

12. Nichol, 34.

13. Nichol, 34.

14. Barrett, "A Survey of the 20th Century Pentecostal/Charismatic Renewal in the Holy Spirit," *Dictionary of Pentecostal and Charismatic Movements,* Table 1.

15. Nichol, 72.

16. E. L. Blumhofer, "Assemblies of God," *Dictionary of Pentecostal and Charismatic Movements,* 23.

17. William Martin, *A Prophet with Honor* (New York: William and Morrow, 1991).

18. Graham's willingness to work with local clergy in liberal churches of the day occasioned a break with theologically conservative Christians, leading to the distinction between "fundamentalists" and "evangelicals."

19. Riss, 112-24.

20. P.D. Hoken, "Charismatic Movement," *Dictionary of Pentecostal and Charismatic Movements,* 132.

21. See Theodore Jungkuntz, *Confirmation and the Charismata* (Lanham, Md.: University Press of America, 1983) as an example of a theologically sophisticated effort at incorporating charismatic experience within an historic church's theological framework.

22. For example, at this Mass, a lay Catholic named Bruce Yocum delivered a prophecy speaking of impending times of increasing darkness for the world, but glory for the church, admonishing the hearers to prepare for a time when social and church structures would suffer considerable collapse.

23. C. Peter Wagner, "Third Wave," *Dictionary of Pentecostal and Charismatic Movements,* 843-44.

24. Nichol, 32.

THREE
Power and Pain

1. Oscar Cullman, *Christ and Time* (Philadelphia: Westminster, 1964), 37ff.
2. Matthew 10:1, 7-8; Luke 10:1, 9; Acts 6:8, 10; Acts 8:4-7; Acts 9:17-18; Galatians 3:5; 1 Corinthians 1:7; 12:9; Philippians 4:9; Hebrews 2:3-4; 6:4-5.
3. See for example John MacArthur, *Charismatic Chaos* (Grand Rapids, Mich.: Zondervan, 1992), 107. We see no biblical support for MacArthur's position. For a thorough dismantling of MacArthur's view that the healing gift gradually disappeared in the New Testament, see Jack Deere, *Surprised by the Spirit* (Grand Rapids, Mich.: Zondervan, 1993), 238-40, 289.
4. The Bible *does* teach that there may be other reasons for a person's lack of healing, including a general attitude of unbelief in a community. "He could not do any miracles there [in Nazareth], except lay his hands on a few sick people and heal them. And he was amazed by their lack of faith" (Mk 6:5-6). Perhaps the "lack of faith" in the western world in general, and our western churches in particular, explains why there seem to be fewer healings here than are reported in the other two-thirds of the world. While we tend to attribute the relative abundance of divine healings there to new church planting, or illiteracy, or their supposed need for the supernatural, it simply may boil down to greater faith in their communities and churches (see Matthew 8:5-13). Other biblical reasons why people don't receive divine healing include: *not asking* God for healing—James 4:2 says, "You do not have, because you do not ask God"; *apostasy* by God's people—"We are given no miraculous signs; no prophets are left, and none of us knows how long this will be (Ps 74:9); and *disunity* in the church—"For anyone who eats and drinks without recognizing the body of the Lord eats and drinks judgment on himself. That is why many among you are weak and sick, and a number of you have fallen asleep" (1 Cor 11:29-30). But the *main* reason why healing is not more universal is simply the "not yet" of the Kingdom of God.
5. Mark 8:22; John 9:6; Mark 1:41; Matthew 8:10-12; Luke 7:11-17; Mark 2:5.
6. Compare Mark 5:41 with Mark 5:27-31 and John 4:43-53. Compare Mark 2:5-12 with John 4:14.
7. Conservative evangelicals have been very helpful in providing the church with such books as C.S. Lewis' *The Problem of Pain* and Philip Yancey's *Disappointment with God.* Charismatics would do well to supplement the reading of books on healing with conservative evangelical works on pain and disappointment.

FOUR
The Supernatural and the Natural

1. J.S. Bruner and Leo Postman, "Experiments," in Thomas S. Kuhn, *The Structure of Scientific Revolutions, Second Edition* (Chicago: University of Chicago Press, 1970), 62-64.

2. But even this seemingly evident idea that one cannot walk through a wall was disproven on at least one occasion. After his resurrection, Jesus was apparently able to walk through locked doors (see John 20:19). Thus even our most basic assumptions about the way reality works must be subjected to the challenge of the Word of God.

3. Os Guinness and John Seel, "Breaking with the Idols of Our Age," *No God, But God* (Chicago: Moody, 1992), 164.

4. Guinness and Seel, 164.

5. Often the attempt to draw certain management principles from biblical texts in recent books on Christian leadership seems to be an artificial overlay over the text. Such principles could not have been in the mind of the biblical author but are instead imposed on the text by modern managerial assumptions. Of course, management consultants are not the only ones sometimes guilty of imposing contrived meanings on a biblical text. Psychologists, economists, political scientists, and literary critics have, at times, fallen into the same trap.

6. Don Williams, "Exorcizing the Ghost of Newton" in Charles H. Kraft, *Christianity with Power* (Ann Arbor, Mich.: Servant, 1989), 39-40.

7. See, for example, Luke 13:10-13, where a woman was crippled *by a spirit* for eighteen years. See also Mark 9:25, where Jesus rebukes a spirit that caused deafness and muteness.

8. Consider, for example, the evangelistic impact of the healing of Aeneas upon two entire villages in ancient Judea (Acts 9:32-35). Contemporary reports from China and India suggest that divine healings can often have a *door-opening* impact for the gospel's presentation.

9. Matthew 10:1; Mark 6:12-13.

10. Krister Stendahl, *Paul among Jews and Gentiles and Other Essays* (Philadelphia: Fortress, 1976), 7, cited in Kraft, 65-88, (italics mine).

11. John 9:16-31.

12. This view was popularized by Benjamin Warfield in his book *Counterfeit Miracles*. There are several problems with this view. Among them is the fact that Elijah and Elisha do not fit into the "fresh epoch of revelation" pattern. While they were prophets, no written revelation came through these two. They are a "poor fit" in most attempts to come up with an overarching reason for miraculous occurrences other than that God is a miracle-working God who regularly works miracles. Moreover, if signs and wonders infrequently occur during a particular period of time it is, from a biblical perspective, not because God has nothing else to say to his people, but rather because of God's judgment and discipline of his people (e.g., Psalm 74:8-10; Amos 8:11; 1 Samuel 3:1). From a biblical perspective, God's *presence* and *blessing* are marked by signs and wonders while God's *absence* and God's *judgment* are marked by the absence of signs and wonders.

13. There is no such thing as a "bare fact or event." Facts do not generally "speak for themselves." Instead, what we have is a fact and an interpretation of the

fact. The interpretation springs from the context of the fact and one's worldview. That doesn't mean that facts carry with them *no meaning;* rather, facts often carry more than one meaning. The appropriate meaning is difficult to establish with *absolute certainty.*

14. Several possible tests of whether a fact ought to be interpreted as having a supernatural cause might include: (1) *momentous timing*—for example, a healing of blindness occurs immediately after a prayer of command "see!" (2) *exceeds natural causes*—a healing so exceeds known natural causes that it is reasonable to attribute it to another cause; (3) *the claims*—the healing is performed entirely in Jesus' name and brings together the qualities of "grace and power" (Acts 6:8).

15. In a lengthy section on *prophecy,* not word of knowledge, the apostle Paul provides the following example: "But if an unbeliever or someone who doesn't understand comes in while everybody is *prophesying...* the secrets of his heart will be laid bare. So he will fall down and worship God, exclaiming, 'God is really among you!'" (1 Cor 14:24-25). Likewise, when Jesus told the woman at the well her secret sins, she did not say, "Sir, I perceive you have the gift of word of knowledge." Rather she said, "Sir, I can see that you are a *prophet*" (Jn 4:19). Thus, we would place all spontaneous revelations under the heading of "prophecy." We were interested to find that our conclusions about the word of wisdom and the word of knowledge are supported by a prominent theologian at Trinity Evangelical Divinity School named Dr. Wayne Grudem. See Wayne Grudem, *Systematic Theology* (Grand Rapids, Mich.: Zondervan, 1994), 1080, 1081.

16. Francis Schaeffer, *The God Who Is There* (Downers Grove, Ill.: InterVarsity, 1968), 78-80.

17. The apostle John speaks of Jesus as the "true light that *enlightens* every man" (John 1:9). This cannot be the enlightening of people to a knowledge of Christ, the Bible, or even a generalized knowledge of God since the Light of Christ is said to enlighten *every man.* Rather, Christ, as the divine Logos, is the mediator of all knowledge that comes to all people, including the knowledge of medicine.

SIX
Dusting off the Gospels

1. George Eldon Ladd, *A Theology of the New Testament* (Grand Rapids, Mich.: Eerdmans, 1974), 57.

2. Daniel Wallace, "Who's Afraid of the Holy Spirit?" *Christianity Today,* September 12, 1994.

3. Wallace.

4. Danny Harrell, "Reaching the First Post-Christian Generation," *Christianity Today,* September 12, 1994.

SEVEN
Worship and the Word

1. Iain H. Murray, *Jonathan Edwards: A New Biography* (Edinburgh, Penn. Banner of Truth, 1987), 169.
2. George Whitefield, *Journals* (Edinburgh, Penn.: Banner of Truth Trust), 487.
3. 1 Kings 8:10-11; Acts 2:1-4.
4. Exodus 33:14-16.
5. The Westminster Assembly was summoned by the English Parliament in 1643 to advise Parliament about restructuring the Church of England along Puritan lines. After completing work on a confession, the Assembly wrote a Shorter Catechism designed for children in 1647 and a Larger Catechism designed for the pulpit in 1648.
6. 1 Timothy 5:17; Titus 1:5; Hebrews 13:17; 1 Peter 5:1-4.
7. Mark 12:32-33.
8. Jeremiah 29:11.
9. Richard Lovelace, *Dynamics of Spiritual Life: An Evangelical Theology of Renewal* (Downers Grove, Ill.: InterVarsity, 1980), 279.

EIGHT
Hearing God's Voice

1. Alan Burgess, *The Small Woman* (Ann Arbor, Mich.: Servant, 1985). Originally published in 1957 by E.P. Dutton & Co., Inc.
2. For an excellent treatment of hermeneutics see Gordon D. Fee and Douglas Stuart, *How to Read the Bible for All It's Worth* (Grand Rapids, Mich.: Zondervan, 1982).

NINE
Receiving the Spirit: An Empowered Evangelical View

1. Nichol, 28.
2. Thomas C. Oden, *Life in the Spirit* (San Francisco: HarperCollins, 1992), 156-58, 180-83.
3. D.L. Moody, *Secret Power* (Ventura, Calif.: Regal, 1987), 135-51. Excerpted from R.A. Torrey, *What the Bible Teaches* (Old Tappan, N.J: Revell, 1898).
4. Moody, 17.
5. While the New Testament treatment of tongues is not honored in the conservative evangelical avoidance of tongues, neither is the charismatic overemphasis on this gift reflected in the New Testament record. For example, many charismatics actively encourage speaking in tongues to the

point where those who do not have this experience feel that they are missing something essential. Tongues is portrayed as the doorway into a broader experience of the charismatic gifts. In some charismatic circles, various techniques to "help" people speak in tongues are employed. The references to tongues in the Book of Acts, by contrast, are simply a matter of telling the facts, the historical account. And Paul's teaching on tongues is restricted to one letter (1 Corinthians) addressed to a church which had been abusing this gift. A conservative evangelical approach to tongues should reflect both the biblical guidelines regarding tongues and the biblical emphasis, which is modest.

6. See Jonathan Edwards, *Treatise Concerning the Religious Affections* (London: Banner of Truth, 1961).

7. Edwards, *Treatise Concerning the Religious Affections,* 59.

TEN
Mind and Emotions: Room for Both

1. Alan Richardson, ed., *A Theological Word Book of the Bible* (New York: MacMillan, 1950). See "Mind/Heart," by E.C. Blackman, 145.

2. Richardson, 144.

3. "The will, and the affections of the soul, are not two faculties; the affections are not essentially distinct from the will, nor do they differ from the mere actings of the will, and inclination of the soul, but only in the liveliness and sensibleness of exercise." Jonathan Edwards, *The Religious Affections* (London: Banner of Truth Trust, 1961), 25.

4. Conrad Cherry, *The Theology of Jonathan Edwards: A Reappraisal* (Blooming-ton, Ind.: Indiana University Press, 1966), 167.

5. "The religion of the most eminent saints we have an account of in scripture consisted much in holy affections." Cherry, 37-43.

6. My thanks to Betty Dresser, from the Metro Vineyard in Detroit, for her insights on this topic from a presentation entitled, "Jesus: A Man of Joy."

7. Edwards, 46.

8. Cherry, 167.

9. Murray, *Jonathan Edwards: A New Biography.* See chapter 8 for a description of Edwards' devotional life.

ELEVEN
The Future of Empowered Evangelicalism

1. Gene Veith, *Postmodern Times: A Christian Guide to Contemporary Thought and Culture* (Wheaton, Ill.: Crossway, Good News, 1994), 39.

2. Sarah Ferguson, "Feel the Pain," *Leadership Magazine* (Spring 1995), vol. XVI, No. 2, 44.

3. William J. Bennett, *The Index of Leading Cultural Indicators* (New York: Simon & Schuster, 1994) provided all the statistics in this paragraph.

4. John MacArthur, *Charismatic Chaos* (Grand Rapids, Mich.: Zondervan, 1992), 40-43.

5. Robert Ferm, *Cooperative Evangelism: Is Billy Graham Right or Wrong?* (Grand Rapids: Zondervan, 1958), 72, 73.

6. MacArthur, 107.

7. The idea for summarizing our goals as evangelicals in terms of "three ends" came from a message by Leighton Ford given at the International Conference for Itinerant Evangelists in Amsterdam, the Netherlands, in 1983.

8. "Mission Frontiers," *Bulletin of U.S. Center for World Missions* (May/June 1995), 5.

9. These statistics are derived from Stanley M. Burgess and Gary B. McGee, *The Dictionary of Pentecostal and Charismatic Movements* (Grand Rapids, Mich.: Zondervan, 1988).